Drug Cartels Do Not Exist

CRITICAL
MEXICAN STUDIES

CRITICAL MEXICAN STUDIES
Series editor: Ignacio M. Sánchez Prado

Critical Mexican Studies is the first English-language, humanities-based, theoretically focused academic series devoted to the study of Mexico. The series is a space for innovative works in the humanities that focus on theoretical analysis, transdisciplinary interventions, and original conceptual framing.

Other titles in the series:
The Restless Dead: Necrowriting and Disappropriation,
    by Cristina Rivera Garza
History and Modern Media: A Personal Journey, by John Mraz
Toxic Loves, Impossible Futures: Feminist Living as Resistance,
    by Irmgard Emmelhainz
Unlawful Violence: Mexican Law and Cultural Production,
    by Rebecca Janzen

Drug Cartels Do Not Exist

Narcotrafficking in US
and Mexican Culture

Oswaldo Zavala

Translated by William Savinar

Vanderbilt University Press
Nashville, Tennessee

Originally published in 2018 as *Los cárteles no existen. Narcotráfico y cultura en México* by Malpaso Editorial.

Copyright 2022 Vanderbilt University Press
All rights reserved
First printing 2022

Library of Congress Cataloging-in-Publication Data
Names: Zavala, Oswaldo, 1975- author. | Savinar, William, 1990- translator.
Title: Drug cartels do not exist : narcotrafficking in U.S. and Mexican culture / Oswaldo Zavala ; translated by William Savinar.
Other titles: Cárteles no existen. English
Description: Nashville : Vanderbilt University Press, [2022] | Includes bibliographical references and index.
Identifiers: LCCN 2021050482 (print) | LCCN 2021050483 (ebook) | ISBN 9780826504661 (paperback) | ISBN 9780826504678 (hardback) | ISBN 9780826504685 (epub) | ISBN 9780826504692 (pdf)
Subjects: LCSH: Drug traffic—Mexico—History—20th century. | Drug control—Mexico—History—20th century. | Drug traffic—United States—History—20th century. | Drug control—United States—History—20th century.
Classification: LCC HV5840.M6 Z3813 2020 (print) | LCC HV5840.M6 (ebook) | DDC 364.1/33650972—dc23/eng/20211021
LC record available at https://lccn.loc.gov/2021050482
LC ebook record available at https://lccn.loc.gov/2021050483

For Ignacio Alvarado and Julián Cardona,
who knew it first and better than anyone else.

Contents

Acknowledgments

This book would not have been written without the indispensable work of juarense journalists Ignacio Alvarado and Julián Cardona, whom I was fortunate to learn from during my years as a reporter for *El Diario* in Ciudad Juárez. With them I first comprehended the scope of the official discourse and mythology surrounding the "cartels." I appreciate their generosity, friendship, professional integrity, and combative reporting, which continues to be one of the best examples of investigative journalism in Mexico and Latin America to this day.

Journalism has been and will always be a crucial function of my intellectual work. The ideas on these pages have been inspired and improved upon—perhaps for them inadvertently—by the dialogue and friendship of the journalists of *Proceso* magazine, especially Homero Campa, Rafael Rodríguez Castañeda, Alejandro Gutiérrez, Arturo Rodríguez, Alejandro Saldívar, Álvaro Delgado, and José Gil Olmos.

I also appreciate the stimulating exchange of ideas and the friendship of journalists Sergio Rodríguez Blanco and Federico Mastrogiovanni, who offered me the invaluable opportunity to teach journalism and literature seminars at the Ibero-American University during the 2016–2017 academic year. These seminars, addressed in part to the intelligent and inquisitive journalists of Ibero's extraordinary Press and Democracy (PRENDE) program, were key to the development of many of the ideas put forth in this book.

This project is also a direct result of my academic work as professor of contemporary Latin American literature and culture at City University of New York (CUNY). My ideas owe much to the generous support, rich dialogue, and insightful observations of my colleagues and friends Magdalena Perkowska, José del Valle, Fernando Degiovanni and Álvaro Baquero. In the academic world outside of CUNY, my work has benefited from the bright conversation and friendship of Ignacio Sánchez Prado, Oswaldo Estrada, Irma Cantú, Cristina Carrasco, Tamara Williams, Viviane Mahieux, José Ramón Ruisánchez, Dante Salgado, Marta Piña, Jorge García, Mabel Moraña, Sara Poot-Herrera, Raquel Serur, Jacobo Sefamí, Stuart Day, Pedro Ángel Palou, Sophie Esch, Brian Price, Rafael Acosta, and Bruno Ríos.

In Mexico City, while I was finishing the manuscript, my main interlocutors were Juan Villoro and David Miklos. Their comments gave my book intellectual depth, and their friendship made the writing experience significantly happier.

I am grateful for the friendship, camaraderie, and brilliant editorial work of Rafael Lemus, which substantially improved every page of the original manuscript in Spanish.

This book could not have found a better editorial home than Vanderbilt University Press. I am indebted to the brilliant and tireless work of Ignacio Sánchez Prado and feel fortunate to be part of the Critical Mexican Studies series. I am equally grateful for the professionalism and commitment of Zack Gresham, acquisitions editor at Vanderbilt, whose kind support and guidance brought new life to this book in its English-language avatar. This translation was made possible in part thorough the generous funding of the PSC-CUNY Research Award Program.

My teachers are always present in my writing: Rosario Espinoza, Rosendo Zavala, and Ricardo Zavala.

Without the love of Sarah Pollack, Ximena Zavala, Mateo Zavala, and Diana Zavala, not a word would ever make sense.

Drug Cartels Do Not Exist

I don't believe in fucking conspiracy theories.
I'm talking about a fucking conspiracy.

Gary Webb

The Invention
of a Formidable Enemy

On February 19, 2012, then President Felipe Calderón gave his final speech while in power on the anniversary celebration of the founding of the Mexican Army and Air Force. Something extraordinary happened that day that Luis Astorga, a sociologist and expert in drug trafficking and security issues, noted. A group of soldiers acted out the procedure for checking a car for drugs. Astorga writes:

> In a vehicle where marijuana was presumably concealed, the soldier who played the trafficker was dressed according to his archetypal image, an image that is shown even in the [National Defense Secretariat] (SEDENA) museum dedicated to drug trafficking; cowboy boots and a sombrero, listening to *narcocorridos*: "The scene made Calderón, his wife Margarita Zavala, and the secretaries of National Defense and Navy, General Guillermo Galván, and Admiral Francisco Saynez, burst into laughter," according to the newspaper story covering the event.[1]

The military carried out a performance of their activities against drug trafficking, embodying the figure of the trafficker that the Mexican political system has constructed for a specific purpose: a man dressed as a cowboy listening to *narcocorridos*, or drug ballads. That image, as Astorga points out, has been built into SEDENA's Museo del Enervante (Museum of Drugs). In this museum, popularly known as the narco museum, a mannequin is dressed like that same narco that the military put on display that day: a rancher vulgarly flaunting his sudden wealth generated by drug trafficking in the form of the unavoidable Versace shirt, crocodile skin boots, and that ever-present sombrero, without which his image would not be recognizable. The museum even adds objects to strengthen the legendary Mexican narco character: gold-plated, diamond-encrusted weapons with the drug lord's engraved initials.[2]

This military performance gives us a rare glimpse into how the Mexican political system has created a formidable enemy in these times of permanent national security crisis. The narco imagined by the military is, in theory, the opposite of the soldier: undisciplined, vulgar, ignorant, violent. For the Army, however, the narco requires, if not a uniform, a *uniformity* that distinguishes the soldiers from the narcos whom, in the name of government, the soldier must eliminate.

Astorga observes that the archetypal clothing of the narco coincides with many of the inhabitants of rural Mexico. How does the military manage to distinguish criminals among the country's ranchers? During President Calderón's "war" against the narco, according to official data, around 121,683 people were murdered.[3] But if the narco staged by the military provoked the laughter of the president, his wife, and the Defense of Navy secretaries, it was due to the *caricature* of the phenomenon, with obvious similarities to narcos in movies or television series. In reality, the average appearance of both victimizers and victims of the alleged war is radically different. A November 2012 study conducted by the independent think tank México Evalúa showed that the recurring profile of victims of intentional homicide during the Calderón administration was that of single, poor men between twenty-five and twenty-nine, with little to no formal education. Far from being ranchers or cowboys, they resided in cities such as Ciudad Juárez, Monterrey, or Tijuana. The usual perpetrator during the alleged clashes between "cartels" did not resemble the narco played by the soldiers. It wasn't the country drug trafficker who killed his enemy in cowboy boots and a ten-gallon hat while listening to Los Tigres del Norte as a soundtrack to a low-budget film directed by the Almada brothers. Instead, we see that same poor, uneducated man living a criminal lifestyle in the country's northern cities with one major difference: he was often five years younger than his victim.[4]

Before Calderón, the military simultaneously played the role of the hero and the violent enemy of the state and civil society. They had to play both roles because behind the curtains they didn't exist as they were represented. Where does that recurring narco archetype come from then?

To answer that question, we need to go back in time. In 1989, just at the end of the Cold War, the political scientist Waltraud Morales wrote an article that is fundamental to understanding the new world order after the fall of the Berlin Wall, "The War on Drugs: A New US National Security Doctrine." For half a century, anti-communism occupied the center of the US national security policy.[5] The National Security Act, enacted in 1947, was the mechanism by which the US Congress gave legal status to the global strategy that polarized the planet after World War II. During that year, two key institutions of the new security era were founded: in the United States, the Central Intelligence Agency (CIA), and in Mexico, the Federal Security Directorate (DFS). The Cold War, of course, directly involved Mexico. Over the next three decades, both agencies joined efforts to contain the alleged communist threat in the hemisphere. Their collaboration deepened as the US government deployed Operation Condor, an aggressive interventionist policy on the continent during the mid-1970s. A separate Operation Condor, however, was designed solely for Mexico, keeping the same name but with a different focus on drug trafficking and not on the fight against communism. The thousands of soldiers and Federal Police officers who destroyed drug plantations between 1975 and 1987 (when it officially ended) also produced the mass displacement of peasants, drug producers, and drug traffickers. By the end of the 1970s, the Mexican drug trade not only continued to exist, but moved its center of operations to the city of Guadalajara and proceeded to dominate the international trade by charging Colombian organizations up to 50 percent of profits on cocaine that went through Mexico.[6]

The most feared traffickers of that time, Miguel Ángel Félix Gallardo, Ernesto "Don Neto" Fonseca Carrillo, and Rafael Caro Quintero, took on mythical status. Félix Gallardo, for example, had been a Sinaloa judicial police officer and, until the mid-1980s, lived in the public eye, often seen with well-known politicians. Catching onto the term US officials used to describe the organizations headed by these larger-than-life characters, the Mexican media also started using the word *cartel*. But the word *cartel*, like practically all vocabulary associated with the *narco*, has an official origin. Luis Astorga emphasizes the contradiction in referring to drug trafficking groups as *cartels* because, according to official intelligence, far from collaborating to enhance their profits, the cartels act as rivals who are willing to eliminate each other.

In his book, *El siglo de las drogas* (The century of drugs), Astorga discusses another event of narco political history. In a 1994 interview between *Time* magazine and Gilberto Rodríguez Orejuela, the Colombian trafficker who allegedly led the Cali cartel with his brother Miguel, the trafficker states that the Cali cartel simply does not exist. "It's an invention of the

DEA [Drug Enforcement Administration] . . . There are many groups, not just one cartel. The police and the DEA know. But they prefer to invent a monolithic enemy."[7] The British journalist Ioan Grillo was given the same response in Colombia when interviewing the "narco-attorney" Gustavo Salazar, the legal representative of the alleged Medellín cartel. The lawyer repeated what Rodríguez Orejuela said: "Cartels do not exist. What you have is a collection of drug traffickers. Sometimes, they work together, and sometimes they don't. American prosecutors just call them cartels to make it easier to make their cases. It is all part of the game."[8]

The title of this book comes partly from these statements; but above all from a critical reflection on the official language that insists on mythology when discussing organized crime. The cartels do not exist: that is the early lesson learned by the drug traffickers themselves. There is a market for illegal drugs and people who are willing to work in that market. But there is no such division that Mexican and US authorities use to try and separate these groups from civil society and government structures. Trafficking organizations may generate violence, but, as I will argue throughout these pages, this violence is more a symptom of state policing strategies than the criminal action of the narcos themselves.

Before I was an academic and essayist, I was a reporter. My research is the product of a long intellectual journey that began in the 1990s while writing for *El Diario de Juárez*, one of the most well-known newspapers in northern Mexico. There, I had the good fortune of completing my professional education under the mentorship of the investigative reporter Ignacio Alvarado and the photojournalist Julián Cardona. For decades, long before I even dreamt of this book, these two journalists began a powerful decentering of narco news coverage. For both, the cartels are a symbolic device whose main function is to hide the real networks of official power that determined the flow of drug trafficking. Their work was, and continues to be, revolutionary and has had a profound impact on a new generation of Mexican and foreign journalists and academics who have built on their contributions. The remarkable work of Alvarado and Cardona has been indispensable throughout my career as a journalist and academic. Thanks to their critical insight, I have been able to develop the central ideas of this book: ideas that I have corroborated, over five years of research, with other sources that have separately reached similar conclusions.[9]

Another one of the fundamental sources of my research has been, as I have mentioned, the crucial work of the Mexican sociologist Luis Astorga. In his early book, *Mitología del narcotraficante en México* (Mythology of the drug trafficker in Mexico), Astorga first observed the symbolic construction of what we think we know about drug trafficking. According to him, the drug trafficker is a myth based on a "matrix" of language whose rules and meaning have been determined by the state: what we call the *narco*.[10] This matrix does not explain the actual activities of traffickers, but symbolically codifies the epistemological limits with which we involuntarily represent traffickers and the drug trade. Astorga explains:

> The distance between the real drug traffickers and their world and the symbolic construction that we use to speak about them is so great that there seems to be no other current and feasible way than to refer to this subject in a mythological way, whose antipodes are represented by legal code and drug ballads.[11]

The importance of Astorga's conclusion cannot be overstated: we know little to nothing about the phenomenon of drug trafficking, since their social space and the public sphere are separated by a dense structure of meaning that has been conceived for the political purpose of concealment and non-understanding. But if, on the contrary, our impression is that we know all too well the life and death of the narcos, their family relationships, their uncontrolled ambition, and their psychopathic violence, it is because for decades we have been accustomed to that system of official representation that contradictorily reveals the cartel flowchart but is clearly unable to stop them.

Now, it must be emphasized that this matrix of narco discourse had its origin in the complex binational relationship between Mexico and the United States. As Waltraud Morales recalls, when US anti-drug policy replaced communism as the new doctrine of national security, the US public was already prepared to confirm the invasion of the drug cartels: a CBS survey conducted in 1988 showed that US citizens believed that the trafficking and consumption of prohibited drugs posed a greater threat to national security than terrorism or arms trafficking.[12]

This change in perception among the US public was not the result of an accurate understanding of the issue of drug trafficking. On the contrary, the belief in drug cartels as the new national security threat was the direct effect of the implementation of a state policy based, in part, on the conception of a permanent enemy that allows the justification of actions that would otherwise be illegal and immoral. To make the security agenda legal, President Ronald Reagan signed the National Security Decision Directive 221 in 1986, which designated the illegal drug trade as a rising threat to US national security. The War on Drugs, which began in the 1970s during the

Nixon administration as a domestic strategy to combat leftist dissent and exert social control of racialized minorities, would now take the place of communism to legitimize US intervention. Waltraud Morales's prediction in her 1989 article is still as impressive and pertinent now as it was then:

> The "evil empire of drugs" has the potential to evoke that fear of the enemy so basic and powerful in the doctrine of anticommunism. The danger therefore is that one more generation of US foreign policy will be rooted in hatred of a mythical enemy, in conspiracy and not democracy, and ideological doctrines of national security.[13]

Anti-drug policy as the new security doctrine since the 1980s produced one of the most significant political scandals in the history of the United States. Although some journalists had approached the subject before, the revelation was made full force, with national and international fanfare, by the investigative journalist Gary Webb in a series of three news articles published in the *San Jose Mercury News* between August 18 and 20, 1996. Webb revealed direct links between the so-called "crack cocaine epidemic" in the black neighborhoods of South Central Los Angeles and the CIA-backed counterinsurgency strategy in Nicaragua to subvert the Sandinista government. According to Webb's reporting, the CIA allowed Nicaraguan Democratic Force (FDN in Spanish) operatives, otherwise known as the Contras, to finance their guerrillas with profits obtained from the sale of crack cocaine in California:

> While the FDN war is barely a memory today, black America is still dealing with its poisonous side effects. Urban neighborhoods are grappling with legions of homeless crack addicts. Thousands of young black men are serving long prison sentences for selling cocaine—a drug that was virtually unobtainable in black neighborhoods before members of the CIA's army started bringing it into South-Central in the 1980s at bargain-basement prices.[14]

Webb's reporting profoundly damaged the credibility of the CIA's counterinsurgency operations in Central America. In response, the government unleashed a brutal smear campaign against the journalist, a campaign backed by the mainstream media, including the *New York Times*, the *Washington Post*, and the *Los Angeles Times*, which preferred to privilege official sources who questioned Webb rather than give credit to a colleague for the risk he took. The national newspapers pettily refused to investigate simply because Webb's work had been done for another news outlet. This onslaught ended Webb's journalistic career when even his own newspaper retracted his reports. Finally, Webb's life ended when, unemployed, marginalized, and betrayed by his colleagues, he committed suicide in 2004.

In 1998, the CIA admitted in a report from its inspector general that the agency "had only worked with 58 contras involved in the trafficking of cocaine, but also hid its criminal activities from Congress," according to Alfred McCoy's classic study, *The Politics of Heroin: CIA Complicity in the Global Drug Trade*.[15] That same year, the celebrated journalist Charles Bowden met Webb in Sacramento, California. Bowden stressed Webb's resolute confidence while defending the validity of his reporting when he brought up the fact that Webb's work had been discussed alongside conspiracy theories. Webb stated, "I don't believe in fucking conspiracy theories. I believe in fucking conspiracies."[16]

This book strives to build on the critical potential of the brave work of reporters like Webb. Throughout these years of research, I have found other reporters who, without the prestige of awards or lucrative international scholarships, have raised the same red flag that Webb did concerning state culpability within the supposed War on Drugs. One of them is Terrence E. Poppa, who wrote a book fundamental to my research: *Druglord: The Life and Death of a Mexican Kingpin*. As Charles Bowden has noted, this book can be read as an instruction manual for understanding drug cartels. Reporting for the *El Paso Herald-Post*, Poppa embarked on a lengthy investigation into drug trafficking along the border when a fellow photographer was kidnapped for taking pictures of the construction of a hotel in Ciudad Juárez, allegedly owned by a local drug trafficker. Through skillful reporting, Poppa managed to perceive the control that the Mexican political system exercised over organized crime, subjecting it to its power structure. This control is expressed, for example, in the notion of the *plaza*. Most reporters in Mexico think of the plaza as the domain of a trafficker. Poppa's investigation, following the life of the trafficker Pablo Acosta in the town of Ojinaga, discovered something much more complex:

> Traffickers like Pablo Acosta operated under a system that was almost like a franchise. They had to pay a monthly fee to their managers for the right to work in a specific area. It was a form of private tax based on sales volume, with the money going to those in power. As noted in the book, traffickers frequently received badges from the Federal Police. The army, the Attorney General of Mexico and its Federal Police, the Ministry of the Interior and its secret police, several governors, and many more powerful people were involved.[17]

Poppa carried out his research in the late 1980s, the same time the Mexican political system began a transformation of its security system that Waltraud Morales warned us about. Between 1975 and 1985, between Operation Condor and the assassination of Enrique Camarena, a DEA special agent in Guadalajara, the political system absolutely overpowered organized crime, limited its operations to specific cities, regulated its trafficking routes, and, even more importantly, separated it from political, civil, and military power. Not until the open adoption of the US national security discourse of the following decade, especially with the creation of the Center for Investigation and National Security (CISEN) in 1989, did the Mexican political system gradually employ a violent militaristic strategy that culminated with the daily horrors of Ciudad Juárez, Monterrey, or Tampico, and all the crimes against humanity committed during Felipe Calderón's presidency and onward.

The supposed national security crisis that Calderón said justified the War on Drugs is based mainly on a discursive strategy without material foundation. The sociologist Fernando Escalante Gonzalbo already showed, with a simple analysis based on official figures, that the country's violence began after the militarization ordered by Calderón in 2008.[18] In the previous decade, between 1997 and 2007, the homicide rate was in fact decreasing in the country's main cities, including Ciudad Juárez. Violence only returned in those areas of the country where Calderón sent thousands of soldiers and federal agents. Calderón and his cabinet wanted to militarize the country to contain a supposed war of cartels that produced no violence. Cities where there was no crisis were taken over by the army and federal agents. The state went in to stop a non-existent cartel war because cartels do not exist.

In 2007, a year before Calderón's war began, Luis Astorga published one of his most important books, *Seguridad, traficantes y militares* (Security, traffickers, and the military). During the first years of the twenty-first century, national security became a central theme in Mexican drug policy. This is surprising because, once again, there was no valid reason to assume that drug traffickers posed a threat to civil society or to the viability of the state. One year before the "joint operations" of the military and Federal Police began in the states of Chihuahua, Nuevo León, Guerrero, and Veracruz, among others, Astorga wrote:

> In the field of power, traffickers have historically been subordinate to the government. They have not been in competition with it or have tried to compete by creating associations or political parties; nor have they developed a

far-reaching "infiltration" strategy to reverse this subordinate relationship. There is isolated corruption, especially within police departments, but not an agreed-upon plan between criminal organizations or a conspiracy to drive a systemic change that would "test" the president. In other words, the traffickers are some of the social actors whose activities and actions undoubtedly hinder governance, but do not pose a threat to political power or the direction of the state.[19]

If drug traffickers, as Astorga explains, had neither the long-term capacity nor the political determination to threaten the sovereignty of the state, then what motivated the War on Drugs, and where did the violence attributed to the alleged drug cartels come from? I go back to the journalist Ignacio Alvarado to begin to answer this question:

> Violence in Mexico is not explained by a war between drug traffickers or a dispute over plazas. Moreover, there is no single drug trafficker with the capacity to challenge institutions such as the Army, the Navy or the Federal Police; not even the recently [imprisoned] Joaquín "El Chapo" Guzmán. Nothing supports the government's story. Drugs are only the pretext at the heart of the violence. The US State Department's influence on this issue is crucial. Mexico's judicial, energy, tax, and education reforms are being driven by actors at the highest levels of US government —with capital interest in mind— and the Mérida Initiative is the perfect instrument for the social and political manipulation of the country. The goal of this system of terror is exile: the depopulation of immense territories that are rich in hydrocarbons, minerals, and water. Today we can see how the energy sector has been affected by such reforms. Private and foreign capital that has been waiting on this moment for two decades can now exploit these natural resources.[20]

The important investigative work of the Italian journalist Federico Mastrogiovanni as well as Canadian academic and journalist Dawn Paley have separately come to the same conclusion: the federal government's energy reform is one of the central explanations for the current violence in Mexico. Mastrogiovanni writes: "Both processes —the gradual opening of the energy sector to private capital and the intensification of violence and terror— have developed in parallel."[21] Paley views anti-drug policy in the United States and Mexico as a direct expression of capitalism in the neoliberal era benefitting the global energy sector and expanding economic opportunities in the manufacturing and transportation industries, from mining and hydrocarbon exploitation to the opening of new Walmart locations. Paley writes:

> The war on drugs is a long-term fix to capitalism's woes, combining terror with policymaking in a seasoned neoliberal mix, cracking open social worlds and territories once unavailable to globalized capitalism. This project is about re-thinking what is called the war on drugs: it isn't about prohibition or drug policy. Instead, it looks at how, in this war, terror is used against the populations in cities and rural areas, and how, parallel to this terror and resulting panic, policies that facilitate foreign direct investment and economic growth are implemented. This is drug war capitalism.[22]

Without crossing paths, Alvarado, Paley, and Mastrogiovanni embarked on research that led them to the same conclusion: the War on Drugs is a cipher that masks the political strategy of large-scale community displacement for the appropriation and exploitation of natural resources that, if not for the War on Drugs, would remain unattainable for national and transnational capital.

In one of his columns, the prominent Mexican author Juan Villoro analyzed the tension between Mexico and the United States caused by the unexpected election of Donald Trump. When discussing the infamous border wall proposed by Trump, Villoro recalls an episode from *The Sopranos*. As it is known, the protagonist Tony Soprano is a New Jersey gangster that faces the challenges of everyday family life in US society while engaging in violent, illegal activities. In the episode discussed, Tony Soprano's neighbors cannot hide the fear brought on by their coexistence with a criminal. Villoro writes:

> To satisfy his neighbors' morbid curiosity, Tony Soprano wraps a package full of sand and asks his neighbors to keep it for a while, as if they're his accomplice. They cannot refuse. They accept the box, thinking it contains something illegal, not just sand. In a single gesture, Tony asserts his power over them while injecting poison into their lives.[23]

The narco in Mexico and the United States works like Tony Soprano's clever trick. The narco appears in our society as a fearsome Pandora's box that, we believe, would unleash endless death and destruction if opened. If we could overcome that fear and confront what we call the narco by finally opening the box, we would not find a violent trafficker, but the official language that invents him: we would hear words that would slip through our fingers like sand. Let's open the box then.

CHAPTER 1

Narco Culture Depoliticized

CORPSES WITHOUT HISTORY: NARCO NOIR NOVELS AND THE MYTH OF THE CARTEL KINGDOM

One of the most famous pieces by the Oaxacan street artist known as Yescka is a stencil mural on exhibition inside the Oaxaca Museum of Contemporary Art. It sums up the dominant narco imagery of Mexico perfectly. It is a scathing riff on the Last Supper: taking place of Christ is a faceless narco wielding an AK-47; this weapon, nicknamed the "goat's horn," is a weapon of choice for both narcos and the military. He sits at the table surrounded by Mexico's political and business elite. To the left of the narco-Christ is former President Felipe Calderón. Other dinner guests include the owner of Televisa, Emilio Azcárraga Jean; former president, Carlos Salinas de Gortari; one of the richest businessmen in the world, Carlos Slim; the former president of the National Education Workers' Union (SNTE)—formerly in prison for embezzlement, Elba Esther Gordillo; and the former Governor of the Bank of Mexico and former Secretary of Finance in Felipe Calderón's cabinet—Agustín Carstens. On a tray in the center of the table rests the head of Benito Juárez —the first and only indigenous president of Mexico— as if it was the severed head of John the Baptist. In the lower right corner, a masked prostitute turns to us with a smile that could also be a face of disgust.[1] At first glance, the mural could be interpreted as the elite's submission to a narco who asserts himself as the highest authority in the country. It seems that at the final gathering, this elite brotherhood has chosen him as their savior; has embraced his teachings of a theologically post-political world intersecting with relentless globalization. Thus, drug trafficking rises above state structures, and armed with the transnational flow of capital, violently imposes its will over the broken-down political order.

FIGURE 1. *The Last Supper* by street artist Yescka depicts an archetypal drug trafficker with a golden AK-47, surrounded by elite political and business figures in Mexico, including former presidents Carlos Salinas de Gortari, Felipe Calderón, and Enrique Peña Nieto, Catholic Church and military leaders, Uncle Sam (holding a watch), a helicopter in the distance, and what seem to be the heads of former President Benito Juárez and President Andrés Manuel López Obrador. Courtesy of the Museum of Contemporary Art, Oaxaca, México and artist Yescka.

Yescka's critical take is consistent with the narco's representation in practically all known Mexican discourse. Journalists, filmmakers, musicians, novelists, and visual artists all share the same epistemological platform that places the narco in the center of a post-sovereign pact. When looking at the devastating figures attributed to drug trafficking—over 350,000 murders and nearly 80,000 disappeared from 2006 to 2021—how can we imagine that the drug lords sit anywhere else than at the center of the oligarchy's table?[2] If we believe that drug cartels operate in a country where we are told the state has lost all sovereignty, where government institutions have been displaced by the power of impersonal, private, and depoliticized global capital, how can we not confirm—with the historian Carlo Galli—that contemporary society's concept of the political is outdated?[3]

Notions of the state, sovereignty, and political divisions appear in academic debates as obstacles to understanding the emergence of drug trafficking in Mexico. Gareth Williams's book *The Mexican Exception* is symptomatic of this problem. Williams makes the argument that the "War on Drugs is a conflict that is internal to capital, rather than being a conflict between external sovereign domains or distinct ideas of social organization."[4] According to Williams, the narco is essentially a phenomenon internal to the logic of economic capitalism, which presupposes its position outside the power structure of the state. His analysis is consistent with the work of academic critics, journalists, and intellectuals inside and outside of Mexico, such as Sergio González Rodríguez, Rossana Reguillo, Herman Herlinghaus, Rita Segato, and Gabriela Polit, who interpret drug trafficking as an unpredictable phenomenon that is constantly transforming the illegal drug market and can only be understood through a post-state lens.

Currently, the most commercial crime novels consequently represent this vision of a post-sovereign Mexico in which a multiplicity of cartels control entire regions completely overpowering the weak state organizations who have been ruined by the corrupting power of global organized crime. Like the vast majority of journalistic investigations, songs, films, and conceptual art about the narco, this type of novel focuses on the violence acted upon the corpses through ahistorical and mythological narrative strategies: in short, a depoliticized interpretation. In this sense, I am interested in discussing how some of the most celebrated Mexican crime novels strengthen the post-political perspective by choosing the victim's body as the base for their representation of the narco. The corpse is found in the main narrative arc of these novels, constructed as an exercise in semiosis that unnecessarily transforms the victimized body into an empty vessel. In it is deposited all kinds of arbitrary interpretation that moves away from the historical conditions of the narco and instead produces a depoliticized narrative fantasy. Finally, and against the tide of post-political criticism, I am interested in pointing out how the drug phenomenon in Mexico is in fact decidedly political—according to the term as conceptualized by Carl Schmitt, as I will discuss later—with notions of state and sovereignty more relevant than ever.

The Mexican crime novel is dependent on the conventions of the British police detective novel (Arthur Conan Doyle, Agatha Christie), the US hardboiled novel (Dashiell Hammett, Raymond Chandler), and the bestselling crime novels of more recent generations (Henning Mankell, Rubem Fonseca). However, to acquire the symbolic capital of these conventions and formulas, the Mexican narco-narratives of the last decade have had to get rid of their domestic and political contexts and produce archetypal characters with plots that can be transferred to foreign cultural spaces. Transforming the historical and political dimension of the narco into a series of mythological attributes that naturalize violence and moralize criminal actions, these novels offer a decontextualized caricature of the narco that minimizes, or even erases, its most complex elements of greater literary interest.

The other influence on these novels comes from the popular Mexican practice of the journalistic chronicle. As I will discuss in detail in the following chapter, the work of renowned reporters such as Diego Osorno, Anabel Hernández, and Alejandro Almazán has popularized a narrative form that exoticizes the violence and squalor attributed to drug trafficking. Often drawing from the nineteenth-century *costumbrismo* tradition, these writers have created quite a trend among young journalists who seek to make a name for themselves by moving away from journalism in search of the alarmist police report or the activist's outrage with the relaxed subjectivity of the narrative chronicler who misreads the legacy of US New Journalism. Look at the journalistic chronicle anthology, *Generación ¡Bang!* (Generation bang!, 2012) compiled by Juan Pablo Meneses, for example, whose sensationalist title perfectly captures the frivolous superficiality of this curious trend of journalism. In this way, between the predictable dramatics of the best-selling police detective novels and a doubtful understanding of journalistic narrative, the Mexican crime novel is committed to retaining the reader's attention by mythologizing a violence whose political history is simply ignored.

Elmer Mendoza's career singularly depicts this phenomenon. In his first novels, *Un asesino solitario* (A lone assassin, 1999) and *El amante de Janis Joplin* (Janis Joplin's lover, 2001), Mendoza sets the action in the murky political context of 1990s Mexico. Its characters confront the main facilitator of crime in the country: official power. Drug traffickers, government or mob hitmen, common criminals, and even white-collar professionals—are all pawns in the game run by the political and government elite. The elaborate plots of these early Mendoza novels feature innovative characters who have little to do with the mythological narcos in his later novels. Jorge Macías, the protagonist of *A Lone Assassin*, for example, is a professional thug who works for a shadowy government agency. Far from the stereotypical character who slams tequila and listens to drug ballads all day, "Yorch" surprises the reader by preferring Coca-Cola and saltines while listening to Creedence Clearwater Revival's classic, "Have You Ever Seen the Rain?"

Upon achieving greater visibility, however, Elmer Mendoza radically shifted his literary work to police mystery novels starring the agent Edgar "El Zurdo" Mendieta, whose picturesque adventures exploit bloody narco deaths for the national and international audience. *Balas de plata* (*Silver Bullets*, 2008), the novel that won him the Premio Tusquets de Novela, a Spanish language literary prize awarded by the publishing house Tusquets Editores, shows this. It was his first book to feature agent Mendieta. Early in the novel, the protagonist goes to the site where a corpse wrapped in a blanket has been found:

The blanket was brown and blood-soaked, emblazoned with a stag between two peaks, on it lay the body of a man, forty-five or fifty years old, the detective calculated, five foot nine, Versace shirt, barefoot, castrated, and with a bullet in his heart. One of the officers scouring the place returned with an ostrich-leather cowboy boot, Mendieta made a face. Let's hand the case over to Narcotics, he ordered his partner, several cell phones rang out. We don't need his name to know his line of work. Not only did they castrate him, Zelda said, they also cut out his tongue, we haven't found the casings, which makes you think they killed him someplace and brought him here. It makes no difference, any case that involves narcos has already been solved.[5]

The man found wrapped in a blanket wears the standard clothing of narco mythology (Versace shirt, ostrich-skin boots) and the violence of the trade is manifested on his body (detached genitalia and tongue, a coup de grâce to the heart). The corpse here is not the metonymy of the narco but instead is the condition of the narco's possibility. The corpse creates the narco's very existence. The mutilated body is the most tangible manifestation of a phenomenon that would hardly be recognizable if it wasn't for these violent forms of its representation. The reader needs no more information to conclude he was a narco, and along with Mendieta, deems it unnecessary to investigate any longer. The case has been solved without even the victim's name being known: He is, obviously, a narco executed by other narcos.

Toward the end of the novel, another narco, executed and wrapped in a blanket, seems to have bought his clothing from the same store as the other one: "Garza lay riddled with bullets in his Versace shirt and his ostrich-leather belt."[6] The novel ends with two more executions that hitmen carry out as if following the same instruction manual: "two unfamiliar faces came in, they looked sunburned, one was carrying an AK. I'll get the blankets, the other grumbled as he climbed the stairs to the second floor where the bedroom had to be."[7] Alive, the narcos imagined by Mendoza are unrecognizable from each other: "The bodyguards, two guys about thirty years old, Versace shirts, gold chains, baseball caps, were leaning against their black dual-cab Lobo. They must buy them by the lot, the detective thought."[8] Perhaps unintentionally, even the agent Mendieta seems to criticize the cliché of the narcos always wearing the same clothes and driving the same trucks in novels. Whether the reader is aware or not is irrelevant: the universal traits of narcos, alive or dead, are repeated in the journalistic chronicles of Diego Osorno, Anabel Hernández, and Alejandro Almazán; and in films such as *El Infierno* (2010)—or in *Saving Private Pérez* (2011) though as an intelligent parody—, in television series such as *Narcos* (2015), in the drug ballads of Los Tigres del Norte, and even in Teresa Margolles's supposedly sophisticated conceptual art.[9] Any narco is all narcos.

Another crime in the novel, and the core of *Silver Bullets*, echoes Elmer Mendoza's problematic view. Bruno Canizales, son of the former Secretariat of Agriculture who is running for president, is shot in the head with a silver bullet which is, as recalled in the novel, what is usually used to kill werewolves and vampires according to European folklore. Noting the bizarreness of the crime, Mendieta's partner, Gris Toledo, hypothesizes about the murderer's profile: "You know what I think, only the narcos could use silver bullets, if they put diamonds in their teeth and wear those bizarre jewels, why wouldn't they use silver bullets?"[10] The question that Agent Toledo puts forth is less the result of a brilliant detective deduction and more the most basic popular image of narcos in Mexico. Without police training, it will make sense to most readers to assume that narcos are capable of using silver bullets and firing solid gold pistols all the while grinning with diamond-encrusted teeth. So obvious is this image that Mendoza uses it as a strategy to make the reader doubt the very identity of the possible murderer.

The novel, however, ends in an even more absurd way: a couple admits to having killed Canizales in an unimaginable plot of insatiable sexual appetite, a tone that borders on homophobia: the son of the presidential hopeful, frequent participant in sexual roleplaying encounters, and fascinated by the idea of dying from a silver bullet, is murdered by his own sexual partners. The novel ends up contradicting its own narrative logic when Samantha Valdés, daughter of the powerful drug lord, Marcelo Valdés, avenges the death of Bruno Canizales (who had been her partner) by ordering the murder of those responsible despite the fact that at the beginning of the novel she herself had considered assassinating Canizales.

The novels of Elmer Mendoza, like many famous Mexican writers who address the issue of drug trafficking, were deeply affected by the unprecedented success of *La reina del sur* (*The Queen of the South*, 2002), written by Spaniard Arturo Pérez Reverte. The incredible story of a beautiful Sinaloan woman who goes from being the lover of a local drug dealer to commanding her own international drug cartel excited Mexican novelists who were willing to exploit the subject without having to worry about narrative or conceptual limits. The novels written after *The Queen of the South* set out to reproduce a character as attractive and fantastical as Pérez Reverte's, deliberately imitating the most outrageous aspects of the supposed narcos. Faithfulness to the formula established by Perez Reverte yielded success for numerous novels published in that next decade: Yuri Herrera tells the story of a drug ballad composer and mythological "lord" of narcos in

Trabajos del reino (*Kingdom Cons*, 2004); Heriberto Yépez invents a new type of drug for his violent and marginalized city in *Al otro lado* (On the other side, 2008); Orfa Alarcón tells, to the rhythm of reggaeton, of the criminal education of a young lover of a hitman in *Perra Brava* (Brave bitch, 2010); Bernardo "Bef" Fernández follows the life of a privileged Mexican woman who stops her art studies abroad to inherit a drug cartel in *Hielo Negro* (Black ice, 2011).

In his review of Black Ice, the critic Geney Beltrán Félix stresses the structural contradiction of this type of crime novel: "it seems that certain authors, while demanding artistic status for themselves, do not find it unworthy to perpetrate books that reinforce macho stereotypes. They use language poorly and recycle narrative conventions that reduce the vision of reality."[11] This can also be said about the imagined biography of a powerful drug lord named "El Chalo Gaitán" in *El Más Buscado* (The most wanted, 2012) by Alejandro Almazán. The historian Froylán Enciso offers an ambiguous compliment about these types of novels: "when it comes down to it, we need to admit that we like narco-mythology and power, and Alex [Almazán] knows how to feed that guilty pleasure."[12]

In certain novels written before the enormous influence of Perez Reverte's established formula, the mythological characterization was decidedly absent. This is partly due to the fact that, before *The Queen of the South*, the narco theme enjoyed dubious prestige in the literary world. The image of the drug trafficker, originally associated with the unstable and rural states of northern Mexico, for decades was a motif mostly exploited only by low-budget action films, often starring the legendary brothers Mario and Fernando Almada, and by popular northern music such as the band Los Tigres del Norte. But the absence of a narco mythology in these novels is compensated for in other ways. Until *The Queen of the South* turned the subject into a profitable literary motif that relocated the narco to an urban and cosmopolitan context of upper-middle-class interest, the writers used multiple high-brow references to validate the narco in their novels. In numerous works about drug trafficking, quotes from canonical authors are strewn throughout the novels to validate police detective plots adapted to a Mexican environment, most of the time in northern cities like Culiacán, Tijuana, or Ciudad Juárez.

Such is the case in *Mi nombre es Casablanca* (My name is Casablanca, 2003) by Juan José Rodríguez. Although it manages to demythologize its drug trafficking characters, it transfers that need for mythology to its canonical crime novel and film references. The beginning of the novel is a perfect example. While arresting a criminal, a character cleverly asks the protagonist, Agent Luis Ayala Marsella, an agent with the public ministry: "Have you read *The Godfather*?" As the investigation of a series of seemingly unrelated murders unfolds, Agent Marsella constantly references famous police mystery novels, mentioning the works of Arthur Conan Doyle, Agatha Christie, and Mario Puzo. Also significant is the emphasis placed on famous US mafia films such as *The Godfather* and *Goodfellas*, as well as the US espionage film, *Casablanca*, which the novel gets its title from. These references are used in the novel as narrative markers that distinguish criminals with ethical codes (*The Godfather* and *Casablanca*) from those with a greater propensity for unscrupulous brutality (*Goodfellas*). At the same time, such references allow the Mexican author to establish a link between his distinguished mentions and his novel, as if this is the only way his story could be considered high literature.

One should contrast the use of these references with how Rodríguez demythologizes his narco characters. When the murders commence, Marsella meets with the bosses of the two main drug trafficking groups, who at no time call themselves cartels. The first of the two, Don Armando Ibarra Borbón, identifies himself as a humble country man: "The men of this profession, before having trucks or airplanes, distributed milk on horseback, oak firewood, or marijuana in sacks."[13] At the dealer's property, as Marsella notes, there are no weapons or threatening bodyguards in sight. And even though his garage is filled with luxury cars (including the obligatory Lobo truck from *Silver Bullets*), the drug dealing rancher prefers a small, beat-up Nissan pickup. Ibarra Borbón explains: "I like it. It's comfortable, doesn't need a lot of gas, and is unassuming. Whenever I go out with a friend, nobody looks at me. They think I'm a vender heading to the market, discretion is vital."[14] In contrast, the other drug trafficking group's boss, Don Genaro Barreto, does want to live the high life, and has invested large amounts of money toward an expensive art collection. But, as Marsella notes, his terrible taste and ignorance have led him to buy counterfeit masterpieces, such as the painting of a geometric apple "signed by a painter named Pissaco."[15] Among these humorous aspects, however, Rodríguez is careful not to make a caricature out of him. He lives in an understated and quietly built house "thanks to the prudence of a young architect from Monterrey, who didn't ruin it with the typical domes and glass used in the area."[16] Between these two characters, Rodríguez makes a realistic portrait of the common drug trafficker: men with little education, originating from rural communities who maintain their rustic way of life, as in the case of Ibarra Borbón, or like Don Genaro Barreto, who questionably aspire toward a new life of high class.

Another of the novel's important achievements is the intimate relationship portrayed between organized crime and the police department. Marsella knows the two bosses closely and is able to locate them at any given moment, establishing a cordial relationship and relative trust between the men. The agent notes that the drug traffickers do not intend to "confront the whole system" by breaking "the rules of the game."[17] By mentioning "the system" Marsella understands that, sooner or later, the will of official power is imposed on organized crime. We also see this when Agent Marsella tells Jorge Maytorena, gunman for Don Armando Ibarra Borbón, a story about the legendary US policeman Elliot Ness devastating the poorest part of a city to arrest a serial murderer. By telling him that, Marsella sends a tacit warning to the traffickers that, if they don't comply, "the institutional power will deal with them accordingly: review bank accounts, make arrests, all the machinery of the Mexican system, Interpol, or whoever is close to the shooting."[18]

Although *My Name is Casablanca* was published a year after *The Queen of the South*, it is clear that the mythological appeal of the latter did not in any way influence the writing of Juan José Rodríguez. However, also evident is the fact that the novel cannot completely avoid the common pitfalls that come with representing the drug trafficking world: the person who ends up responsible for the apparently random crimes is a powerful Colombian drug dealer who tries to create a war between the two drug trafficking groups in order to take control of the Sinaloa plaza. Here, Rodríguez includes the typical plot device of the canonical crime novels: the psychopath with a brilliant criminal mind who, as in Conan Doyle's novels, is the only one equal to a detective of the stature of Sherlock Holmes. The Colombian narco explains to Marsella how each one of the murders symbolizes a chess piece: among the victims are construction workers who symbolize pawns, burning castles (rooks), and slaughtered knights. Unbeknownst to him, Marsella is in the center of the board representing the bishop. This fantastical criminal character who lacks the depth of all the other characters is, in part, the effect of a certain discourse on drug trafficking that not even such an intelligently thought-out novel like this one managed to avoid. The absolute evil of this character only allows an oversimplified image of good and evil that the novel had skillfully managed to avoid until this character's appearance. The Colombian narco is somehow more interested in a complex police detective plot than in the success of his drug business. Predictably, the narco is killed by a police raid after a stripper tells the police that Marsella and other agents were kidnapped. The novel weakens its achievements with its hurried, action-packed outcome, more typical of an Almada brothers film than the carefully constructed novel it had been up that point. In the end, the heroic Agent Marsella re-establishes the social order ruined by the mad criminal genius, defeated not by the persistent intelligence work of the "Mexican system," but by a stripper's well-timed glance as she somehow managed to stay alert while dancing nude in a nightclub.

Beyond the problematic narco representations discussed so far, it is important to consider the notable exceptions of a few writers who have managed to critically address the issue. I refer in particular to Víctor Hugo Rascón Banda (1948–2008), César López Cuadras (1951–2013), Daniel Sada (1953–2011), Roberto Bolaño (1953–2003) and Juan Villoro (1956), whose works I will discuss in detail in the following chapters. For now, it is imperative to point out that the work of these writers has initiated a valuable critical discussion in Mexico that, although infrequent and anomalous, has allowed us to reformulate our literary conception of the narco. Despite this, the persistent narco mythology in most of the crime novels that I have discussed in this essay still dominates the literary world. This is the direct result of the discourse that has permeated society for decades, which positions organized crime as an enemy that permanently challenges state sovereignty with the latent threat of a post-political interregnum. This narrative, as the work of Luis Astorga shows, originated in an ideological matrix constructed by the same state that, "with pretensions of universality," imposes one definitive meaning onto the narco, creating the basic coordinates of its representation by *inventing* said mythology.[19] Similarly, Fernando Escalante Gonzalbo points to this state-sanctioned language as the power behind a "'standard knowledge' of organized crime, capable of explaining the whole process, every event, with two or three easily understandable broad strokes."[20] This official monopoly on the discourse of the narco is possible because the history of drug trafficking in Mexico is derived from the history of state prohibition. In other words, state prohibition is the condition of possibility for the existence and development of organized crime; all the more reason for the state to invent the language we use to describe it. Astorga has aptly documented how the Mexican state disciplined and subordinated criminal organizations during the second half of the twentieth century, forcing them to operate under the control of the Institutional Revolutionary Party (PRI) until the mid-1990s. With drug trafficking deemed a national security issue under absolute state control, the military and police conceived of a smooth and orderly drug trafficking system with a reduced rate of violence.

With the fall of the PRI, the police state was gradually dismantled during Vicente Fox's presidency, whose inability to articulate a national security policy allowed new criminal associations between governors, local businessmen, and drug traffickers in states such as Chihuahua, Michoacán, Nuevo León, and Tamaulipas. It was in this context that during Felipe Calderón's presidency, the so-called "War on Drugs" was put into place. To understand Calderón's crusade, I return to the theory of sovereignty laid out by the German political theorist Carl Schmitt. Correcting Max Weber and his influential definition of the state as the "human community that (successfully) claims the monopoly of the legitimate use of violence within a given territory," Schmitt explains that the state actually holds the monopoly of the *exception*, which he defined:

> not as the monopoly to coerce or rule, but as the monopoly to decide. The exception reveals most clearly the essence of the state's authority. The decision parts here from the legal norm, and (to formulate it paradoxically) authority proves that to produce law it need not be based on law.[21]

The unprecedented levels of violence in Mexico during Calderón's presidency, especially in the north, must be understood as a desperate attempt to reclaim state sovereignty. Calderón attempted to discipline the criminal groups working within state power structures who had established their own exceptions and self-regulation independent of the federal government. And although several researchers inside and outside Mexico speak of a "failed state," Escalante Gonzalbo affirms that the most recent national security policies in both Mexico and the United States have created state disciplinary controls that are, in fact, mightier than ever. This point demands a careful re-reading of the Schmittean idea and a decisive caveat in the face of the more radical currents of post-political thought. Drug trafficking is frequently imagined as an illicit activity derived from a form of global capitalism that has transcended national borders. Echoing neoconservative arguments in books such as Francis Fukuyama's *The End of History and The Last Man*, it is too easily thought that the narco, like transnational capitalism, has triumphed over all state control. But let us remember that even Fukuyama has already distanced himself from his celebration of the free market, considering in *The Origins of Political Order* that his claim of a supposed "twilight of sovereignty" as a result of globalization is simply "an exaggeration."[22] The state's sovereignty over the narco, I want to stress, is far from going away.

At the beginning of 2014, three events separated by a few days allow me to justify the previous point. Taken together, these events hinted at the way in which the narco continues to be an object of official power. First, on

February 13 of that year, *Time* magazine put President Enrique Peña Nieto on the cover of its international edition with the headline, "Saving Mexico," giving him credit for "sweeping reforms [that] have changed the narrative in his narco-stained nation."[23] Just six days later, President Barack Obama held a private meeting with Peña Nieto in Mexico during the North American Leaders Summit. In a press conference on February 19, Obama praised the same reforms as *Time* magazine, saying he was "very interested in hearing President Peña Nieto's strategies as he embarks on dealing with some of the reforms in the criminal justice system and around security issues."[24] Three days later, these security issues would materialize with irrefutable effectiveness: on the morning of February 22, Mexican Navy troops and Federal Police officers arrested Joaquín "El Chapo" Guzmán, head of the Sinaloa cartel who, if we trust the United States and Mexico authorities, led a multi-million dollar global empire with a presence in fifty-four countries. And although, according to diplomatic cables leaked to the media, El Chapo usually surrounded himself with three hundred guards for his protection, he was arrested without a single shot. This is how the surprised *New York Times* correspondents state it:

> This time Mr. Guzmán . . . did not slip out a door, disappear into the famed mountains around his northwest Mexico home, or prove to be absent, as he had in so many previous attempts to apprehend him. He apparently had no time to reach for the arsenal of guns and grenades he had amassed or dash into a storm drain or tunnel, as authorities said he recently did minutes ahead of pursuers.[25]

Rather than speculate, as the vast majority of researchers and journalists did at the time, on an unlikely arrest of a body double or on his successor in the cartel, it is necessary to understand that El Chapo's capture—the second of three arrests until his extradition to the United States—was a clear political demonstration of the sovereignty of the state over criminal organizations.

The rise and fall of the Zetas or the armed conflict in the Tierra Caliente ("hot land," an area of Mexico comprised of parts of Guerrero, Michoacán, and the State of Mexico) must be understood in the same way. As with El Chapo, Heriberto Lazcano, the vicious boss of the Zetas, was assassinated in October 2012 while watching a baseball game in the company of a bodyguard. In the case of Michoacán, the defeat of the criminal group called the Knights Templar and the conversion of community self-defense groups into a rural police force by order of the federal government is recognized by two *Proceso* magazine covers. The first headline on January 12, 2014, describes

the Michoacán conflict as "Peña Nieto's War," specifying the federal government's manipulation of the self-defense groups to decimate organized crime
and local power. The second headline, on May 18, 2014, eloquently summarizes the conclusion of this episode just fifteen months after it began: "The
Domesticated Self-Defense Groups." Here we see what depoliticized crime
novels miss the most: that the narco is reducible to state security strategies.
The state is the *true* power—both legal and illegal in a country that exists
in a permanent state of exception—that we must put to the test. To do this
we must set aside the endless repetition of absurd stories about the rise and
fall of presumed drug lords, their cartels, and their plazas. Misunderstand-
ing and not accepting this assertion prevents us from articulating an effective critique of the official power, whose criminal brutality is hidden in the
false narrative of the cartels and their supposed endless reign.

I return to Yescka's *Last Supper* and now find a different and disturbing
new reading: the faceless narco in the place of Christ is the archetype of *all*
the narcos that have been manufactured by official power over the decades.
His false apostles will remain hidden in the background so they can take
advantage of their so-called lord's martyrdom. They will turn him in and
then deny it; they will let him be crucified. After his most humiliating torture and death, his apostles will forever preach the victory of his resur-
rection and his implausible triumph over Caesar and the Roman Empire,
over all Caesars and all empires. The operational fable of drug trafficking in
Mexico is that only literal and symbolic sacrifice means victory, and along
with it comes the inexhaustible genealogy of drug lords who die and rein-
carnate as is required by the state. It is also the inexhaustible source of most
narco noir novels. But the face of the narco remains anonymous because
he is the metaphor for all the narcos who can and will indistinctly occupy
the place in the narrative that already predisposes his rise and fall. Knowing the true identity of that forever resurrected corpse is the still-waiting
cry for our best literature yet.

NEUTRALIZED CHRONICLES: THE JOURNALISTIC IMAGINARY ON DRUG TRAFFICKING

In the first decade of the twentieth century, a Mexican national debate crys-
talized over an alleged crisis of violence that, according to the federal government, affected entire cities in which different forms of organized crime
had been established. The question of drug trafficking took over the popular
imagination, which saw the issue traditionally belonging to the rural areas
in the north of the country with little relevance to the large urban centers,

now gained traction in cities such as Monterrey, Tijuana, Culiacán, and Ciudad Juárez. At the end of the 2010s, works on drug trafficking appeared in practically all disciplines. Along with numerous novels, films, songs, and conceptual art, books of journalistic chronicles such as *El cártel de Sinaloa* (The Sinaloa cartel, 2009) by Diego Enrique Osorno, *Los señores del narco* (*Narcoland*, 2010) by Anabel Hernández, and *Huesos en el desierto* (Bones in the desert, 2002) and *El hombre sin cabeza* (The headless man, 2009) by Sergio González Rodríguez—among the most visible—occupied a central place on the subject. Among this generous output, what has been called "narrative journalism" has had particular relevance as a device of cultural interpretation in the articulation of strategies for representing the current violence.

I now propose to review these journalistic forms as intellectual contributions that, in more than one way, have repositioned the coordinates of the analytical discourse regarding violence in Mexico, with profound repercussions in the field of contemporary cultural production. In my analysis, journalistic chronicles will read as a symptom of a complex epistemological problem that neutralizes journalism in general, turning it into the source of the dominant imaginary about violence. Finally, I will point out how the work of journalists such as Diego Osorno, Anabel Hernández, Sergio González Rodríguez, and Alejandro Almazán, among others, is founded on a radical practice of cultural interpretation that diminishes our understanding of the historical transformations of the official discourse of violence that depoliticizes the most urgent discussions related to social inequality, the criminalization of poverty, and the advent of police discipline that manifests itself in a permanent state of exception unprecedented in the history of modern Mexico. Thus, this exercise of journalistic chronicle has direct implications on the systems of representation of organized crime in general, since it is assumed to be the authentic access material to the real narco that appears in the symbolic works of novelists, musicians, filmmakers, and conceptual artists who assimilate that mythological and depoliticized condition of the dominant imaginary about drug traffickers.

The Invention of the National Security Crisis

Before examining the limitations of narrative journalism, it is important to understand that the prevailing discourse of violence in the dominant imagery of cultural production in the last decade is of recent invention. As explained by Brian Bow and Arturo Santa-Cruz, national security had not historically been a prominent issue in modern Mexico because, "[through] most of the post-revolutionary period, the security of the nation was seen to be essentially equivalent to the security of the ruling regime."[26] Without substantial domestic controversy and with the Army subordinate to political power, during the seven decades of successive PRI governments, "there was no perceived internal enemy to resist."[27] Of course, during the turbulent years from 1968 to 1971 the state attacked different radical leftist groups, student resistance, and rural educator and peasant movements, but that violence was not laid out as a permanent strategy of social disciplinary control, but as contingent actions whose logic was essentially political. It is by no means my intention here to minimize the extermination strategy and brutality conducted by the Mexican state and police agencies such as the Federal Security Directorate (DFS) between the late 1960s and early 1970s that left a catastrophic death toll. My purpose here is rather to point out the decidedly political condition of state violence at the time. This is how Carlos Montemayor's analysis explains it:

> State violence in the Mexican social movements of the twentieth century was deployed in a wide range of regions and social sectors all in the context of prevention, containment, repression or persecution of social nonconformity, as well as channeling against vulnerable social groups, unions, isolated regions, communities, political parties, subversive movements, and working-class demonstrations.[28]

The main point to understand here is that state violence, especially in the sixties, seventies, and eighties, was carried out by a repressive apparatus under the aegis of political conflicts that threatened the integrity of the ruling elite. In other words, until the mid-1990s the Mexican state confronted domestic conflicts as problems of opposition and resistance with a strictly political root, not as the permanent threat and opposition to the state that organized crime now represents. Thus, as the prominent journalist Julio Scherer records, the student and guerrilla movements were accused of "social dissolution," as codified by the Federal Criminal Code during Manuel Ávila Camacho's presidency in the middle of World War II, or, as Carlos Monsiváis recalls—they were accused of being "subversives" in the context of the Cold War.[29]

The landmarks of late-twentieth-century Mexico exist in the same political vein: the armed uprising of the Zapatista Army of National Liberation (EZLN) in Chiapas and its protest of social injustice and historical marginalization of the indigenous communities excluded by the PRI project of modernization; the high-profile assassinations of Cardinal Juan Jesús

Posadas Ocampo in 1993; and then of presidential candidate, Luis Donaldo Colosio and secretary-general of the PRI, José Francisco Ruiz Massieu, both in 1994. Even though some attributed the murders to drug trafficking organizations, an evident political undertone prevailed upon any other hypothesis that could explain the crimes. And finally, the "December mistakes"—so-called for Carlos Salinas de Gortari's accusation that Ernesto Zedillo's policies were at fault for the deep 1994 economic crisis that led to the drastic devaluation of the Mexican peso. Not only was he issue of drug trafficking never mentioned in the context of these political events as a national emergency, but at the time had even been, as Luis Astorga notes, "a protected phenomenon that developed from different spheres of political and police power as part of a power structure, but in a subordinate position, and whose main actors were initially excluded from political power."[30] In other words, while the most shocking problems faced by the state during the 1990s were political in nature, the drug trade had been politically subdued and neutralized by the ruling class.

Astorga explains that the incorporation of a security agenda in Mexico responded to the influence of US hegemony, which designated drug trafficking as a threat to national security in 1986, with a presidential directive signed by Ronald Reagan. The first major effect of this hegemony was the disappearance of the Federal Security Directorate (DFS), which President Miguel de la Madrid (1982–1988) considered a "secret police."[31] In 1989, the Center for Investigation and National Security (CISEN) was created in its place during the first year of President Carlos Salinas de Gortari's presidency (1988–1994). This agency had the key role of implementing the US agenda, adopting the discourse that began thinking of "cartels" as threats to national security.[32] And although the latter chose not to do so, Ernesto Zedillo's (1994–2000) government began to gradually use the armed forces to eradicate drug trafficking. This transformation process culminated with the presidency of Vicente Fox (2000–2006): during his administration, under pressure applied by the US government in the post–September 11 geopolitical landscape, the Mexican state openly adopted a national security policy that placed organized crime at the center of a governability crisis that called for immediate action. Reproducing disciplinary strategies first on the narco and later on terrorism and immigration in the United States, drug trafficking in Mexico was laid out as the greatest threat to national sovereignty. Fox's transition team had initially considered drug trafficking "purely a police matter" which, unlike the case in Colombia, had neither the capacity nor the intention to destabilize the state.[33] However, and after a series of high-level meetings with US officials, Adolfo Aguilar

Zinser, then National Security Adviser—a position created by the Fox presidency—began to refer to the narco without mentioning "the links between PRI political groups and traffickers" and instead highlighted the alleged threat to national sovereignty that, according to the new government, drug trafficking now implicated.[34]

This security transformation produced two effects of radical importance: first, it allowed the depoliticization of immediate domestic conflicts such as marked economic and social inequality, endemic government corruption or the creation of private fortunes as a result of neoliberal policy; and second, it made the official discourse turn toward a supposed permanent emergency independent of any specific political coordinates of organized crime. The narco then became a primary object of national security: a permanent enemy, without real political objectives, its only interest being economic domination through illegality and violence. In this way, the state conveniently stopped recognizing the political specificity of the opposition and resistance movements and instead constructed and disseminated national security discourses of organized crime groups that supposedly threaten civil society in general and not just the government elite. In other words, the state came up with a national security strategy *devoid of political content* in order to consider political grievances no longer relevant.

This new definition of the narco, as we know, did not produce the violent military and police mobilizations in urban areas of the country, but Felipe Calderón's (2006–2012) government security strategy did. The state of exception created by Calderón between 2006 and 2012 was justified by his government as a reaction to an alleged escalation of violence attributed to organized crime. But, as Fernando Escalante Gonzalbo demonstrates, homicide rates nationwide had consistently shifted toward a "slow and steady decline" during the twenty years prior to Calderón's anti-drug strategy.[35] For this reason, the "explanation of 1990s largescale violence was, according to the numbers we know, a fantasy."[36] Escalante Gonzalbo sees this false national security discourse as the articulation of a "phantom crime," a phenomenon "made largely of inventions, prejudices, imaginations, unfounded conjectures, incomplete, impossible to verify, or directly false information."[37] Calderón's strategy shows a causal relationship different from the one he publicly defended. Not only was the escalation of violence attributed to drug trafficking nonexistent, but the decline in the homicide rate sustained for two decades was reversed in the exact areas where the Army and Federal Police were sent to fight cartels, according to the new federal strategy. The total number of murders across the country during his government alone is staggering: 121,683 murders recorded by the National

Institute of Statistics and Geography (INEGI)—more than four times the number of victims caused by the "dirty war" of Argentina's military dictatorships during the 1970s and 1980s—and almost 30,000 disappeared persons registered by the Secretariat of the Interior.

At the discursive level, the notion of the narco in Mexico as a real threat to the state and national security has permeated the national imagination. Astorga observes: "The invention of a monolithic enemy, organized hierarchically, with a bureaucratic and economic rationality, which dominates all phases of the trade and is at least in a position to control the market and prices, fascinated politicians, police, and journalists."[38] When that fascination became the hegemonic discourse, the question of national security was justified, and since then has conditioned, a priori, all reflection on drug trafficking—especially in journalism.

The Political Neutralization of the Narrative Journalism

As in practically all disciplines that approach the drug trafficking phenomenon in Mexico, journalism is deeply mediated by hegemonic discourses laid out by official power. Before referring to the case of Sergio González Rodríguez, Alejandro Almazán, Diego Enrique Osorno, or Anabel Hernández, it should be noted that the depoliticization found in narco chronicles is also present in the work of the most experienced and established journalists, even those with great political commitments. Perhaps the most visible example can be seen in the works of Carlos Monsiváis. As Ricardo Gutiérrez Mouat points out, the works on violence published by Monsiváis at the end of the 1990s "represent a new chapter of secular confrontation in Latin America between the intellectual and violence," whose objective is to intervene in the most urgent sociopolitical processes of the immediate present with the repressive force of the state as the central problem.[39] In a text published in 1999, for example, Monsiváis includes in his definition of urban violence:

> conflicts, tragedies, extreme behaviors caused by the crisis of the rule of law, the perpetual outbreak—economic, social and demographic—of cities, and the impossibility of effective public security, either due to the inefficiency of the groups in charge or by the prevailing "feudalization" of neighborhoods. Urban violence is the wide spectrum of criminal situations, exercises of male supremacy, ignorance and contempt for human rights, traditions of terrified indifference to abuse of power, wild anarchy and ignorance of the norm.[40]

This broad definition highlights the intrinsic systemic nature of violence, where common crime is aggravated by specific political, economic, and cultural conditions. In 2013, however, when he reissued his book *Los mil y un velorios: Crónica de la nota roja*, (The thousand and one wakes: A chronicle of crime news in Mexico) Monsiváis's analysis appears mediated by the prevailing official discourse that, by then, had already consolidated the national security agenda to define drug trafficking as the greatest criminal emergency in Mexico. Monsiváis writes: "Suddenly, drug trafficking is the great sideshow that society views with terror and morbidity, with relief ('they didn't kill me today') and depression ('today they kept killing')."[41] He continues: "Since the 1990s the presumption of a narco-state has grown in the midst of a circular journey from fear to terror, from suspicion to panic, from resignation to paranoia."[42] And although at times the text indicates the corrupt relationship between the state and drug trafficking groups, Monsiváis mainly limits himself to the impression of a national emergency solely carried out by the drug traffickers: "War breaks out between the cartels at a very high cost of lives"; "The groups are declared: the Zetas, the Familia Michoacana, the Gulf Cartel, La Línea"; "Three years of confrontations between narcos and the Army, between narcos and the Federal Police, between narcos and the local police."[43] The narrative exhibited by Monsiváis coincides with the official version, the repeated explanation that President Calderón offered about the escalation of murders during his term: "The territorial dispute is the factor that triggers the wave of homicides and violence in Mexico and that continues to this day."[44] At this point the central problem of narco chronicles in Mexico appears more clearly: it deals with texts dependent on official sources that circulate a narrative originally configured by and disseminated from multiple state agencies and spokespersons, assimilated without criticism by the vast majority of the media and later reiterated by the fields of cultural production, especially by television, cinema, music, and literature.

According to Susana Rotker, since the end of the nineteenth century the "definition of the journalistic chronicle genre as a meeting place for literary and journalistic discourse is as central to the renewal of Latin American prose as the modernists."[45] But, as Rotker also advises, privileging the narrative resources of the chronicle from a subjective point of view certainly did not imply that the genre was politically neutral, but rather that it made a point to distinguish itself from strict news reportage. As the wave of New Journalism emerged in the United States with work from journalists and writers such as Truman Capote, Norman Mailer, and Gay Talese, among others, the use of literary sources reappears with greater strength and from a more intimate and personal point of view. However, as Tom Wolfe emphasizes, the innovation was not only in the technique, but in the reporting procedures themselves:

> I'm sure that others who were experimenting with magazine articles, such as Talese, began to feel the same way. We were moving beyond the conventional limits of journalism, but not merely in terms of technique. The kind of reporting we were doing struck us as far more ambitious, too. It was more intense, more detailed, and certainly more time-consuming than anything that newspaper or magazine reporters, including investigative reporters, were accustomed to. We developed the habit of staying with the people we were writing about for days at a time, weeks in some cases. We had to gather all the material the conventional journalist was after—and then keep going.[46]

In Mexico, the tradition of journalistic chronicles has evolved by combining the founding legacy of the modernist chronicle with the subsequent influence of US New Journalism. In the 1970s, journalistic chronicles reached a new level due to the relevant political agency in the works of figures like José Pagés Llergo (founder of *Siempre!* Magazine), Julio Scherer (founder of *Proceso* magazine), Miguel Ángel Granados Chapa, Elena Poniatowska, and Carlos Monsiváis, among others. It goes without saying that without the sharp critical power of this journalism we wouldn't have such an understanding of the political crises of the sixties, seventies, and eighties—from official responsibility for the Tlatelolco massacre of 1968, the evolution and debacle of undemocratic presidentialism and centralism, to the official incompetence surrounding the 1985 earthquake. The influence of this narrative journalism can clearly be seen in the recent work of chroniclers born in the second half of the twentieth century; notably José Joaquín Blanco, Juan Villoro, and Fabrizio Mejía Madrid, who have absorbed the critical and political aim of those before them. Villoro, for example, defines the chronicle as a form that is as "[c]ommitted to the facts as it is to the truth," while for Mejía Madrid, the chronicle represents "the meeting of a look and a date, a mood with the flow of time."[47] Both of them establish a demand for rigor and commitment to the immediate present regardless of the formal techniques of their chronicles.

Mediated by the damaging hegemonic discourse that relocates drug trafficking to the center of a national security crisis, the narco chronicle of the last two decades, however, departs from the critical tradition of journalism that historically confronted the official power of Mexico. Instead, the narco chronicle hinges on a politically configured official discourse and is not the result of an independent journalistic process. When examining a subject whose epistemological coordinates have been shaped by the state, this type of chronicle is automatically limited to the analysis of the alleged cartels as the main factor of crime, completely ignoring the historical relationship between the political class and organized crime.

The neutralization of the narco chronicle is thus the effect derived from a habitus, which, according to the sociologist Pierre Bourdieu, is a system of principles that generate and organize certain practices and forms of representation in a given environment. This habitus essentially renounces an analytical process to comprehend for the conditions of the possibility of the narco—in particular its economic existence disciplined by a state geopolitics. The journalistic problem then lies in what Bourdieu conceptualized as a form of "state thinking." That is, the epistemological limitation that explains why "the very structures of consciousness by which we construct the social world and the particular object that is the state, are very likely the product of the state itself."[48] Bourdieu's analysis expands Max Weber's famous definition by considering the state as the "monopoly of legitimate physical *and symbolic* violence, inasmuch as the monopoly of symbolic violence is the condition for possession of the exercise of physical violence itself."[49] When examining Bourdieu's influence in Latin America, Mabel Moraña highlights how this state monopoly on symbolic violence penetrates all social spaces, from the domestic environment to the work place, to the cultural productions and the institutions that normalize citizen space. Moraña explains:

> As already indicated, for its implementation, symbolic violence often relies on the acquiescence and loyalty of the dominated to the dominator and is supported, in many cases, by the fact that both share the same form of knowledge and interpretation of social reality that prevents a free thought in the one who is subjected to the power of the strongest.[50]

In this point, Moraña notes how, despite admitting to the possibility of artistic resistance to the state monopoly of symbolic violence, Bourdieu is rather pessimistic, considering the media as a "mechanism of oppression and social domination."[51]

In the same way, Jesús Martín Barbero analyzes the ideological function of the media and recalls the crucial role it played in different historical transformations of modern societies. Not only did the media fail to critically report on the political processes of each era, but they were instrumental in the very construction of those exact processes. With its apparent neutral language, the media operated—and continues to operate—as a representation of immediate reality even though it conceals the reality with previously established meanings. Explains Martín Barbero:

> I refer to "formulas" by the means of which words give meaning regardless of context or content. The contexts are always particular, partial, temporary; they are the forms, or rather the formulas of jargon that introduce the claim of universality, of being outside of space and time. The formulas are "clean" with the purity provided by the new secularized religion of "objectivity." *The conversion of form into formula* is the way in which the operation is expressed, the demand that consumption poses in terms of a mass public becomes language: the operation of conformity, trivialization, depoliticization.[52]

The dominant discourse on the narco has produced a formula whose lexicon and designated meaning allow for only one specific narrative. In journalism, as Martín Barbero argues, "meaning does not exist without form," that is, "the form of myth forging history and imposing meaning."[53] We write *drug trafficker, hitman, plaza, war, cartel*; and with those words the same universe of violence, corruption, and power immediately reappears and fills the pages of a novel, newspaper columns, the lyrics of a drug ballad, a narco's clothes in an action movie. The language to describe this reality is unavoidably colonized by that habitus of official origin that can only be cracked on rare occasion.

Without moving toward a critique of the conditioning effects of this power, narco chronicles then operate as a symbolic shift in two directions: first, toward genealogies of drug traffickers and the supposed national security crisis they instigate, a narrative we have seen created and disseminated by official sources; and second, toward a reiteration of the resignified body of the victims and their violence, reducing the complex phenomenon of drug trafficking to an artificial and ahistorical continuity of death and destruction. Both shifts formally maintain the legacy of the modernist chronicle, the combative impulse of Mexican journalism in the second half of the twentieth century, and the literary appeal of US New Journalism, but don't include the political dimension and journalistic rigor of either of them. That being said, I do not intend to argue that narco chronicles completely lack political background, but it's that their critical will, from the outset, appears neutralized by the influence of official discourse on drug trafficking. By focusing the narrative only on the pockets of violence attributed to a permanent cartel war, narco chroniclers only superficially examine the violent and illegal security policies undertaken by the government.

Let us consider the essays of Sergio González Rodríguez, one of the most prominent journalists and intellectuals in Mexico until his sudden death in 2017.[54] His work operates as an exercise in excessive narrative imagination conditioned by the official discourse of that phantom crime ideology promoted by the Mexican state. In González Rodríguez's perspective, violence is not a phenomenon circumscribed by political vectors, but it is reduced to an empty signifier that erases the concrete materiality that produces it. It is this interpretation that gives shape and meaning to his most known texts on violence: *Bones in the Desert* and *The Headless Man*. Critic Ignacio Sánchez Prado points out a difference between these books and the rest of González Rodríguez's work, such as *El centauro en el paisaje* (The centaur in the landscape, 1992), and *De sangre y de sol* (Of blood and sun, 2006). The latter, according to Sánchez Prado, represent "the central nucleus of his work: a cosmopolitan and erudite practice of the essay, which seeks to use a vast and peculiar cultural archive as a repository of languages for the configuration of a contemporaneity whose uncertainty resists representation."[55] On the contrary, I don't consider there to be any substantial difference between González Rodríguez's reflections on violence and the rest of his essay production. Sánchez Prado describes, for example, *The Centaur in the Landscape* as an exploration of "the relationship between the city and literature; the interaction between the sacred and the technical; the relationship between art, memory and desire; and the trope of the monster in connection with modern norms."[56] That same reading can essentially be found in both *Bones in the Desert* and *The Headless Man*. In fact, the biggest problem with these two books is precisely that they are structured like his cultural interpretive essays. By refusing to examine violence in its historical and political immediacy, González Rodríguez writes as if violence were just another cultural object, awaiting another elucidating think piece. After reading any of his books such techniques are recurring and even predictable. On this point, Sánchez Prado is right when he affirms that González Rodríguez's work is "a new affirmation of literature as an epistemologically privileged territory to decipher contemporaneity, given the exhaustion of paradigms that have defined the Mexican intelligentsia since the eighties, in the so-called 'transition to democracy.'"[57] But, rather than just the restoration of literature as a vehicle for the interpretation of violence, González Rodríguez's work assumes the drug phenomenon as an object of cultural significance at the cost of eliminating its political and historical specificity.

Through an artificial connection of meanings extracted from journalism, official records, the memoir, the narrative strategies of the detective novel, and the misreading of multiple historical, economic, literary, and philosophical references, González Rodríguez positioned himself in the literary world as one of the most relevant cultural interpreters of violence in Mexico. His vision appeals, above all, to a certain international audience that reads the works from the Spanish publisher Anagrama, but is also fully in line with the national security discourse promoted by recent government strategies in Mexico. His celebrity is explained by the symbolic prestige of having written two of the most representative books of the change in mentality on the subject of national security. Both *Bones in the Desert* and *The Headless Man* suggest cultural practices supposedly endemic to a lax contemporary society (serial killers, radical gender violence, the rise and dominance of organized crime) that, although intersected tangentially with domestic and global political and economic phenomena, imply a permanent national security threat to the social fabric, its political content having been erased by the ruling elite.

Let's discuss *The Headless Man* for now, as I will take up *Bones in the Desert* later. The catalog of vague anecdotes collected by González Rodríguez only lists drug traffickers identified by the state and whose names we see constantly repeated in the media: "El Chapo" Guzmán, Heriberto Lazcano, the Sinaloa cartel, the Zetas, etc. These references coincide exactly with those provided by the state and, in fact, repeat verbatim the official explanation of what has supposedly happened in Mexico during the first decade of the twentieth century: the country has been taken over by known intruders, drug traffickers, and they are the ones responsible for the wave of violence that President Calderón's security strategy set out to confront. The narrative structure conceived of by González Rodríguez thus produces what appears to function as an intellectual history of beheadings and a more or less journalistic commentary. The focus of the book is the violence related to "the drug trafficking war," a phenomenon that, according to González Rodríguez, "reached its climax here when the remains of dismembered bodies and the beheadings appeared."[58] Without including any journalistic investigation into specific beheadings, the book dwells on the multiple levels of significance that the motif of beheading inspires, producing a web of supplementary explanations ranging from pre-Hispanic witchcraft practices to stories from "the crusades, [King] Richard the Lionheart, and Sultan Saladin."[59]

Dazzled by the "complex" mix of references in the book, writer Bernardo Esquinca notes that being beheaded is, for González Rodríguez, the unequivocal metaphor that indicates how Mexican society "has lost its way in an overstimulating world, where every time it becomes more difficult to separate reality from fiction."[60] Thus, not being able to separate reality from fiction, González Rodríguez's representation of drug trafficking requires supplementing reality with an exercise in narrative fiction that produces two fallacies: the first indicates that drug trafficking operates as an entity *outside* of the state and that the Mexican government is its main enemy, posing as an immediate national security emergency; the second, that in order to understand drug violence one requires a complex theoretical framework of cultural interpretation that goes beyond immediate historical circumstances. Both fallacies produce an emptying of the political that nullifies any critique of the historical causality of the state in relation to drug trafficking.

González Rodríguez's essays are thus problematic based on a double paradox: first, to try to unravel the phenomenon of contemporary violence, what begins as an effort to historicize and document soon reveals itself as an indulgent overinterpretation of those same acts of violence. The different layers of meaning that derive from this overinterpretation are observed as cultural practices throughout history that go beyond the immediate circumstances of drug trafficking in Mexico and that, organized as a fictional narrative, also somehow serve to explain the invention of the guillotine or the letter Z that "a criminal group" marks on the foreheads of its victims, as well as the excessive violence of US soldiers in Vietnam and Iraq.[61] The narrative structure of the essay contradicts itself between an eagerness to describe the actuality of the drug trade and its compulsion to insert itself into a context of global cultural impact.

It is precisely this depoliticization that González Rodríguez carries out in his analysis of violence that allows him to transform the *discontinuity* of history into an imagined *continuity*. Consider the following excerpt from the book:

> Mexican history has three icons linked to decapitation: the *tzomplantli*, the Aztec palisades that held the skulls of victims who were decapitated with obsidian knives and sacrificed to the gods; the mutilated head of the clergyman Miguel Hidalgo y Costilla, who proclaimed war for independence at the beginning of the nineteenth century, which was placed inside an iron cage by the Spanish troops as a lesson to the rebels; the revolutionary bandit Francisco Villa of the last century, whose tomb was violated and his head cut off a few years after his death. It is rumored that the skull is part of a Skull and Bones collection, a university secret society in the United States.

> Or it remains buried in a Mexican mountain. In any case, his memory floats
> around from here to there in the imagination of many.[62]

Here, the Aztec sacrifices, the executions of insurgents in 1810, the assassinations of revolutionaries in 1910, and beheadings attributed to the narco
are all the product of a single impulse for death and destruction that seems
to be intrinsic to the history of Mexico. González Rodríguez, then, must
be the most faithful follower of Octavio Paz's aporia on what he calls "the
double reality" of October 2, 1968, which, consisted of being "a historical
fact" and "also a symbolic acting-out of what could be called our subterra-
nean or invisible history."[63]

In *The Limits of Interpretation*, Umberto Eco argues that one of the most
pernicious patterns of interpretation, which he calls "hermetic semiosis,"
has structured Western thought since the Middle Ages to promote a paradigm of similarity. That is, "the relationships of sympathy that link micro-
cosm and macrocosm to one another. Both a metaphysic and a physic of
universal sympathy must stand upon a semiotics (explicit or implicit) of
similarity."[64] According to Eco, this metaphysics of correspondence is still
active in modern thought in certain contemporary critical theories that
draw reality as an organic system determined by analogy. González Rodríguez's essays resort to similar narrative procedures in their representation
of violence. Due to an overload of analogous meanings, his reflections
work from interpretations of interpretations, producing chains of meanings that distance themselves from the immediacy of the initial references
toward cultural symbols that take on only a remote meaning under the
system of free association that is brought together under the general form
of the essays.

The case of González Rodríguez is certainly unique in that his dual
profile as a journalist and intellectual with international renown is based
on his ability to go beyond the parameters of journalism through literary and philosophical references. But it is this singular international success that has confirmed the profitable value of his journalistic technique.
It is in this same way that the narco chronicles of Diego Enrique Osorno,
Anabel Hernández, Marcela Turati, and Alejandro Almazán appear among
the most visible. The case of the first of them is perhaps the most significant: in his best-known book, *The Sinaloa Cartel*, Osorno recounts the
well-known history of drug trafficking in the "golden triangle" region during prohibition in the first decades of the twentieth century based on the
research of Luis Astorga, among others. When he writes about present-
day drug trafficking in Mexico, however, Osorno faithfully reproduces the

state's account of the supposed national security crisis. In the first chapter of his book, he addresses the generalized violence in the city of Monterrey and writes:

> So far, what seems to best explain the out-of-control situation in Monterrey is what some security advisers that usually visit the official residence of Los Pinos say. In short, that two groups, the Sinaloa Cartel and the Gulf Cartel, began to fight for the city in blood and lead and that in the middle of that battle is everyone from small time drug dealers to politicians who have been overtaken by the tempting cloak of drug trafficking.[65]

By accepting the official explanation of violence, Osorno's book can proceed in only two ways: narratively delving into that alleged cartel struggle and then articulating a critique of the state's strategy to confront it. The main problem is that both routes favor and legitimize the actions of the state in the face of the narco, not only justifying their necessity but also their lack of success—since in the end, the cartels are always imagined to be much more powerful than the state.

To narrate the alleged cartel struggle, Osorno privileges official sources that corroborate the alleged confrontation between drug traffickers following the development of a narrative logic. A significant example illustrates this point: in 2013 Guillermo Valdés Castellanos, director of CISEN for five of the six years of Felipe Calderón's presidency, published the book, *Historia del narcotráfico en México* (History of drug trafficking in Mexico). In the introduction, he notes that the escalation of violence during the Calderón government "has been generated and carried out mainly by criminal organizations that participate in the illegal drug market" and that "there is sufficient evidence of this."[66] To prove this, Valdés claims to have used both official government information and other independent sources that supposedly corroborate his investigation. Among these sources are the renowned work of sociologists such as Luis Astorga and journalists such as Terrence Poppa, whose analysis Valdés accepts and confirms, especially when it comes to the historical account of the relationship between the PRI and narco at that time:

> The plaza does not exist without the complicity of the authorities. It is not just about drug traffickers corrupting police and soldiers, but about a scheme of coexistence of a political system with organized crime, devised, endorsed and operated by high-level federal authorities. Although at the local level the drug lord is untouchable and a public figure who does not hide and can

even be the head of state agency representatives and command over them, he knows that compared to the federal government he is subordinate and his power depends on who maintains the concession of the plaza.[67]

Between 1990 and 2006, however, Valdés records "the disappearance" of political barriers to enter the market, so that "the drug trafficking map spread over more territories of the vast national geography" allowing for "increasingly fragmented organized crime who confronted each other, but also extremely widespread, powerful and violent."[68] This occurred, according to his analysis, for three reasons: 1) the growth and diversification of the consumer market in the United States, 2) the disappearance of the "'board of directors' of drug trafficking under the direction of the Federal Security Directorate," which led to 3) the fragmentation of the "federation," the monopoly of drug lords from Sinaloa headed by Miguel Ángel Félix Gallardo.[69] It is in this context, according to Valdés, that the numerous wars between cartels and their open defiance of the Mexican state take place. The Valdés investigation, however, is based on a deceptive circularity: although he cites academic and journalistic sources outside CISEN, it is important to note that *their* sources were primarily official sources in the first place. Valdés attributes much of his information to the journalistic work of Diego Enrique Osorno, but it is enough to consult the sources of both to note that the information comes from state agencies. When reporting on the first tensions between the Sinaloa cartel and the Zetas, Valdés notes, for example, that Osorno "located three operators of the Sinaloa organization in Tamaulipas who crossed drugs into the territory," but in his book, *The Sinaloa Cartel*, Osorno states that this information comes from the Army and the Attorney General's Office (PGR). The circularity of information has a fundamental political use: it validates the official narrative by attributing it to the supposedly independent reportage of journalists like Osorno, whose work, reducible to the transcription of official reports, becomes an involuntary object of power.[70]

The assimilation of hegemonic discourse in journalism is also visible in the manufacturing of genealogies of drug traffickers that take on a central role within the narrative structures of narco chronicles. The most significant example here is the supposed biography of Joaquín "El Chapo" Guzmán. The works of Anabel Hernández and Alejandro Almazán advance the most recurring theme in narrative journalism about El Chapo. In *Narcoland*, Hernández summarizes this thesis as follows:

> The story of how Joaquín Guzmán Loera became a great drug baron, the king of betrayal and bribery, and the boss of top Federal Police commanders

[. . .] Joaquín Guzmán Loera alone will quit when he feels like it, not when the authorities choose. Some say he is already preparing his exit.[71]

According to Hernández, El Chapo was protected by the Vicente Fox and Felipe Calderón administrations so he could carry out his war with rival cartels. But by doing so, El Chapo was no longer relegated to the subordinate position that the Mexican state historically kept the traffickers to, and instead was in a position of undisputed leadership. His power reached such a degree, "that the AFI [Federal Ministerial Police] began to operate fully as El Chapo's army."[72] In open defiance to official state power and displaying an irrefutable supremacy, Hernández attributes to El Chapo's organization for example, the 2008 plane crash in which then–Minister of the Interior, Juan Camilo Mouriño, died. Hernández concludes that El Chapo and the main bosses of his organization, Ismael "El Mayo" Zambada and Juan José Esparragoza Moreno, "El Azul," "are firmly in control of an empire. Between them they have achieved a virtual monopoly of narcotics trafficking in Mexico and the United States, a dominion based on blood, sweat, and tears."[73]

At first reading, Hernández's work appears to be critical journalism combating official power, but its political neutralization occurs for two reasons: the first is due to its interpretation that categorizes El Chapo's supposed power the same way that the state sources do. Hernández points to El Chapo as one of the main figures responsible for the violence during Calderón's administration in the same way that the former director of CISEN analyzes it. It was exactly this type of analysis that allowed the Calderón government to justify its supposed War on Drugs and at the same time excuse its failure. Valdés takes this logic to its ultimate conclusion:

In 2006, Felipe Calderón's government encountered a problem of national security, not of public safety. The clearest and most evident symptom was not the worrying increase in drug use in Mexico [. . .] What was crucial was the territorial expansion of the organizations and their diversified criminal activities, the increasing violence of the confrontations between them and, above all, the weakness and process of capturing state institutions in the area of security and justice. [. . .] There was criticism of President Calderón's decision to take action against drug trafficking organizations under the conditions in which the institutions were. However, a president cannot politically or legally argue the inaction of the state and ask the populations subjected to violence and insecurity to wait fifteen or twenty years for the institutions to be rebuilt.[74]

As in the most critical pages of Anabel Hernández's book, the former director of CISEN does not hesitate to acknowledge the vulnerability of the state
and even notes that the alleged empowerment of the drug trafficker goes
"hand in hand with a long history of corruption, complicity and inability
of state institutions to prevent such strengthening."[75]

The second reason why Hernández's work is politically neutralized is
strictly journalistic in nature. Her lack of rigor in the sources of information
she uses makes her research simply unverifiable. Her most serious accusations
of government corruption are mostly attributed to "living sources of information" that ask the reader for an act of faith without real journalistic support.
The activist and political scientist Andrés Lajous recalls how, in his *Reforma*
newspaper column, the journalist Miguel Ángel Granados Chapa commented
on Anabel Hernández's version of El Chapo's escape from the Puente Grande
Prison, which was based according to Hernández, on what the drug lord himself told "his close friends, and even negotiators sent by the President of the
Republic." Faced with such vagueness, Granados Chapa noted: "The readers
of the book can trust what the journalist said or not." And Lajous continues:
"Despite sympathizing with the argument, Granados Chapa did not dare take
the detailed description given by Hernández about how El Chapo Guzmán
allegedly escaped from the Puente Grande prison as his own."[76]

Finally, it is recent events that refute the work of Anabel Hernández and
Osorno: El Chapo's supposed empire collapsed in an unexpected way, and
with much significant political context. After a long period as the most
famous fugitive from international justice, El Chapo was arrested for the
second time on February 22, 2014, three days after the meeting in which
then-President Barack Obama celebrated President Enrique Peña's security policy, as I mentioned before. His spectacular escape on July 11, 2015,
through that incredible tunnel (which I will discuss later in another essay)
was for many the confirmation of his immeasurable power. But his third
and final capture on January 8, 2016, was accompanied, as we know, by a
humiliating interview with US actor Sean Penn and Mexican actress Kate
del Castillo in *Rolling Stone* magazine and with an extradition trial to the
United States that ended in his imprisonment for life.

All that remains of El Chapo's empire now are the narco chronicles that
helped invent it.

Less Journalism and More Narrative

The narco chroniclers frequently privilege their narrative techniques over
their journalistic rigor. Lacking any criticism from the media or their pub-

lishers, the books by Sergio González Rodríguez, Diego Enrique Osorno, and Anabel Hernández have received numerous awards, scholarships, and national and international media attention. Given the epistemological conditions in which the hegemonic discourse on drug trafficking is structured, it is not surprising that the world of cultural production rewards the most superficial and reiterative versions of that official narrative. Despite being independent from the federal government, the National Prize for Journalism has consistently recognized narco chronicles and the supposed national security emergency that the official story promotes. One of the most exceptional cases in this regard is that of Alejandro Almazán, who has received the award three times for his narco chronicles. In 2013 he also received the Gabriel García Márquez Prize awarded by the Foundation for a New Ibero-American Journalism (FNPI, in Spanish), which was created to highlight the intersection of literature and journalism in reference to the US New Journalism's legacy mentioned earlier. The case of Almazán is significant because it is perhaps the most extreme: in narrative journalism, Almazán has made ventures into literature with two novels about the narco, *Entre perros* (Among dogs, 2009) and *El más buscado* (The most wanted man, 2012). The latter is an imagined biography of "El Chalo" Gaitán, whose criminal power surpasses the state's until he hatches a retirement plan, resembling Anabel Hernández's speculative exit for El Chapo, faking his own death at the end of the novel. It should not surprise us that Almazán's fable and Hernández's reporting overlap: El Chapo's power, at least at the level attributed to him by journalists such as Almazán, Hernández, and Osorno, can best be expressed in the pages of a novel. In fact, it is important to note the increasingly frequent crossover between literary and journalistic figures as a validation for both forms. Let's look at the publication of books of narrative journalism with prefaces by fiction writers. Among the most recent are: *La guerra de los Zetas* (War of the Zetas, 2012) by Diego Enrique Osorno, prefaced by Juan Villoro; *Entre las cenizas: Historias de vida en tiempos de muerte* (Among the ashes: Stories of life in times of death, 2012) by Marcela Turati and Daniela Rea, with a prologue by Cristina Rivera Garza; and finally, *Narcoleaks: La alianza México–Estados Unidos en la guerra contra el crimen organizado* (Narcoleaks: The Mexico–United States alliance in the war against organized crime, 2013) by Wilbert Torre, prefaced by Yuri Herrera. In 2012 an anthology compiled by Juan Pablo Meneses gave an eloquent name to this emerging form of narrative journalism. The book, which brought together texts by Almazán, Osorno, Turati, and Rea is entitled, perhaps with involuntary irony, *Generation Bang!* The volume opens with an epigraph by Chilean novelist Roberto Bolaño. It thus becomes understandable and logical for Osorno, in his *War of the Zetas*, to describe his work as "infrarealist journalism."[77]

The celebrated trajectory of awards, recognitions, translations, and media attention that narco chroniclers have received has been complemented by the disproportionate success of so-called narco literature, written by novelists such as Yuri Herrera, Juan Pablo Villalobos, Élmer Mendoza, and Bernardo "Bef" Fernández. Journalism and literature are both offered as textual complements to a reality that confirms the alleged drug cartel violence and the weakness and victimization of an apparently defeated and even, for many, failed state. The core of these books, journalistic and fictional, is the exhaustive anxiety of narrative significance that their authors produce in order to account for a phenomenon that should be understood primarily within political parameters. By this, I mean the critical possibilities that emerge when politicizing the historical conditions of violence in unstable cities like Ciudad Juárez. By leaving aside the mythologies of violence that generate great symbolic capital but a poor understanding of why it occurs, perhaps the next task of our critical intelligence lies in the analysis of positively identifying that unstable life, where political agency patiently waits for its moment to emerge.

I have tried to point out the pernicious influence of the hegemonic national security discourse on how our narrative journalism represents and addresses the issue of drug trafficking in Mexico. But the main critical point that I am interested in promoting lies not only in showing the political neutralization of narrative journalism, but in denouncing the fact that the prevailing national security agenda completely contrasts with the relocation of organized crime to the center of political power where it belongs. As an integral dimension of a new national political project, Enrique Peña Nieto's presidency effectively continued the violent restoration of the sovereignty of official state power over the drug trade that Felipe Calderón's presidency desperately attempted. I am not referring to the true fight against the alleged drug cartels, but to the incorporation of groups of drug traffickers for specific political purposes. Beyond the corrupt despotism and the illicit enrichment of politicians, police, and military, what this agenda offers to state power is the advantage of a vast underground economy of violence with deep geopolitical implications between Mexico and the United States first, and in the rest of Latin America after. Understood in this way, the state's strategy is to operate a transnational political framework that returns decision-making to the federal government in the face of a labyrinth of interests hidden behind a vague national security discourse.

This labyrinth often coincides with the recent exploitation of natural resources in the regions where the greatest violence attributed to the "cartels" is concentrated, as the important work of journalists such as Ignacio Alvarado, Dawn Paley, and Federico Mastrogiovanni has shown. In my view, the Peña Nieto presidency tried to use the drug trafficking issue as a profitable object of international policy demarcated by and for the particular interests of the Mexican ruling class as well as looting by transnational conglomerates. Taking the criticism of this strategy to its ultimate logical conclusion continues to be the pending instruction of national journalism. To think *politically* as a journalist can be an essential operation to visualize and critically assess the monopoly of symbolic and real state violence. Journalism can express the global world and make the representational tensions typical of neoliberalism known, but it will not be able to aspire to a true political dissidence until it disposes of its hegemonic official discourse on organized crime. Most of our novelists are not up to the challenge. Our journalism cannot afford the same failure.

The Cartel, Narcos, Sicario: National Security Discourse in US Movies and Television

One of the most surprising narco related events in recent years was undoubtedly the maximum-security prison escape of Joaquín "El Chapo" Guzmán, the man considered by the Mexican authorities as the head of the "Sinaloa Cartel." The drug trafficker, as was widely reported by the national and international press, escaped from his cell on July 11, 2015, through a one-mile long tunnel about thirty-two feet deep under his cell that led to an under-construction safe house. The tunnel measured five and a half feet high and about two and a half feet wide, just enough room for the drug trafficker to walk through it without having to bend down. It was equipped with lighting, oxygen tanks, and even a rail-mounted motorcycle to speed up his escape. According to an expert's assessment consulted by the media, the work must have cost around five million pesos (more than $300,000 dollars) and required the work of excavators, surveyors, and civil engineers.[78]

Two days after the escape, US writer Don Winslow presented a new novel, *The Cartel*, in a Washington, DC bookstore. In an interview discussing the events, Winslow attributed El Chapo with a disproportionate role within power relations in Mexico:

This is a very smart man, a survivor, a man with billions of dollars at his command, a man who can reach out and kill almost anybody he wants to kill, to have killed, and a man who knows secrets about high levels of the Mexican government. There's a reason why they didn't extradite him to the United States — principally because he could afford high-level lawyers to block that. He could afford bribes to block that. But also because if he were extradited to the United States, his only deal-making ability now [would be] to start telling those secrets and telling those stories.[79]

Later in the same interview, Winslow claimed that even the self-proclaimed Islamic State (ISIS) is embracing the violent strategies of the Mexican drug cartels:

[The Mexican cartels] are sophisticated. They know that they need, not only to control the action on the ground, but also the narrative, [to] control the story. I think ISIS is just taking a page from their playbook.[80]

A few weeks earlier, on June 28, the *Washington Post* published Winslow's "An Open Letter to Congress and the President." The letter criticized the United States's anti-drug policy. The novelist noted that the War on Drugs—conceived during Richard Nixon's presidency (1969–1974)—is destroying the social fabric of the United States with a massive and racist prison system, militarized police, and failed foreign policy, all while US consumers continue to "finance the carnage" in Mexico. The letter generally maintains a progressive stance, calling for drug legalization. Referring to Mexican traffickers, however, Winslow re-emphasized the supposed power of the "cartels" as a source for terrorist inspiration:

You're so concerned about terrorists thousands of miles away that you don't see the terrorists just across our border. The cartels are more sophisticated and wealthier than the jihadists and already have a presence in 230 American cities. The cartels were running the ISIS playbook—decapitations, immolations, videos, social media—ten years ago.[81]

Winslow's political views, of course, reappear in his fictional works. Two books prior to *The Cartel* cast him as an international connoisseur of organized crime in Mexico: *The Power of the Dog* (2005), which I will discuss in depth in the next essay, and *Savages* (2010), the latter made into an Oliver Stone film in 2012. In both novels, the drug traffickers' capacity to act is demarcated by geopolitical factors in which state power—whether it be the Mexican Army or Federal Police, the DEA, or the CIA—ends up prevailing. In *The Cartel*, however, Winslow puts forward a very different

treatment of the subject. The novel tells of the confrontations between cartels that, according to the official story, worsened under President Felipe
Calderón (2006–2012). In the center of the plot is Adán Barrera, a powerful
drug trafficker—apparently protected by the Calderón government—who
confronts the Juárez cartel by invading its stronghold border city.[82] The war
generates such chaos that not even the ones causing it understand the logic
of the daily occurring and increasingly cruel and brutal massacres. However, Art Keller, DEA agent and protagonist of the novel, is convinced that
the Mexican cartels have extended their business to various countries in the
hemisphere and even Europe.

Winslow's works of fiction and political commentaries, along with other
writers of comparable success, have become some of the main cultural references in the United States and Mexico on issues of security and organized crime. In the midst of a wave of novels about drug trafficking in the
region, the view of writers like Winslow is also undoubtedly emblematic
of a hegemonic discourse that *imagines* drug trafficking as a permanent
national security emergency that is represented equally in narrative fiction as it in the narrators' own analysis of the phenomenon. With Art
Keller, the avenging DEA agent obsessed with capturing Adán Barrera,
"the most wanted" of the drug lords, Winslow reproduces a recurring perception of drug trafficking as the primary cause of rising violence and
political instability. This perception, of course, is of recent invention, but
its ramifications have profound implications on the anti-drug policy of
Mexico and the United States and ultimately in the transnational imaginary that informs most of the cultural production on drug trafficking in
both countries.

I now want to examine three works that broke into the cultural mainstream in the last few years that caused a shift in the global cultural production concerning drug trafficking, all with the same central theme: drug
trafficking from the perspective of the US security discourse. Along with
the novel *The Cartel* by Don Winslow, I am referring to the television series
Narcos (produced by Netflix) and the film *Sicario*, directed by Denis Villeneuve. The three narconarratives are cultural products whose protagonists are US agents who see drug trafficking as an *external* national security emergency that threatens the *internal* integrity of US civil society. Far
from a simple thematic coincidence, the novel, the film, and the television
series should be understood as a *representation* of a political security agenda
within the world of global cultural production that reproduces the US hegemonic agenda in around the phenomenon of drug trafficking. At the same
time, I am interested in questioning the materiality of the security discourse

itself and the way it feeds back from the cultural objects it configures. With this, I would like to point out toward the end of this essay that the security agenda, like the cultural imaginary that it invents, lacks direct, real references, and instead only appears to be supported by the same strategies of representation held up by the official power.

In the United States and Europe, the security crisis is studied as the result of the new neoliberal order that has radically transformed state structures at the global level. Prominent academics such as Wendy Brown and Carlo Galli warn of the security agenda as the further effect of a twenty-first century "global war" waged by non-state actors within a setting of decimated sovereignty.[83] On the contrary, I propose to understand the security discourse as a peculiar reconfiguration of state power as the revival of twentieth century political antagonisms. I refer here to the power relations of Western politics that have been the key legacy of the Cold War and that, in my opinion, are relevant to understanding drug trafficking outside of the problematic neoliberal post-political condition that informs much of the academic debate on the matter. In this sense, the supposed weakening of the state with the advent of neoliberalism is mainly seen at a discursive level that, beginning in the second half of the twentieth century, allows the state's disciplinary control strategies relating to organized crime to be invisible. The emergence of the security discourse in the public sphere correlates to the dismantling of state sovereignty produced by the rise of neoliberalism since the late eighties. But drug trafficking is not a causal factor of the security discourse, but rather an *objective* of that discourse. In other words, what we commonly call "narco" is the invention of a state policy that responds to specific geopolitical interests.

With the help of 1.6 billion dollars in US aid— distributed during the first three years of the Mérida Initiative—President Calderón mobilized thousands of soldiers and Federal Police in various areas of the country for his anti-drug strategy.[84] As I discussed previously, this resulted in 121,683 homicides and more than 30,000 forced disappearances, according to official data. Among others, a recent statistical study carried out at Harvard University showed that militarization in cities like Juárez is directly linked to the radical increase in violence.[85] Prior to Calderón's War on Drugs, according to the figures, there was no national security emergency. Thus, the only material reference to narco activity is the wave of violence attributed to it by the federal government. But if the national security discourse has maintained its hegemony, it is because since the mid-1970s the federal government has imposed an entire vocabulary and an essential narrative with which to give it its name.

The three cultural objects that I am interested in commenting on resort to this vocabulary and narrative as strategies that alone establish, a priori, the power relations and violence of drug traffickers. First, let us consider the curious transformation of this vocabulary in the literary world. In a *New Yorker* magazine review, Laura Miller notes that Don Winslow's *The Power of the Dog* shows important differences from *The Cartel*. In *The Power of the Dog*—published in 2005, a year before Calderón's "war"—drug trafficking is narrated as the direct result of geopolitical issues during the Cold War. The novel proposes that what we now understand as the Mexican "cartels" is the product of DFS and CIA security strategies, while the DEA and US State Department insisted on their naïve but also hypocritical fight against drugs. Such a premise, Miller writes, was only possible at a time "before the slaughter and chaos of the cartel wars reached hallucinatory proportions."[86]

Ten years later, we see how the hallucinatory violence of the late 2000s, assumed to be a true national security crisis, has already penetrated Winslow's narrative in *The Cartel*. In the plot, DEA agent Art Keller pursues drug lord Adán Barrera in the middle of a cartel war that leaves the state out of the picture and more as a rather reactive and even easily manipulated observer. As Miller explains: "The cartels that were mere trafficking gangs in *The Power of the Dog* have become, Keller thinks, 'little states and the bosses [are] politicians sending other men to war.'"[87]

In this way, the drug trafficker who once survived in a designated plaza administered by state actors in *The Power of the Dog* is, now in *The Cartel*, the leader of "all the plazas." The cartel wars, Miller assures us, have escalated into "something extraordinary, something monstrous, a ghost in the machine whose precise origin cannot be traced."[88] It is not a mere coincidence that Miller refers to the narco in practically the same terms that the Mexican academic Rossana Reguillo uses, who has described drug trafficking as a "narco-machine."[89] Both ways of imagining the narco come from the same official epistemological platform that configures the perception— and not the reality—of the supposed security threat the narco poses.

The Colombian critic Héctor Hoyos proposes to understand the "narco-novel" publishing phenomenon within the theoretical model of "world literature," following the academic work of Pascale Casanova, Franco Moretti and David Damrosch, among others. As Hoyos explains, this type of novel "represents an increasingly multipolar and interconnected post-1989 world order" that can lead to an understanding of the cultural influence of neoliberalism in the region through representations of organized crime in countries such as Colombia and Mexico.[90] Similarly, many of the most influential journalistic and social sciences studies understand drug trafficking as a global and transnational phenomenon. From Alfred McCoy's seminal academic book, *The Politics of Heroin: CIA Complicity in the Global Drug Trade* (2003), to Roberto Saviano's celebrated *ZeroZeroZero* (2013), the drug trade has been studied according to the alleged security emergency officially expressed by the United States, Europe, and Latin America after the end of the Cold War. In this context, the international success of novels such as *La reina del sur* (*The Queen of the South*, 2002) by Arturo Pérez-Reverte, *El ruido de las cosas al caer* (*The Sound of Things Falling*, 2011) by Juan Gabriel Vásquez, and of course, *The Cartel* by Don Winslow have only emphasized the supposed threat that drug trafficking organizations pose, a threat that apparently goes beyond international borders and cannot be contained by the police nor the military. In fact, as Hoyos himself cites in his book, drawing from Rebecca Walkowitz's work, most narco novels "are born already translated." But this also implies, in my opinion, that they are written with the same predisposed bias to verify that same global imagination about the narco. It is in this way that most commercial narco novels, academic studies, and investigative journalism on the phenomenon are organically integrated into the same model of "world literature."

This transformation can be found in the Netflix series, *Narcos*. As it is known, *Narcos* is based on *El patrón del mal*, the Colombian telenovela aired by Caracol TV in 2012. In the latter, Escobar makes a slow ascent through the Medellín criminal world during the series's 113 episodes. The drug lord discovers the limits of his criminal agency, learning in the underground economy of small-time drug dealers, scammers, and thieves. With less patience, the US series reduces the first part of Pablo Escobar's story to ten episodes in the first of two scheduled seasons about his life, which ends with his escape from the jail that he himself built as part of his surrender agreement with the Colombian government.

Narcos focuses on the power of corruption and subjugation that the group of drug traffickers led by Pablo Escobar supposedly wielded at the time. We see him intimidate and murder Army commanders and guerrilla members alike. However, as in the Mexican case, the cultural imaginary differs from the real power dynamics documented by experts on the subject. In his book *Systems of Violence: The Political Economy of War and Peace in Colombia*, for example, the political scientist Nazih Richani shows how the Colombian army has historically maintained that traffickers "do not pose a threat to the social order as is the case of the guerrilla groups."[91] Far from the unstoppable corruption of wicked drug traffickers, Richani shows how the military has traditionally operated within a "complacent political culture that accepts smuggling and money laundering as the normal state of affairs."[92] More importantly, Richani explains that the army "had social allies in the rising narco-bourgeoisie who could strengthen counterinsurgency tasks with their vast financial capabilities."[93]

On the other hand, although the series has been discredited due to its ambiguous mythologization of drug traffickers, I am interested in highlighting a positive outcome—perhaps involuntary— of the series that allows us to critically analyze the security phenomenon. *Narcos* clearly points out that the rise in violence was the result of open confrontation between the state and Escobar, after the ruling elite, following DEA advice, chose to reject Escobar's incursion into politics as a congressman and instead declared him a public enemy. Much of the plot unfolds in accordance to the intelligence work of DEA agent Steve Murphy, who along with the support of the United States ambassador to Colombia, methodically meets with figures such as the presidential candidate Luis Carlos Galán, allegedly assassinated on Escobar's orders, and with his successor, President César Gaviria, whom they end up convincing that the Medellín cartel needs to be confronted and Escobar threatened with the possibility of extradition to the United States. In other words, *Narcos* suggests that the alleged national security crisis is the self-induced product of a violent security policy promoted by US hegemonic interest within the Colombian government, and any political alternatives to aggressive militarism were never even considered. At the same time, the series imagines Escobar himself celebrating the "Medellín Cartel" when in reality, as I discussed in the introduction, the notion of any cartel was coined by the DEA in order to attribute to the Colombian traffickers a greater capacity for organization than what had been historically shown. As it is known, Escobar's group publicly called themselves The Extraditables out of fear of US prisons. Since the 1980s, the word *cartel* has always been a part of US anti-drug policy in Latin America, but it was not said or used by drug trafficking groups themselves until much later.

The film *Sicario*, directed by Denis Villeneuve, completes the consolidation of the security imaginary among recent US cultural production. The film narrates a covert CIA operation from the southern border that intends to dismantle the largest Mexican cartel, whose tentacles have already reached several North American cities. As in the novel, *The Cartel*, and in *Narcos*, Latin American drug traffickers appear not only as solely responsible for the production and distribution of drugs between Colombia and Mexico, but also for trafficking and selling in numerous US cities, erasing the large history of domestic organized crime in the US. The same complacency of these cultural products that imagines US borders as fragile and vulnerable also serves to consequently imagine the cartels as holding extraordinary power.

But, as with *Narcos*, *Sicario* has an unexpectedly successful critical side. The film's protagonist, FBI agent Kate Macer (Emily Blunt), initially joins an operation coordinated by Matt Graver (Josh Brolin), first identified as a State Department agent, to arrest a drug dealer responsible for the death of various FBI agents. Toward the end of the film, an unexpected twist occurs: Graver explains to Macer that the operation was actually organized by the CIA to allow a sinister Colombian agent known only by his first name, Alejandro (Benicio del Toro), to assassinate the boss of the cartel that killed his wife and daughter years before. But there is still a greater objective than this settling of scores: according to the CIA agent, the real mission is not to interrupt the drug trade but to subject it to US government control, which, according to Graver had been the ways things used to be done, a reference to the CIA and DEA's role in the fight against the Medellín cartel. Along with the other narco narratives, *Sicario* shows the desire for geopolitical control that is structured around the logic of the security agenda as a state project. The original causality of the film is then reversed, and the plot implies that the loss of US dominance over Latin American drug trafficking was the original condition of possibility for trafficking organizations to reach their northern border. Less interested in fighting drug trafficking in their own hemisphere, the US government is shown in the film as determined to regain the same political and militaristic control over the region as it did in the past, especially during the many global conflicts of the Cold War.

More than just works of fantasy, the three representations that I have discussed here, in the end, reveal a fundamental aspect of the security discourse: the lack of a direct reference to support it. There is no historical materiality underneath these representations pretending to show the *real* of the narco. After that superficial reading, there are only texts that circularly refer to *other texts*, generating the illusion of a world populated by drug traffickers, hitmen, and cartels that never directly appear. In an essential way, this imagined security agenda is built on forms of knowledge that approach the phenomenon independently and sporadically, but with a shared state origin in both Mexico and the United States. The most relevant of these forms is undoubtedly located in the journalistic work of reporters in Mexico and the United States who mainly use official documents and who repeat the same narrative that invented the security crisis. Added to this are interviews with government spokespeople and federal agents, and the testimony of alleged narcos who offer statements in trials that are also mediated by political vectors.

In addition to journalism, the security discourse is fed back to the same cultural objects that it configures: novels, films, and music that have temporarily taken on an advanced position in the world of cultural production in Mexico and the United States. This discourse, finally, constitutes our current perception of drug trafficking as a global threat. By assuming that the sovereignty of the state is in crisis, the waves of migrants, political refugees, volatile flows of transnational capital, and a defeated sense of nationalism stand out as the reality of the twenty-first century.

But what we call *narco* cannot be understood without those geopolitical strategies that have been active in the hemisphere since the Cold War and that have only radicalized in the era of global neoliberalism. As a deliberate effect of a particular *governmentality*, here following Michel Foucault's proposed notion in his seminar *Security, Territory, Population*, at the base of the security agenda is still a form of sovereignty closer to the state decisiveness of Carl Schmitt than to the body of Thomas Hobbes's *Leviathan*.[94] Under the current security imaginary, we will continue to be stimulated by Pablo Escobar and "El Chapo" Guzmán in our cultural productions. We will continue to be fascinated by their mythological lives until the idea of national security and the general narrative of our neoliberal present is challenged by a critical imagination that relocates the history of drug trafficking to the center of state power, as one of the multiple and complex interests and objectives of its government structures and programs, together with its most basic political logic.

CHAPTER 2

Drug Cartels Do Not Exist (but State Violence Does)

THE DRUG WAR AND ITS RAISONS D'ÉTAT: SOVEREIGNTY AND BIOPOLITICS IN THE CONTEMPORARY MEXICAN NARCO NARRATIVE

As it cannot be overstated, let us remember once again: the unprecedented violence attributed to drug trafficking since 2006 has left the monstrous balance of more than 350,000 homicides and nearly 80,000 forced disappearances. The upheaval of those years has mainly been interpreted as the product of a failed state overtaken by organized crime. This vision's blind spot, disseminated equally by journalism and academia, is the specific historical nature of the Mexican state's recent transformations. The main limitation in this vision lies in its inability to determine the narco's *political dimension* in Mexico, that is, following the German political theorist, Carl Schmitt, the distinction between friend and enemy in the administration and regulation of the drug market.

In what follows, I propose a historical digression to reconsider the centrality of the Mexican state and its police regime's role as the condition of possibility of drug trafficking; from the emergence of the so-called cartels in the 1970s to the War on Drugs ordered by President Calderón's government. My intention is to identify three historical periods of *raisons d'état* concerning the narco and discuss the way in which they have been represented in three novels written during those periods: *Contrabando* (Contraband, written in 1991 but published in 2008) by Víctor Hugo Rascón Banda (1948–2008), *2666* (2004) by Roberto Bolaño (1953–2003) and *Entre perros* (Among dogs, 2009) by Alejandro Almazán (1971). By elucidating the specific historical nature of their representation of sovereign power, I will point out how these novels, as cultural artifacts, produce literary works that allow us to visualize and follow the Mexican state's transformation in relation to the drug market. We will see that the drug war *raisons d'état* transform parallel with their literary representation. Ultimately, I am also interested in highlighting the impasse that neutralizes the critical potential of recent narco narratives and the agendas that study them, due to a generalized depoliticization that insists on reflecting on drug trafficking in terms of a dysfunctional democracy or of a seemingly failed state. This will lead me to conclude, with Michel Foucault, that the lack of a rule of law and its subsequent violence actually implies the absolute, orderly, and effective presence of the state. In other words, after the unprecedented wave of homicidal violence, perhaps the most aggressive biopolitical program in modern Mexican history—far from being a failure, the Mexican state has prevailed.

By analyzing the transformations of Mexican state sovereignty and its relationship with drug trafficking, it is necessary to remember, according to Luis Astorga, that drug trafficking in Mexico developed under the absolute disciplinary control of the country's political and police system. To develop the implications of this important point, I propose to discuss three historical moments in the relationship between the narco and the state: 1) the sovereign power of the PRI government that disciplined the narco between the 1970s and 1990s; 2) the power vacuum generated by Vicente Fox's National Action Party (PAN) presidency, from 2000 to 2006, when the sovereign power of the state was challenged by certain governments and their state and municipal police with the consolidation of neoliberalism; and 3) the strategy conceived by the Calderón government between 2006 and 2012 as a war against drug trafficking whose real objective, in my opinion, was to regain the sovereignty of the state over disputed regions of the national territory through what Foucault calls the coup d'état. This concept, contrary to its contemporary meaning, does not mean the overthrow of state sovereignty, but actually the direct and absolute action of the state to preserve its integrity. Both notions—state and sovereignty—have been relegated under the aegis of cultural studies for decades and have only reappeared on the horizon of debate in the last two decades thanks to a revisiting of Carl Schmitt and Michel Foucault's seminal works, as well as through theoretical works on the concept of the state of exception and biopolitics, in particular by Giorgio Agamben and Roberto Esposito. Underestimating the power of the state leads to an erasure of the disciplinary strategies that the PRI maintained over drug trafficking as their internal policy during its decades in power. As will be seen, even after the radical weakening of the state caused by the fall of the PRI in 2000, I note that the effects of this extraordinary policy conditioned the War on Drugs ordered by President Calderón, and no doubt operated in President Enrique Peña Nieto's attempts to recreate part of the police state conceived by the old PRI.[1]

Operation Condor and the Birth of "Drug Cartels"

In the first part of his novel, *The Power of the Dog*, US writer Don Winslow describes what he considers to be the "original sin" of the state's drug trafficking policy: Operation Condor, the binational operation by which the governments of Mexico and the United States destroyed drug crops between 1977 and 1987 in what is called the "golden triangle," the mountainous region located in the states of Sinaloa, Chihuahua, and Durango. Starting in the nineteenth and early-twentieth centuries, this is where some of the first Mexican drug trafficking organizations started operating. The novel's protagonist, Art Keller, is a DEA agent who participates in Operation Condor and who, over the next decade, understands that Mexican drug traffickers led by Miguel Ángel Barrera, an obscure former Sinaloa policeman, will take advantage of this military operation in order to force a generational shift by breaking apart Pedro Avilés's organization, the first drug trafficker to transport shipments by air. With the bosses of the old guard killed or in prison, Barrera and the other young drug traffickers transform the business into a federation, operating in different parts of the country but based in the city of Guadalajara. This work of fiction, based on real events, dramatizes the way in which the very notion of the cartel will gradually occupy a central place in the lexicon developed by the Mexican state in order to refer to drug trafficking, specifically starting in the 1980s.[2] Winslow's novel thus condenses the modern history of drug trafficking into the international geopolitical network, making it one more dimension of official state power.

I summarize this book in order to discuss the cultural imaginary of drug trafficking because a novel with the critical scope of *The Power of the Dog* simply doesn't exist in Mexico. On the contrary, the predominating narrative on this topic in Mexico operates within the parameters of representation that relies on the state's past and current central role within the evolution of the narco—especially since the second half of the twentieth century—being underestimated at best or, more often, completely erased. The case of literature is not isolated. In fact, the discourse that scholars like José Manuel Valenzuela, Juan Carlos Ramirez-Pimienta, Rossana Reguillo, and Gabriela Polit studied as "narcoculture" emanates from a paradigm of representation configured a priori and spread from the power of the state. This paradigm overvalues the relevance of the incorrectly called drug cartels to disassociate official institutions from this criminal activity, and over the decades it has acquired historical validity through a discursive practice that has developed its own inertia.

The official state narrative permeates through various fields of knowledge about the narco, such as journalism, academia, and numerous forms of cultural productions. In a 1997 article, Luis Astorga had already pointed out that the cultural imaginaries about drug trafficking were "for the most part the result of a process of construction and imposition of meaning whose monopoly has been held by the state."[3] In fact, the narco discourse laid out by the state dominates the field of cultural production—as I discussed in the first section of this book—save a few exceptions to which I will refer later. And although this mythology mainly influenced drug ballads and low-budget films in the 1970s and 1980s, it now also operates in the literary world, especially over the last ten years, with the proliferation of narco novels that reproduce the discursive logic by which power relations that subordinate the narco to official power have been erased.

Going back, however, let us remember that, until Operation Condor, what we now vaguely call the narco was once actually made up of scattered and discontinuous networks of criminality, mainly in northern regions, subdued by local officials. The curious apparition of these rudimentary drug traffickers adapted into precarity and backward socioeconomics like what in the US had been mythologized in the legend of Al Capone. Far from the glamour of Chicago bootleggers, Astorga notes that Sinaloan smugglers of the mid-twentieth century, for example, were given the dubious merit of having transformed Culiacán into "a new Chicago with huarache-wearing gangsters."[4]

With Operation Condor, however, the Mexican government carried out the country's largest military and police anti-drug mobilization of the twentieth century, which radically transformed our way of imagining the narco. The figures vary but, according to Astorga, 10,000 soldiers participated under the command of General José Hernández Toledo, a veteran of the 1968 Tlatelolco student massacre.[5] Historian Froylán Enciso records 5,000 soldiers and 350 PGR agents, in addition to 40 aircrafts used in combination with telecommunications, aerial photography, helicopters, and training provided by the United States.[6] US journalist Dan Baum notes that, without any resistance, the Mexican government agreed to spray the Sinaloa drug plantations with 2,4-D, a defoliant chemical similar to Agent Orange. By their own accord, the Mexican government also decided to use paraquat, an herbicide produced in England that has been used for committing suicide and murder in several countries, but which in Sinaloa was used on marijuana crops. And while Jimmy Carter's presidency was held responsible for around 500 tons of tainted marijuana that entered the US drug market, Baum recalls that Peter Bourne, Carter's drug policy advisor, testified in US Congress that he personally tried to dissuade the attorney general of Mexico to stop using paraquat.[7]

Omitting subtle binational politics, Mexican anti-drug policy is often reduced to two options: either it is understood merely as a subordinate relationship to United States hegemony, or it is interpreted as the result of an ineffective political contingency in the face of the threat that organized crime poses. These views overlook the fact that, until the mid-1990s, the PRI effectively managed a network of sovereignty that allowed it to lay out a geopolitical game in which drug trafficking was subject to mechanisms of state discipline and sovereignty. I use the concept of sovereignty here as Carl Schmitt puts it, as the power of the state "to decide on the exception."[8] For Schmitt, the state of exception implies political or economic conflicts that require extraordinary measures which, as in the Mexican case, provoke concrete actions that in little or no way reflect the framework of legality. In this way, it is necessary to understand that, although anti-drug policy in Mexico is deeply conditioned by its US counterpart, that apparent subordination alone does not explain the power dynamics with which both countries operate in relation to the narco.

Note, for example, how the Nixon administration conceived its "War on Drugs" primarily as a domestic strategy to intimidate and dismantle the civil rights movement and the hippie left in West Coast universities, a policy that later only indirectly affected Mexico. "Drugs," Dan Baum explains, "were the only thing that young people, the poor, and blacks seemed to have in common" in the United States in the 1970s.[9] Journalist Ioan Grillo notes that the Mexican government, in parallel but by its own decision, used Operation Condor to attack radical leftist groups during the so-called Dirty War who were within reach of the Army in the Sinaloa and Chihuahua mountains.[10] In this way, through Operation Condor, the Mexican state operated what we could consider a brutal but effective biopolitical program carried out by army intelligence work and the Federal Security Directorate (DFS) since Diaz Ordaz's presidential term (1964–1970). Luis Echeverria's presidency (1970–1976) however, set the stage for the most dramatic effects: first, with Operation Condor came the mass exodus of peasants to the major cities of Sinaloa, in particular to Culiacán. As Judith Butler the-

orizes, those displaced from any armed conflict, both expelled and contained, far from being abandoned by state force, appear rather as the body
"saturated with power precisely at the moment in which it is deprived of
citizenship."[11] Later, and simultaneous to this peasant exodus, Mexican military and police intelligence allowed for the relocation of the main drug
trafficking bosses to form the so-called narco "federation" based in Guadalajara, as dramatized in the novel *The Power of the Dog*.

Journalist Ed Vulliamy explains that Operation Condor and the subsequent War on Drugs are largely the factors that "laid the foundations for
modern drug cartels," allowing the state to manage the drug trade throughout the country by means of the Army and Federal Police.[12] This is how, as
journalist Charles Bowden points out, a "national drug industry" emerges.[13]
Considering the ideas of Roberto Esposito here, it is crucial to understand
this historical milestone as the process by which the Mexican state *immu-
nized* its society from the drug trafficking phenomenon, subordinating it
to political power. This occurred just as, at the time, the civilian PRI elite
subdued military power during the second half of the twentieth century,
immunizing society from the murderous inertia of the 1910 revolution.

Finally, the most lasting consequence of Operation Condor is, in my
opinion, the discursive matrix laid out by the PRI's "perfect dictatorship"
(as Peruvian novelist Mario Vargas Llosa famously called it) in order to for-
mulate the narco's new configuration: a matrix that to this day is the epistemological basis of a phenomenon whose labyrinths of power are mostly
unknown to us but which we imagine in an exceeding number of ways. The
main function of this matrix is to naturalize the idea that the narco exists
outside the state, which automatically turns the drug trafficking organizations into enemies of the state that are symbolically located on the external
borders of civil society. Over the decades, the state's administration of the
drug trade has successfully constructed an empty signifier in the notion of
the "narco," visible in the pernicious network of hegemonic power, and in
most academic studies that validate its assumed ubiquity. This is explained
by sociologist Fernando Escalante Gonzalbo:

> The language that we have all learned to talk about drug trafficking is decep-
> tively clear. We all talk about the cartel, the plaza, the route, the lieuten-
> ant, the sicarios, and we get the illusion that we understand. And it is such
> a simple story, so attractive from a narrative point of view, that it ends up
> being irresistible: they killed a mayor? It was organized crime, fighting for
> the plaza. They killed someone running for governor? It was organized crime,
> fighting for the plaza. An attack against the army, against the federal police?

> Organized crime, fighting for the plaza. It was at a party, in a rehabilita-
> tion center, on a dirt road in the Durango sierra, in the Guerrero moun-
> tains? Organized crime, the plaza. Ciudad Juárez, Apatzingán, Teloloapan,
> Tantoyuca, Huejutla, Zacualpan de Amilpas? Organized crime, the plaza. A
> hundred dead, a thousand, ten thousand, twenty thousand, forty thousand?
> Organized crime, the route, the plaza.[14]

The resonance of this official state imaginary reproduced by the majority
of national and international media is the same platform of meaning where
most cultural productions on drug trafficking begin from, and in particular of what is now known as "narcoliterature," which I will return to at the
end of this chapter.

Counter-Hegemonic Narratives and the Critique of the State

Deconstructing the official state discursive matrix, the novel *Contraband*
by Víctor Hugo Rascón Banda proposes to visualize the power of the drug
trafficker within the power of the state. Narrated in the first person, the
plot is a collection of Rascón Banda's impressions during a trip to his native
town, Santa Rosa, deep in the Sierra Madre Occidental of Chihuahua, surrounded by ranches and drug plantations. During his arrival, the presence
of the state manifested itself when Federal Police officers murdered two
unarmed young men at point-blank range who were fleeing along the plat-
forms of the Chihuahua airport. A group of women confront the officers
searching for the belongings of one of the victims:

> Murderers, a pregnant woman yelled at the men who, pointing their guns,
> approached to check the body, taking out his documents, his wallet, his ciga-
> rettes, his planner, his passport, his ticket. Murderers, an old woman with a
> cane yelled at them. They were narcos, replied one of the men, who turned
> and glared at her. That doesn't take away from you being murderers, a young
> woman told him. Murderers, murderers, other women screamed. There was
> indignation on all the faces. Murderers, murderers, murderers.[15]

This exchange is key to understanding the political dimension of the novel.
Rascón Banda correctly notes that the only ones who call the murdered
youths narcos are the policemen. On the other hand, the women, faced with
the general cowardice of the men, characters that choose to remain silent,
confront the agents and denounce their crime: they are murderers. They
do not ignore that they have witnessed an extrajudicial execution. From its

beginning, the novel unambiguously points out that police officers murdered two young men. Nothing else.

State violence is, in fact, very present throughout Rascón Banda's trip. But it is not a question of cartels that besiege the mountains, but of federal agents and soldiers who maintain their control over all activities linked to drug trafficking. In one of the most revelatory parts of the book, an entire family is massacred by a unit of the Federal Judicial Police that justifies the crime and the occupation of the Yepachi ranch by framing the victims as a drug trafficking clan. Damiana Caraveo, the only survivor of the massacre, recounts how State Judicial Police agents known to her family were also murdered by the federal agents upon arrival to the ranch in order to help Damiana. Damiana is later forced to pose at a press conference with a high-powered rifle while being photographed by journalists. The headline published the next day summarizes the police state's upper hand:

> Hit to drug traffickers; 24 dead and 9 wounded. Confrontation between narcos and the Federal Judicial Police. Massacre at the Yepachi ranch, narco nest. Federal Judicial against State Judicial: the Feds won. Damiana Caraveo, head of a drug gang, captured.[16]

Contrary to the official story, Rascón Banda and the inhabitants of Santa Rosa suffer the effects of brutal Army and Federal Police incursions constantly repressing the civilian population. When Rascón Banda and his father are shot at by soldiers at a military checkpoint, his mother explains the possible reasons: "You have a strange look and a look that hurts you [. . .] you look like a drug dealer or Judicial Police, which is the same for that matter. And, besides, you dress like them."[17]

Despite having obtained the Juan Rulfo award in 1991, *Contraband* remained unpublished until 2008, printed posthumously after Rascón Banda's death that same year. Critic Fernando García Ramírez reads *Contraband* from the immediate context of its publication and affirms that the novel "helps us understand why the 'war' against the cartels waged by the government is a lost war."[18] Rejecting this anachronism, I propose to recontextualize the novel as an obvious product of its time, showing a portrait of the state of exception that prevailed from the 1970s to the early 1990s, when organized crime in Mexico, as security analyst Edgardo Buscaglia explains, "was managed by the Mexican state" assigning illicit markets, goods, and services to each criminal group that worked under official state control.[19] In the society of *Contraband*, state discipline is activated mainly in the rural areas of the country, just like the Dirty War against the radical left guerrilla groups in the 1960s and 1970s. And if, as García Ramírez warns, at the beginning of the nineties "nobody wanted to see [...] what was happening," this was due in part to the fact that drug trafficking was not being represented in literature then as independent *from* state power as it is currently described in official discourse and the popular imagination, as I will analyze toward the end of this essay.[20]

After the adoption of neoliberalism as a model to the new structures of government during the presidencies of Miguel de la Madrid (1982–1988) and Carlos Salinas de Gortari (1988–1994), the gradual dismantling of the police state reached its peak with the defeat of the PRI in the 2000 presidential election. With it came the fragmentation of political power during Vicente Fox's presidency (2000–2006), which resulted in "the absence of a state security policy" that, according to Astorga, allowed for "a greater degree of autonomy for the police, military, and drug traffickers with respect to political power."[21] This reconfiguration of power is one of the main themes that critics have overlooked in Roberto Bolaño's novel *2666*.

2666 can be read as a representation of the crisis of sovereignty that Mexico experienced during the first years of the PAN government. In this sense, and despite the title's play on time, it is also a reflection of its immediate context, in particular its representation of northern Mexico in "The Part about the Crimes." This section, the largest in the book, is structured around the two most important phenomena of systemic violence on the border: the hundreds of murders of women that began to be reported in Ciudad Juárez (called Santa Teresa in the novel) starting in 1993—the last year of the presidency of Salinas de Gortari—and drug trafficking. Femicide is revealed here as the extreme effect of the biopolitics exerted by the neoliberal state that collectively transforms the lives of thousands of female *maquiladora* workers. Confined to slums built around industrial parks, the workers' lives are regulated in order to maximize their productivity with grueling night work hours and the threat of being fired if they become pregnant. Without the protection of the rule of law—which only intervenes in favor of capital—the vulnerability of the women tragically materializes when their bodies, excluded from normative society, become objects of impunity. Returning to the notion of immunity proposed by Esposito, the workers are *separated* from their community toward the margins as if an act of asepsis was performed on the social fabric. Like those who have been *abandoned* by the state of exception, according to Agamben, although the women don't appear to be within the scope of legality, they are instead affected by the logic of immunity created by the local powers. They are then "exposed and threatened on the threshold in which life and law, outside and inside, become indistinguishable."[22] In other words, the bodies of the murdered women, even in the face of the indifference of the state, or precisely because of this indifference that condemns them to that blurred space, are saturated with the power of the state. They are exactly the most concrete form of the materialization of that same power.

On the other side of this immunity, drug trafficking in *2666* hints at an official and unofficial complicit local network that regulates the flow of drugs within Santa Teresa without the intervention of federal forces. An example of this is the episode in which Pedro Negrete, the Santa Teresa police chief, hires the young Lalo Cura to work as a "trustworthy friend" for his "old friend" Pedro Rengifo, a prominent local businessman.[23] When Lalo Cura saves the life of Rengifo's wife during an attack perpetrated by two hitmen, including a state policeman, Negrete decides to turn Lalo into a detective, but it is not until much later that Lalo understands: "So Pedro Rengifo is a narco? asked Lalo Cura. That's right, said Epifanio. I can hardly believe it, said Lalo Cura."[24] Rengifo, in addition to being a businessman, is *also* a drug trafficker. This intimate relationship between local police officers, businessmen, and narcos is alluded to later when another police officer talks with Lalo Cura about the murder of radio reporter Isabel Urrea, whose personal daily planner reveals certain aspects of the local political order in the crime investigation:

> I found the phone numbers of three narcos. One of them was Pedro Rengifo. I also found the numbers of several judiciales, including a big boss in Hermosillo. What were those phone numbers doing in an ordinary reporter's appointment book? Had she interviewed them, put them on the air? Was she friends with them? And if she wasn't, who had given her the numbers? A mystery.[25]

As we have seen, the subtle difference between *Contraband* and *2666* lies in the absence of the federal state within the regional dynamics of the narco, where soldiers and federal agents are replaced by state and municipal police with political pacts that in turn produce new biopolitical forms in their place.

The Critical Impasse of Narco Literature

Following suspicions of fraud in the 2006 presidential election, some analysts suggested that Calderón's War on Drugs, which involved the deployment of tens of thousands of soldiers and Federal Police, was conceived solely as a media attempt to legitimize his authority. But, as Luis Astorga explains, this theory is insufficient as it ignores "that the need to set down order was (is) real and urgent" for the *raisons d'état*, which sought to recover the fragmented sovereignty between the multiple semiautonomous police territories that arose in states such as Chihuahua, Nuevo León, Tamaulipas, and Sinaloa.[26] It is possible to visualize the state's concerted action against specific enemies when noting, as Fernando Escalante Gonzalbo explains, that the murder rate at the national level had shown a significant decrease before the militarization of the country. Starting in 2008, with Army and Federal Police intervention, the murder rate in various areas of the country increased by up to 1,000 percent. A study by the think tank México Evalúa shows that most of these victims were lower class men with minimal education, between twenty and forty years of age, while the profile of the alleged sicarios detained by the authorities only differs from this profile in that they were five years younger on average.[27]

A study conducted by the Drug Policy Program at the Center for Research and Teaching in Economics (CIDE, in Spanish) showed that the armed forces' rate of lethality grew dramatically during the War on Drugs ordered by Calderón. Between 2007 and 2011, according to the study, 86.1 percent of murdered civilians who allegedly confronted the Army and federal police were killed with "perfect lethality," that is, in confrontations where all enemy combatants were killed with no survivors left. All this without Federal Ministerial Police investigations that could prove that the murdered civilians had some link to "organized crime." The Mexican Navy has the highest lethality rate: 17.3 deaths for every civilian injured. This is followed by the Mexican Army with 9.1 deaths per injury and then the Federal Police with 2.6 deaths per injury. CIDE researchers also point out that violence increases by 6 percent with each combat and over a period of three months. And even more serious: of the 3,327 documented clashes, 84 percent were actually *caused* by the Mexican Armed Forces. Only 7 percent were direct attacks against the Mexican Armed Forces. Alejandro Madrazo, one of the CIDE researchers, interprets the data unambiguously: "The high lethality and perfect lethality levels are a very strong indication that we are facing extrajudicial executions or the excessive use of public force."[28]

Contrary to being a failed state, what this information reveals is perhaps the most orderly and shocking biopolitical program in recent Mexican history, which was launched in the context of the worst armed crisis since the Mexican Revolution. The state's strategy shows a directly proportional correlation between violence and the presence of federal forces in the areas of greatest conflict. The recurring typology of the victims and their alleged perpetrators suggests that the objective of this war was mainly focused on the lower ranks of drug sales in the poorest neighborhoods of besieged cities, and not in the financial and business sectors that make the transnational circulation of drug profits possible. It is never explained how it can be that the authorities in states such as Chihuahua, where less than 2 percent of crimes are even solved, have had the ability to correctly determine the guilt of the more than 15,000 presumed murdered narcos when most of the bodies were not even identified and ended up discarded in mass graves.[29]

It is at this point that my writing differs radically from much of the intellectual analysis done inside and outside of Mexico. I am referring to the works mentioned before by Gareth Williams, Sergio González Rodríguez, Rossana Reguillo, Herman Herlinghaus, and Gabriela Polit, among others. The depoliticization that prevents distinguishing friend from enemy in the War on Drugs is the product of a discursive policy that lays out a mythology of drug trafficking as a ubiquitous and adaptable agent that can materialize in all areas of society, with even leading scholars like Williams, whose book included a chapter with the title "Absolute Hostility and Ubiquitous Enmity." These approaches exemplify analytical strategies that, as in the case of most cultural studies, are organically structured in accord with the constitutive logic of neoliberalism: the idea of a society where the decentralization of state power has produced a network of multiple and random vectors in which the distinction of the political is always in a scattered state in the global world. This discussion, which has been explored more pointedly in the work of Carlo Galli, assumes that the concept of the political proposed by Schmitt "is exhausted" precisely because the external/internal spatial division separating friend and enemy has been overtaken by new political categories that decentralize and minimize state action and its very political conditions, which, in the logic of globalization, become a dispersion.[30] Taken up in most studies on drug trafficking, this criticism problematically displays the superficiality of a received knowledge that *imagines* an omnipresent narco, both local and global, reified as the subject and object of all manifestations of violence. This conceptualization of the narco thus corresponds to the dynamics of the global economy, reconfiguring the experience of violence in a rhizomatic model that abandons the hegemony of the state in favor of a discontinuous horizon of experiences of violence that cancels out the clarity of the political.

I argue, however, that the logic of globalization assumed by cultural studies and by conceptualizations of the political as the impossibility of a sovereign state, are insufficient in understanding the presence of the Mexican state as the very condition of possibility of the narco. By returning to the concept of the political as the key distinction between friend and enemy, Carl Schmitt defines the causes of a civil war as the internal antagonism that weakens the state in which "the domestic, not the foreign friend-and-enemy groupings are decisive for armed conflict."[31] This point is crucial because, despite the global reach attributed to the alleged drug cartels, the narco in Mexico has been, and continues to be, an essentially domestic phenomenon. To analyze it, it is necessary to reconsider Schmitt's political thought in the face of conceptual vagueness that abdicates its critical potential by assuming drug trafficking as an elusive and omnipresent threat. Unlike how the Colombian state confronted the threat of drug trafficking, the Mexican state kept criminal organizations under a rigorous subordination until the mid-1990s, in the way violence is described in *Contraband*. Integrated into a new local power structure, as put forth in *2666*, the narco operated with police departments under the political motivations of the political and business class during those governments with the common objective of building semiautonomous and independent jurisdictions independent of central federal power. Calderón's military strategy later tried to impose the same subordination method that allowed for the PRI's hegemony, but this time against the new enemies of the state: the local powers that challenged the now reduced PAN state left by Vicente Fox. And, as I noticed before, that same form of the political took on a greater centrality during Peña Nieto's presidency. To overlook this deep domestic politicization of drug trafficking in the last two decades is simply to misunderstand the nature of the phenomenon.

As I discussed in this book's opening pages, the commercial success of numerous novels that promote the official narrative of the cartel wars and the global celebrity of drug lords like Joaquín "El Chapo" Guzmán, regardless of their level of realism, is largely due to the impossibility of thinking politically about the phenomenon. I delayed discussing only one of them for the purpose of my argument: *Among Dogs* by Alejandro Almazán. It is the story of three childhood friends that survive drug violence and meet again as adults years later in Culiacán. One of them has become a journalist in Mexico City and decides to return to Sinaloa to report on a corpse hanging from a bridge. The journalist will discover that his two friends are now agents of local violence: one is a boxing promoter and the other works as a sicario. Later in the novel, we find out how the President of Mexico makes a pact with the Sinaloa cartel in order to confront the Gulf cartel and its gang of assassins known as the Ms who, in the thin subtlety of this *roman à clef*, correspond to the vicious Zetas, renegade ex-military members who, according to army intelligence analysis and journalistic reports, control virtually the entire border state of Tamaulipas. In the midst of the cartel war, the protagonist discovers that everyone in Culiacán is in some way a facilitator of the drug trade, that everyone, to some extent, works for the cartel.

Scholar Gabriela Polit analyzed the novel a few months after its publication and in an academic article recorded her shock with the headline in the Sinaloan magazine *Ríodoce*: "The Zetas Break Siege." The article included a photo of a man hanging from a bridge with the caption: "[Zetas] enter Culiacán and Fight the Sinaloa Cartel: PGR." According to Polit, the coincidence between fiction and journalism could only be understood in two ways: "the news repeated that outburst of cruelty that characterizes Almazán's novel [. . .] Or, what is worse, it showed that the novel is an imitation of that cruel reality."[32] To Polit and Almazán, "reality"—the supposed cartel wars that, according to President Calderón, produced the high rates of national violence—seems to them an unquestionable material fact. But if the alleged reality of the narco ends up looking like fiction, it is because it is a narrative construct laid out mainly from the state. Polit does not pay attention to the fact that the information about the alleged entry of the Zetas into Sinaloa was disclosed exclusively by the PGR (Mexico's Department of Justice) and that the practice of hanging bodies from a bridge had been almost commonplace since the "war" against the narco began. Both, the supposed reality to which Polit alludes, and the novel by Almazán that represents it, are marked with that same discursive logic by means of which the state distances itself from the drug cartels, positioning them outside their power structure, and also reducing them to the function of an external enemy that threatens civil society and its government.

This exact correspondence between literary and journalistic discourse can be understood, according to Alain Badiou, as an ideological reiteration of the *real*. Using the theatrical summary trials that Stalin used to condemn the dissidents of his regime to death as an example, Badiou refers to the "passion for the real."[33] That is, the need to insist on a system of discursive fiction that allows us to constantly point out the materiality of the *real* that is only perceptible from the *symbolic*. Both the accusers and their victims understood that the human purge ordered by Stalin was a mise en scène, but the ideological ends justified the need for false trials. All manifestations of violence, under this imperative to corroborate the supposed real of the narco that has been enunciated from the state, is arranged in the preestablished official discursive matrix. The symbolic of the narco always emerges identical to itself in journalism, academic research, and the set of cultural productions that alludes to it. Of course, as Jacques Rancière puts it, "the real must be fictionalized in order to be thought," but this fictionalization is constructed from a network of meanings that is established *a priori* in an archive made up of hegemonic discourse.[34]

Among Dogs fulfills here the most basic narrative function that similarly appears in novels such as *Kingdom Cons* (2004) by Yuri Herrera, or *Down the Rabbit Hole* (2010) by Juan Pablo Villalobos. The latter are fictions limited by the impossibility of understanding the political nature of the drug war and incapable of identifying enemies of the state. While novels such as *Contraband* and *2666* correctly distinguish the political dimension of the narco, the more recent narconovels forfeit their critical potential by reproducing the official discourse that denies responsibility, attributing unprecedented violence to imaginary drug cartels that, even in the most militarized cities, always somehow manage to overpower state forces. I return to Carl Schmitt in conclusion:

> Words such as state, republic, society, class, as well as sovereignty, constitutional state, absolutism, dictatorship, economic planning, neutral or total state, and so on, are incomprehensible if one does not know exactly who is to be affected, combated, refuted, or negated by such a term.[35]

Correctly determining the enemy's identity is the result of a representational strategy that produces critical knowledge about the narco and clearly visualizes the confronted parties in that antagonism. When reviewing the representational strategies practiced by the novels mentioned here as cultural artifacts of their respective times, I notice that narco-fiction in contemporary literature is dominated by an official imaginary that remains comfortably invisible and safe from any critical perspective. One of our permanent tasks to overcoming this impasse is to accept that determining the materiality of the political is an agenda that cannot be abandoned under the conceptual rhetoric of so-called globalization, as decentralized and unproductive as the world model it imagines. Beyond the current theoretical vocabulary, the specific identity of the enemies of the state must be assumed as the agenda whose fundamental objective will be to name, as Schmitt requested, who among us will be fought, and who, for what *raisons d'état*, will prevail.

THE RECAPTURE OF "EL CHAPO" AND THE STATE'S MEDIA CONQUEST

In one of the many legendary scenes from *The Godfather III*, Vincent Corleone (played by Andy García) meets Don Luchessi, one of the shadowy gangsters who stalks his uncle, Michael Corleone (Al Pacino) in the final part of Francis Ford Coppola's famous trilogy. When Vince admits he does not understand politics or finance, Don Luchessi uses an eloquent metaphor to educate an impulsive and rash man who knows only violence: "You understand guns! Finance is a gun. Politics is knowing when to pull the trigger!"

It would do well to use these famous lines in the context of the final recapture and extradition of Joaquín "El Chapo" Guzmán. In the middle of the supposed "war" for the border plaza of Ciudad Juárez, El Chapo was the boss of the "largest cartel in the world."[36] According to *Fortune* magazine, the Sinaloa cartel was, in 2014, among the five main criminal organizations on the planet—along with the Russian, Italian, and Japanese mafias— with an annual income of three billion dollars, according to US intelligence calculations.[37] In May 2017, with Guzmán extradited to the United States, Mexico's Attorney General Raúl Cervantes, apparently puzzled, declared in a television interview: "As of today, US authorities have not found even one dollar of El Chapo's assets. His money hasn't been found because he didn't use the financial system." Then he affirms: "There are no cartels dominating territories."[38] How can we explain the insurmountable contradiction between the official discourse that claims Guzmán's immense economic and political power and the reality of his poverty and insignificance once in prison?

El Chapo was arrested for the third and final time after escaping twice from maximum security prisons. Although the drug lord's fall has been discussed in political and police terms, the majority of analyses have reiterated the absurd mythology that views El Chapo as the greatest criminal in the history of global drug trafficking even after being humiliated and shown up by the Mexican state on his third capture. Adding to this is the now-classic Rolling Stone article published on the morning of January 10, 2016—a day after El Chapo's arrest —by US actor Sean Penn about the meeting he and Mexican actress Kate del Castillo had with the drug trafficker in Sinaloa on October 2, 2015.[39] Penn's text was disparaged and condemned by various writers, journalists, and academics as a risky exercise in egocentrism and a supposedly wasted journalistic opportunity. Going against this view, I want to discuss El Chapo's capture and the timeline of his interview with Sean Penn and Kate del Castillo as significant events that allow us to approach the reality of drug trafficking differently, and that raise certain questions about the operation to capture El Chapo itself and the role that *Rolling Stone* magazine had in the incident. More than the mere superficial reading that has been made of both episodes, I consider El Chapo's arrest and his encounter with the actors as singular sightings of the actual reality of organized crime in Mexico.

Let's consider the time sequence in which they occurred. Peña Nieto's government not only admitted to having monitored the actors' secret journey, but that, according to reliable information that I had access to at the time, the federal government would have also known in advance the precise date of the publication of "El Chapo Speaks," Penn's article for *Rolling Stone*. The unusual proximity between the military operation to recapture El Chapo at dawn on January 8—President Enrique Peña Nieto announced the capture on his Twitter account at 10:19 a.m.—and the publication of the article a day later give us two possibilities: either the federal government intended, among other reasons, to *control* the context in which Penn's article would be published, or it was published as a media counterpoint to accompany the capture, which would imply a certain level of coordination between the state and the US magazine itself. It is important to emphasize that the *Rolling Stone* article was dated early January 9 on the website, but earlier that day, the *New York Times* already had news of El Chapo's capture on both its online and print versions. In other words, *Rolling Stone* editors included news of the arrest less than twenty-four hours before sending the magazine out to print and before the *New York Times* shared the news. It is unclear exactly what day the print magazine was published—various news sites indicate it was printed either January 9 or 10—but that process requires at least one day in advance for most printed publications. It is unlikely then to suppose that *Rolling Stone* would have simply reacted to the news of El Chapo's capture by releasing the article since they would not have had enough time, with less than a day to print, to prepare the cover article, and reorder the total content of that issue of the magazine. Penn not only reflects on the drug trafficker's arrest but sarcastically predicts his probable extradition: "It won't be long, I'm sure, before the Sinaloa cartel's next shipment into the United States is the man himself."[40] (In an official video released by the PGR on January 27, it is even stated that the operation to recapture El Chapo occurred "at dawn on January 9," that is, when the *Rolling Stone* article had already been printed and the *New York Times* had already leaked it on its website). In any scenarios about this close timing, the possibility of a simple coincidence between the capture and publication of Penn's article would be, in my opinion, naïve and overtly ignore the Mexican state's—and its US counterparts—media strategy.

By recapturing El Chapo before his *Rolling Stone* appearance —even if it happened just one day in advance—the Mexican state inverted the order of events surrounding the drug trafficker's second capture almost two years before. As you will recall, President Barack Obama held a private meeting with Peña Nieto in early 2014 during the North American Leaders Summit. In a joint press conference on February 19 of that year, Obama praised Peña Nieto's government, echoing *Time* magazine's "Saving Mexico" headline dedicated to the Mexican president in its controversial cover story six days earlier.[41] Barely three days after that encounter, on the morning of February 22, Mexican Navy Marines and Federal Police officers detained El Chapo without releasing a single shot. Though this time around the trafficker's arrest occurred *before* the publication of the magazine article, the same goal was achieved: the Mexican government reclaimed its sovereignty in recapturing El Chapo. Both captures have been symbolically and literally complemented by US magazines. *Time* seemed to prepare for the triumph of the federal government, while *Rolling Stone* convincingly and retroactively explains El Chapo's defeat. Did it matter that such an influential newspaper like the *New York Times* reported on the fantastic escape of El Chapo—through that impossible mile-long tunnel—as a "government humiliation" with irrevocable geopolitical consequences?[42]

The federal government's masterful move is confirmed by revelations made by the drug trafficker himself in the interview with Penn. El Chapo is far from being the brilliant criminal genius as reported at the time by journalists like Anabel Hernández, Diego Enrique Osorno, or Alejandro Almazán. Joaquín Guzmán appears in Penn's text rather as a clumsy criminal surrounded by a limited group of collaborators who do not have a single English interpreter to translate the actor's questions nor the minimum technology to get online to send a simple cell phone video of himself with his answers. All this despite the inordinate fortune that the world's media took as fact and that was supposedly built on a criminal structure that "sent tons of drugs to more than fifty countries around the world," reiterates the same *New York Times* correspondent who months before reported on the irreparable blow to the Mexican government caused by El Chapo's escape.[43]

The capture itself actually highlighted the capo's limited survival options. According to the federal government, his presence was confirmed in the safe house where he was located after an emissary of his bought a large order of to-go tacos. Finally, like Jean Valjean, the protagonist of Victor Hugo's *Les Misérables*, El Chapo, "[s]tripped to his undershirt and covered in filth" opted to literally cover himself with shit by attempting one last escape through a sewer before being arrested in the street.[44]

It is surprising that certain analyses overlook this fact, even the very reporters who released the information. As the news was breaking, there were those who saw El Chapo's capture and the *Rolling Stone* article as a mere game of simulations that only revealed the supposed failure of the Mexican State. The anthropologist Natalia Mendoza, for example, in a *Milenio* article, dismissed the importance of Penn's text and his interview with El Chapo, considering them "irrelevant from a judicial investigation and security studies point of view."[45] Along the same lines, Steven Dudley wrote on the website *InsightCrime* that "Chapo is in complete control" during the encounter with Penn and Del Castillo and that the article simply "trafficks in cheap useless, macho-man tropes."[46] Finally, a text by the US writer and journalist Francisco Goldman in the *New Yorker* summed up the most prevalent popular opinion by rejecting even the possibility of the drug trafficker's defeat and instead interpreted the capture as a Hollywood "gringada" that, according to him, served only "as a reminder of how he humiliated the Mexican government by escaping in the first place."[47]

It is curious to observe, then, how these opinions coincide with certain analyses that seek to emphasize the supposed national security crisis of the Peña Nieto government. The attempt of Guillermo Valdés Castellanos, former CISEN director during Felipe Calderón's presidency, to reconcile the precariousness of El Chapo and the intelligence reports where CISEN designates the same druglord as one of the most powerful and "most wanted" borders on absurd. In an article published in *Milenio*, Valdés speculates on even the most absurd contradiction: first he explores the possibility that Guzmán feigned his ignorance and poverty to avoid incriminating himself in front of a camera (which he himself chose to turn on for the voluntary interview with Sean Penn); then he entertains the possibility that El Chapo was actually "one more member" of an organization so enormous to the point that he himself was unaware of its scope and did not really enjoy its profits.[48] Then, refuting the two previous points, Valdés affirms paragraphs later:

> The golden age of narcos, when they could live without hiding, would appear in the social section of the newspapers and be able to work as a bank director, as was the case with Miguel Ángel Félix Gallardo in the eighties, that time is over. First, pressure from the United States, and then persecution from the Mexican government starting in 2006, forced them into hiding.[49]

If the "golden age of narcos" already ended in 2006, then why did there have to be a bloody "war" to fight them? Valdés fails to recall that the PRI kept organized crime on the margins of political power for decades by using a violent repressive police system as I have already discussed in this book. The Peña Nieto government also detained or assassinated the largest organized crime bosses within a significant political context, such as the assassination of Heriberto Lazcano, head of Los Zetas, and managed to neutralize the Michoacán *autodefensas* groups, as I pointed out earlier.

Our best journalism indicates with increasing clarity that state forces—from the Federal Police to the Army—bear a great responsibility in the disappearance in 2014 of the forty-three *normalistas* in the state of Guerrero. Up until the national demand for justice for Ayotzinapa, the Peña Nieto presidency had successfully reconfigured the parameters of the national security agenda. Thus, it is an intellectual and critical abdication to assume from the outset that El Chapo's escapes and arrests are indicative of a state overtaken by organized crime. On the contrary, by holding a monopoly on legitimate violence, as Max Weber explained in his time, the state is the main condition of possibility for organized crime in Mexico, either by managing it or destroying it according to contingent political needs.

As in the famous interview that Ismael "El Mayo" Zambada gave to journalist Julio Scherer in 2010, El Chapo hinted at the true limited size of his power.[50] Humble and aware of these limits, El Chapo responds simply when Penn asks him if he considers his organization to be "a cartel": "No, sir, not at all. Because people who dedicate their lives to this activity do not depend on me."[51] Without a "cartel" at his command, El Chapo wanted to do a film with actress Kate del Castillo that would fulfill the impossible fantasy of being that "boss of bosses" promoted by the state. This was also reflected by Juan Villoro in an article published in *Reforma*:

> It is hard to see El Chapo as responsible for money laundering schemes that pass through London banks, go to offshore paradises in the Caribbean and return to Mexico thanks to apparently legal companies. If he controlled this network, he would be the most powerful narco of all time. He seems to be rather at the mercy of that network.[52]

That network, it is undeniable at this point, refers again and again to the state. Assuming that men like El Chapo occupy positions of true power is to underestimate the capacity of the state of exception in Mexico and the capacity of our government to illegally make use of much of the public and private businesses of the political class.

In his capture, escape, and extradition, El Chapo has been both the fetish of official corruption and also of the amazing symbolic power of the state, which has managed to impose its reality on drug trafficking. Ciudad Juárez journalist Ignacio Alvarado, perhaps one of the most astute researchers and experts on the subject, explained this phenomenon to me in a personal conversation as the state's media conquest, which greatly limits the understanding of journalists, novelists, and academics when it comes to drug trafficking and instead establishes the epistemological coordinates that condition the way in which we even *imagine* the narco. It is therefore necessary to understand drug violence less as an endless cycle of personal vendettas between psychopaths and more as the cold geopolitical calculation between states of exception in our hemisphere. It's not personal, it's business, insist the bosses of the *Godfather*. And in order to place the rise and fall of El Chapo in the correct context, it is essential to accept, as Don Luchessi would posit, that politics consists of the art of determining when to finally pull the trigger.

A LATECOMER TO THE END OF THE WORLD: TRUMP, THE US, THE "NARCO" AND THE MEXICAN ENERGY REFORM

On Sunday, February 5, 2017, at 4:00 p.m. eastern standard time, Fox television broadcasted an interview with former President Donald Trump as part of a pre-show leading up to the Super Bowl. The content of that interview, which should have alarmed all who had the opportunity to see it while awaiting the game, had a minimal impact on the Mexican media, although it was a cause for astonishment in the United States. The difference between Mexican and US reactions revealed dangerous geopolitical implications for our present and immediate future.

Trump decided to continue a tradition started by President Barack Obama, who since 2009 gave interviews ahead of each Super Bowl in front of a massive television audience. But, unlike Obama's often measured and conciliatory tone, Trump's remarks should have caused a national political shock in Mexico. Instead, they went unnoticed by a depoliticized Mexican public who excitedly applauded a game played between two teams whose names accurately symbolize the current political state of the neighboring country to the north: the New England Patriots and the Atlanta Falcons. The unintentional eloquence of that game could not have been more perfect. As it is known, US government officials prone to war policies are called "hawks," while for the right wing that controlled the presidency and US Congress at that time, being a "patriot" fully corresponded to the anti-immigrant, nationalist, and white supremacist sentiment of those in power during the Trump years.

In this context, the most serious statement occurred three minutes into the interview. News anchor Bill O'Reilly asked Trump if he had really threatened Mexican President Enrique Peña Nieto with sending US troops to contain drug trafficking.[53] According to information obtained separately by Mexican journalist Dolia Estévez and the AP news agency, that threat occurred during a phone call that Trump and Peña Nieto had on January 27, 2017. Estévez confirmed that Trump's tone was humiliating and offensive.[54]

o'reilly: Did you say that?

trump: We have to do something about the cartels. I did talk to him about it. I want to help him with it. I think he's a very good man. We have a very good relationship, as you probably know. He seemed very willing to get help from us because he has got a problem, and it's a real problem for us. Don't forget those cartels are operating in our country. And they're poisoning the youth of our country.[55]

There are two extraordinary points in this exchange that, to me, went unnoticed by the public opinion of Mexico. First, at no time did Trump deny having mentioned the possibility of sending US soldiers to fight drug trafficking in Mexico. Spokesmen for the Mexican government and the Ministry of Foreign Relations claimed that Trump and Peña Nieto never talked about it, and rejected less so the use of any offensive tone during the conversation. The White House chose not to make any official statement until Trump's interview. His response did not dispute either the veracity of the two newspaper reports that discussed the alleged threat. Second, and perhaps even more serious, is Trump's statement about Peña Nieto's supposed willingness to receive "help" from the US government. The key here is to determine what Trump meant by "help."

There is no reason to suppose that Trump was not really referring to the dispatch of US soldiers to fight drug trafficking on Mexican soil. In the age of constant national security emergencies, from terrorism to cyberattacks, Trump has not hesitated to take immediate action, however controversial and even illegal it may be. In addition to his repudiated immigration suspension against citizens from seven countries with a Muslim majority, Trump signed three new executive orders on February 9, 2017, to tackle the crime wave that, according to him, afflicts the entire social fabric of the United States. One such order is designed to "break the back of the criminal cartels that have spread across our nation and are destroying the blood of our youth and other people, many other people." He later affirmed: "A new era of justice begins, and it begins right now."[56]

Mexican writer Valeria Luiselli summarized the feelings of terror that Donald Trump winning the presidential election produced inside and outside the United States. In an article titled "This is How the World Ends," published in the newspaper *El País*, Luiselli feared the dismantling of some of the most progressive policies of President Barack Obama. "Endings are slow, gradual, and almost always bureaucratic," she writes. "This ending begins with treaties that will not be signed, agreements that will not be respected, decrees that will be revoked." At the end of the article, Luiselli pessimistically quoted these famous T. S. Eliot verses: "This is the way the world ends/ Not with a bang but with a whimper."[57]

As reported to the point of paranoia in the media, Trump's unexpected electoral victory caused massive protests and uncertainty at the national and international level. His presidential bid—conducted with expressions of fascism, xenophobia, racism, and misogyny—legitimized hate speech with the terrible repercussions of hundreds of reported incidents of harassment and aggression against minorities across the country. On top of that, the questionable appointments of openly racist and xenophobic political figures who are part of Trump's presidential cabinet also coldly confirm the worst promises of his campaign. For Latino, Black, Muslim, and LGBT minorities, the world certainly appears to be entering a sudden collapse.

It is crucial, however, to understand that the transnational political and economic system leveraged by the US brought Obama's administration close to Trump's in more than one way. In their domestic agenda as in their foreign policy, US governments frequently establish a constant that responds positively to the interests of global capital, large transnational corporations, and geopolitical strategies of domination, which vary minimally between political parties and even between such seemingly dissimilar presidents as Obama and Trump.

But it is even more important to understand that the harsh radicalism of Trump's national security discourse on drug trafficking, immigration, and terrorism, as well as his extractivist energy projects, are nothing more than the clear continuity of geopolitical strategies set in previous administrations, including those of supposed progressives like Bill Clinton and even Obama. Understood in this way, the rhetoric that fears the end of the world overlooks that the most destructive impulse of US governments has always been at work. Rather than tremble at the danger of the Trump presidency, we should have always feared the pernicious prevalence of the US political system.

Hydrocarbon and the Mexican Energy Reform

On May 6, 2014, Rice University's Baker Institute for Public Policy published a brief study on the hydrocarbon boom in northeastern Mexico.

The research, carried out by academics Guadalupe Correa and Tony Payán, explains how the Burgos Basin—which crosses the states of Tamaulipas, Nuevo León, and Coahuila—has become one of the main areas in the world for hydrocarbon exploration, extraction, and refining. With the fall in oil prices and the gradual dismantling of Petróleos Mexicanos (PEMEX), the Felipe Calderón and Enrique Peña Nieto governments promoted an energy reform that would grant private and foreign interests that enormous wealth that was yet to be exploited. As Correa and Payán noted, Mexico actually ranks fourth in the world in natural shale gas reserves.[58]

To this point, the report notes a huge inconsistency: although according to authorities on both sides of the border, Los Zetas—the ex-military group that formed its own cartel—controlled the territory where these important natural resources are located, the Mexican government continues to finance investment projects, and public spending on transportation infrastructure has, in fact, increased. How is it possible for the state to finance projects in territories fully controlled by drug traffickers?

The key is to understand energy reform and its relationship to the national security discourse between Mexico and the United States. More than well received by the Obama administration, Mexican energy reform was *promoted* by his government. As diplomatic cables published by Wikileaks revealed, it was the US Department of State headed by Hillary Clinton that offered direct assistance to the Mexican government to free up oil and gas reserves to be exploited by transnational corporations. In 2009, just a year after Obama's election, the US Department of State created the position of Special Envoy and Coordinator for International Energy Affairs for David Goldwyn, who, together with Carlos Pascual, appointed ambassador to Mexico that same year, created the Bureau of Energy Resources in 2011. One of the most revealing diplomatic cables was sent from the US embassy in anticipation of Goldwyn's visit to Mexico: "We should retain the [US government's] long-standing policy of not commenting publicly on these issues while quietly offering to provide assistance in areas of interest to the [Mexican government]."[59]

This policy led to the implementation of the Yacimientos Transfronterizos de Hidrocarburos (Cross-Border Hydrocarbon Deposit Agreement) between Mexico and the United States in July 2014, which overturned the legacy of Cardenista oil expropriation to allow for the exploitation of oil and natural gas to transnational corporations such as ExxonMobil, BP, and Chevron, among others. It is estimated that in the border area between the two countries there are deposits of up to 172,000 million barrels of crude oil and 304,000 million cubic feet of natural gas. Under this agreement, the companies will use extraction tools such as the controversial fracking, which has highly damaging effects on the environment.

Pascual was forced to resign as ambassador to Mexico when other diplomatic cables leaked by Wikileaks revealed his critical stance on the so-called war against drug trafficking waged by then-President Felipe Calderón. Without reprimand, Obama relocated Pascual to be Goldwyn's replacement as the new Special Envoy and Coordinator for International Energy Affairs.

Mexican energy reform has been supported by progressive billionaire George Soros. And although he decidedly opposed Donald Trump's candidacy, they both have a mutual interest in taking advantage of foreign corporations being able to enter the Burgos Basin. Among other energy companies, for example, Soros has invested millions of dollars in call options for Noble Energy, which is dedicated to oil and gas extraction in Mexico, the United States, West Africa, Cyprus, and Israel.

In the midst of the Obama administration's interventionist strategy, Mexico waged the supposed War on Drugs ordered by President Calderón. As journalists Ignacio Alvarado, Dawn Paley, and Federico Mastrogiovanni have reported, the location of the violence attributed to cartels coincides with the sites of large natural resource deposits. The specific areas where the government denounces a war between drug traffickers are often the places of massive looting of energy-rich lands. There is no cartel war, these journalists say, but rather transnational corporations laying siege, along with the interested cooperation of the Mexican political class.

During her presidential campaign, Hillary Clinton chose not to comment on her Department of State strategy to influence Mexico's energy reform, but that policy was exposed by the Wikileaks revelations as well. With this in mind, Trump's extractivist policy is not surprising either. To top it off, Trump withdrew the United States from the Trans-Pacific Partnership for trade cooperation, which includes twelve countries in that region, and from the Paris Agreement on climate change. The only distinguishing feature between the Obama presidency and Trump's is that the latter would no longer continue the contradiction between aggressive extractivist policy and supposed efforts to alleviate the global crisis of climate change.

Deportation, Xenophobia, and "Bad Hombres"

Érika Andiola tries to wipe her tears as she begins to record a video denouncing how undercover immigration agents entered her home without a warrant and arrested her mother and brother. Andiola is a prominent activist in the Dreamers movement, made up of undocumented youth who were brought to the United States at an early age. Her immigration status and her high visibility in the media due to her political activism made her and her family the targets of an unprecedented strategy of mass deportations in the history of that country. The video shows her defeated and powerless in the face of the relentless immigration agents. "This needs to stop," says Érika. "They are separating families and this is real."[60]

This scene could very well have been a prelude to the worrying immigration policy announced by Trump in his first interview after the presidential election on the news program *60 Minutes*. In the interview, Trump stated that his administration planned to deport "between two and three million" undocumented persons with criminal records.[61] But this immigration raid at the Andiola home was carried out on the night of January 10, 2013. This event added to the violent anti-immigration policy undertaken by the Obama administration, unprecedented in the modern history of the United States. According to official figures, the Obama presidency was responsible for the deportation of three million undocumented immigrants, a figure greater than the balance of deportations of any US president in the twentieth century.[62]

Andiola's family was released the next day after enormous media pressure. Érika continued her activism and joined the Bernie Sanders campaign against Hillary Clinton as the Democratic candidate in 2016. In several interviews, Érika denounced the empty rhetoric of the Democratic Party, its broken promises and, worse still, President Obama's brutal deportation policy.

It is true that Obama's admirable efforts to help the Dreamers materialized with the DACA (Deferred Action for Childhood Arrivals) executive order to suspend the deportations of young people who live and study in the US without immigration documentation. Around 650,000 young people have received temporary amnesty. But, even the total number of Dreamers who could benefit from DACA, 1.7 million according to data from the Migration Policy Institute, pales in comparison with the nearly three million deportations ordered during the Obama presidency. In 2012 alone, his administration deported a record 409,849 undocumented immigrants.[63]

"What people don't know is that Obama got tremendous numbers of people out of the country, Bush the same thing. Lots of people were brought out of the country with the existing laws. Well, I'm going to do the same thing," Trump told Bill O'Reilly in another interview on his Fox news show.[64]

According to Héctor Sánchez, then president of the National Hispanic Leadership Agenda (NHLA), Obama was never able to justify his deportation policy to the demands of the Latino lobby on a national level. For his part, Clinton pledged to review that policy only after intense pressure from Latino civic organizations. In the face of Obama's bleak record, Trump's promises not only didn't make a difference, they attempted to replicate the same goals: two to three million deportations. Trump called those who were subject to deportation "bad hombres," assuring that all had criminal records, especially as drug traffickers. Obama made the same guarantee.

The Security Agenda and Interventionism

The security discourse around terrorism and drug trafficking, often deliberately conflated by US rhetoric, has triggered interventionism in regions such as Latin America and the Middle East. Nothing Trump announced should horrify the victims of his US foreign policy or that of his successor, President Joe Biden. For the Mexican intelligentsia that feared Trump's advancement as a new imperial presidency, it should not be a secret, for example, that the governments of George W. Bush and Obama openly supported and financed President Calderón's criminal security policy to carry out his War on Drugs. As Wilbert Torre discusses in his book *Narcoleaks,* the destructive strategy to combat the alleged cartels was directly influenced by the Bush administration and its militaristic agenda. "We want Mexico to take off its gloves to fight the cartels," wrote Tony Garza, the US ambassador to Mexico during the Bush administration.[65]

As Torre recalls, United States support for the Mexican government's war against the narco was agreed upon in a meeting between Calderón and Bush on Tuesday, March 13, 2007. At that meeting in a henequen agave plantation near Uxmal, in the state of Yucatán, Calderón asked for and obtained US political and financial backing. But contrary to what even President Calderón has argued, a source close to him told scholars Guadalupe Correa and Tony Payán that the US manipulated the president into adopting the language of war for his antidrug policy.[66] The Bush administration thus conceived of the Mérida Initiative, continued by the Obama presidency, which to date has provided over $2.3 billion for training and combat equipment for the Mexican Armed Forces. The bloody balance of the war against the narco did not prevent President Obama from continuing his aid and recognition of Calderón's anti-drug policy. The Obama presidency, let us remember, never considered the probable crimes against humanity committed during Calderón's government reported by 23,000 Mexican citizens—from activists, academics, artists, and judges, to the International Criminal Court in The Hague— as worrisome.[67] It was only until October 2015, a year after the disappearance of the forty-three *normalistas* from Ayotzinapa, that Obama penalized the Mexican government by withdrawing 15 percent of the annual funds provided for the Mérida Initiative. In total, Mexico lost five million of the 148 million dollars allocated for that year.[68]

Just like with Mexican energy reform, the US Department of State led by Hillary Clinton was linked to the concession of Honduran mining reserves and hydroelectric resources to transnational corporations. This was denounced by environmental activist Berta Cáceres, who was assassinated in March 2016 in her home while fighting the construction of a hydroelectric dam in the indigenous territory of Lenca. The dispute over Honduras's natural resources was heightened by the 2009 coup that overthrew the democratically elected president Manuel Zelaya. Clinton backed the coup and repeated the baseless accusation that Zelaya could be a new Hugo Chávez-style Venezuela dictator. Although the coup was deplored by the European Union, the United Nations (UN), and the Organization of American States (OAS), Clinton supported the call for a new electoral process and refused to promote Zelaya's presidency.[69]

During his Democratic presidential campaign, Bernie Sanders repeatedly denounced Clinton's personal and ideological proximity to Henry Kissinger, the sinister Secretary of State who, during Richard Nixon's presidency, supported the 1973 coup against President Salvador Allende in Chile in support of General Augusto Pinochet's subsequent dictatorship. At the end of his presidency, Trump's security policy regarding Mexico and Latin America was not too different from the recent history of US interventionism. The same comparison applies to his successor, president Joe Biden, who even extended some of Trump's harshest anti-immigrant policies, including the Migrant Protection Protocols, known as the "Remain in Mexico" policy, which denies entry to refugees from Central America, forcing them to seek asylum in dangerous conditions south of the border.[70] Trump ultimately limited himself to proposing greater security at the borders of his country and, to the scandal of Mexico's political and intellectual class, the construction of new sections of a wall between Mexico and the United States that has existed since the 1990s.

As the Spanish journalist Jacobo García reported, there is already a physical wall to approximately one third of the 3,200 kilometers of the border between Mexico and the United States. That wall covers 1,100 kilometers and runs from Tijuana to Arizona and New Mexico. The original construction of this first wall is the result of the Clinton administration's security agenda. In 1994, his administration toughened immigration policy, sealing border crossings for undocumented immigrants, pushing them further into the extreme desert where they are forced to risk their lives in order to get across the border. As García records, the iron plates that were nailed vertically to separate the two countries during the Clinton administration were brought in from Kuwait, where they functioned as a landing strip for US aircrafts during the 1991 Gulf War. García points out: "The Democrats quietly put up the controversial wall without fuss in the same way that Barack Obama has been the president who has deported the most undocumented immigrants during his almost eight years in office."[71]

The second third of the border contains a virtual wall with cameras, motion and thermal sensors, X-ray devices, and more than twenty thousand Border Patrol agents who belong to the Department of Homeland Security, one of the largest US government agencies with about 240,000 employees. Vigilante groups, such as the Minutemen, are unofficially in charge of the last third of the border, but the desert climate is the biggest deterrent, which has claimed the lives of more than 8,000 migrants. By comparison, as García points out, the Berlin Wall killed between two and five hundred people who tried to escape political repression.

Given the Democrats' proven antiimmigrant inclinations, it should not come as a surprise that the thirteen border security companies that dominate along the US-Mexico border —Deloitte, Elbit Systems, CoreCivic, GEO Group, General Atomics, General Dynamics, G4S, IBM, Leidos, Lockheed Martin, L3Harris, Northrop Grumman and Palantir—contributed more than $40 million to the Republican and Democratic parties during the 2020 election. Contrary to conventional thinking assuming a more progressive political stance on the part of the Democrats, those thirteen companies contributed three times more to Joe Biden's campaign ($5,364,994) than to Trump's ($1,730,435). In exchange, US agencies of Customs and Border Protection (CBP) and Immigration and Customs Enforcement (ICE) issued 105,997 contracts worth $55.1 billion to these and other corporation between 2008 and 2020, according to reporting by Todd Miller and Nick Buxton.[72]

Trump's immigration policy, when fully considered, is not far from the ordinary US national security agenda. His deportation plan did not beat Obama's all-time high, while his vision for a wall between Mexico and the United States comes too late, with a material wall that he did not really conceive and that does not match the money-making opportunities of the virtual wall.[73] Clinton and Obama had an early vision of a security agenda and have already made many of the nightmares bragged about by Trump's presidential campaign a reality. The same goes for US foreign policy and its systemic interventionism to drive extractive projects through various regions of Latin America. In the worst case scenario, Trump aims to continue the US imperial agenda.

In an interview with Reuters news organization, Enrique Escalante, CEO of Grupo Cementos de Chihuahua, scandalized the Mexican public by declaring his intention to take advantage of the profits that the construction of the border wall would generate by selling then-President Trump the necessary materials.[74] But those who screamed in outrage at this casual joining of forces forget that no one in the Calderón of the Peña Nieto governments were able to successfully resist the interventionist strategies of the United States government—Democrat or Republican—that have influenced the deplorable and bloody war against the narco, led to the deportation of more than three million immigrants, and promoted the dispossession and exploitation of our natural resources without the slightest regard for the environment or the local interests of the inhabitants of those regions.

It is in no way my intention to minimize the dangerous political effect that the racist, xenophobic, and misogynistic discourse adopted by Trump had on US society even after his defeat in the 2020 US presidential election. By reversing just two of Obama's most important progressive policies, his healthcare reform and his amnesty for undocumented youth, millions of people would pay dire consequences. The United States' social and cultural regression alone is collateral damage from one of the most divided electoral processes ever. However, it is important to remember that the possibility of such a threat had actual precedent in decades of identical domestic and foreign policy that already caused death, plundering, and destruction—both inside and outside of the United States—and was led by the most benign of US governments, the first black president in US history, Barack Obama, and his Secretary of State, Hillary Clinton.

It is ironic that just now, with Trump's toxic political speech, apocalypse is feared. Only with a short and partial historical memory of US *realpolitik* is it possible to affirm that. Let's accept that Trump has a lot to learn from his predecessors in the White House, predecessors whose security discourse has always been a brutal reality for Mexico and the rest of Latin America. Trump, if anything, was a latecomer to the end of the world.

CHAPTER 3

Four Writers Subverting the Narco Narrative

CESAR LÓPEZ CUADRAS AND THE PRECARIOUS LIFE OF THE DRUG TRAFFICKER

In April 2013, Spanish publisher Ediciones B released the novel *Cuatro muertos por capítulo* (Four deaths per chapter) a few days after the death of its author, the Sinaloan writer Cesar López Cuadras (1951–2013). From the very beginning, the book breaks from the profitable mythology that dominates the current narrative by instead offering one of the most fascinating literary interpretations about the narco phenomenon in the last decade. It is about a young US woman who travels to Sinaloa to interview Pancho Caldera, who had once been the chauffer for the Simental family, a powerful clan of drug traffickers. The *gringa* wants to write a film script narrating their epic catastrophe. With each chapter, however, Pancho Caldera demystifies the power of the drug traffickers and warns of the political limits of organized crime.

The Simental family functions as a metaphor for the generations of drug traffickers whose rise and fall inhabit the narco mythology. They are cornered with only a few options for survival and are finally destroyed by tragedy and state violence but, above all, by the very precariousness of their existence. Pancho explains to the young *gringa*:

> The interesting thing about the story is not the murder between brothers, my güera. Horrendous events of that caliber happen every day; just open the crime section of any newspaper to soak your hands in the blood of the most

horrible crimes themselves, then, in the next delivery, they'll be beaten in the top ten of the blood show by even more horrific crimes.[1]

Although he constructs the story based on the most fundamental narrative motif of violence (the biblical murder between brothers), López Cuadras moves away from the usual journalistic sensationalism of the vast majority of narco novels. Without the absurd fantasy of cartels, drug lords, and sicarios who subdue police, military, and politicians alike, *Four Deaths per Chapter* masterfully recreates a world independent of the official imaginary that insists on a country controlled by drug traffickers, but in reality was always governed by official state power and its monopoly on legitimate violence. Thus, Pancho advises the *gringa*: "Don't trust those who speak in the name of the law."[2]

The novel structures the representation of the narco itself as a problem. Caldera must explain the nature of the business to the *gringa* accustomed to the hegemonic mythology that a priori assumes that any story of drug traffickers will primarily be a heinous catalog of crimes. Let us remember that the *gringa* seeks to write a film script and that Caldera, in order to obtain sexual favors, is willing to entertain her expectations of violence in the story they craft. Cleverly, López Cuadras formulates a novel to satisfy a double desire: that of the *gringa* in search of a myth and that of Caldera in search of sex. Every vision of organized crime, López Cuadras seems to say, is based on an unsatisfied desire to perceive something more than its simple reality.

In this problem of representation, two principal mediums compete for the narco narrative: the film and the novel. But, from the perspective of López Cuadras, both complement each other to generate a plausible interpretation of drug trafficking. As the narrative progresses, however, Caldera admits that he must resort to showy storytelling in order to keep the suspense going. Hence the title of the novel: as a tabloid rule to produce narrative tension, Caldera includes four deaths per chapter.

The experiment, of course, fails. The novel and the screenplay must soon confront the reality of the narco that Caldera cannot ignore. Although it includes gratuitous action, violence, and sex, the novel and screenplay's critical knowledge of the narco and the Simental family ends up undermining its own mythology. The first effect of Caldera's demystification operates on the common language used to refer to the narco. From the beginning, Caldera deconstructs the story "that the newspapers call 'drug trafficking,' but those of us who have lived it in its guts, have been gobbled up, regurgitated by it and swallowed up again, if not spewed through its ass, just call 'the business.'"[3] After that lexical reconfiguration, López Cuadras transforms the well-known universal history of drug trafficking in Mexico that is repeated in biographies so blown out of proportion of figures like Rafael Caro Quintero, Amado Carrillo Fuentes, and Joaquín "El Chapo" Guzmán. Different from the drug lords who star in countless corridos, movies, and novels, López Cuadras critically imagines the lives of provincial traffickers limited by the real powers of the state.

In order not to reveal key plot points, I limit myself to discussing three crucial lessons that Pancho Caldera offers the *gringa* toward the end of the novel that allows her to understand the narco: 1) "It is no longer possible to distinguish between good and bad" because narcos and the police "work together openly"; 2) the alleged "cartels" do not have the international power attributed to them and none "exercises, even in confined spaces, absolute control of the market"; and 3) "all drug traffickers lose, from the smallest to the largest, either because they go to prison, they're killed or they're displaced by the true centers of power."[4] The sharp condemnation of these "true centers of power" is combined in the novel with a memorable cast of characters that show the narrative strength of López Cuadras, only comparable, in my opinion, with books such as *Contraband* (2008) by Víctor Hugo Rascón Banda, *El lenguaje del juego* (The language of the game, 2012) by Daniel Sada, *Septiembre y los otros días* (September and the other days, 1980) by Jesús Gardea, and even *2666* (2004) by Roberto Bolaño.

The remarkable achievements of López Cuadras are, for the most part, as unknown in Mexico as Rascón Banda and Gardea are, and as superficially read as Sada and Bolaño. Winner of the Sinaloa Prize for the Arts, López Cuadras is the author of four novels and a book of short stories, a bibliography that for now is admired only by a small audience, mostly writers and academics. As critic Geney Beltrán Félix has pointed out in a review, López Cuadras is perhaps "one of the most inexplicably relegated secrets of Mexican narrative fiction."[5] Looking in a bookstore for a copy of his first novel, *La novela inconclusa de Bernardino Casablanca* (Bernardino Casablanca's unfinished novel, 1996) is as fruitless as finding Gardea's books, even those published by the Fondo de Cultura Económica (Economic Culture Fund), the state-run prestigious publisher. *Contraband* by Rascón Banda suffered a similar fate, which won the Juan Rulfo novel prize in 1991 but had to wait until 2008 to be posthumously published by the Mondadori publishing house.[6]

In Mexican literary circles, so accustomed to bullets and squalor, novels that do not resort to the profitable clichés of drug violence, marginalization, and poverty lose their place of enunciation and even the editorial label of "northern literature," as if Mexico's north were only understandable through

AK-47's operated by outlandish sicarios and drug lords who feast on blood while caressing a Bengal tiger in their living room. If Spanish author Ramón María del Valle-Inclán had lived in our time, he would have found the *esperpento* (the grotesque) redundant and would have realized that innovative depictions of violence now lie in merging Golden Age meter with popular speech, as Daniel Sada did, in Jesús Gardea's unusual baroque desert, in Víctor Hugo Rascón Banda's political sobriety, and certainly in López Cuadras's representation of rural communities in Sinaloa.

In one of his most celebrated stories, "El león que fue a misa de siete" ("The lion that went to seven o'clock mass"), a village church is besieged by a lion who decides to rest in the cold humidity of the church, "abruptly breaking his elemental routine, desolate and dusty."[7] After the lion is merciless killed by an incompetent policeman, a distorted newspaper story has to rewrite the pathetic and anticlimactic ending of the circus animal that walked out of a cage left open. The town is the mythical Guasachi, invented by López Cuadras, whose originality turns the insufferable hell of Comala into a bearable wasteland of beautiful women, baseball, and Pacífico beer, including a spineless and not so malicious drug trafficker down on his luck. This is also the setting for *Bernardino Casablanca's Unfinished Novel*. Different than the endless list of "chroniclers" who limit themselves to plagiarizing Truman Capote, López Cuadras actually appropriates Capote as a character and takes him to Guasachi to help a young writer solve the puzzling murder of the owner of a brothel. The business is called Casablanca because Bernardino, according to one of the prostitutes, gives off an air of Humphrey Bogart. But, in the work of López Cuadras we will always have a beer on hand to fend off the heat and help investigate a crime where the official powers and facts converge, in which the narco is just another small reason that justifies the criminal networks of Sinaloa. Bernardino may seem like a cinematic icon, but he never takes on that worn out image of the narcos that appear in *The Queen of the South* by Arturo Pérez-Reverte, the best-selling archetype of all narco novels.

Truman Capote gets drunk in Guasachi, takes an interest in its unusual characters and guides the young writer to finish his novel: "Maybe it has nothing to do with the truth. But it is a possibility. That is the important thing: you have a brilliant hypothesis, and you can make a good novel with it; the rest, the truth even, throw it away. Don't let the truth disappoint you."[8] A story of love and betrayal, inserted into a story of power and corruption, makes the murder of Bernardino Casablanca the symbolic core of a way of life that goes beyond the eternal war of cartels fighting for the plaza. It peeks out into a lively city captivated by the inertias of power that refute the idea that everything in Mexico is merely reducible to drug trafficking. It shows instead episodes of robbery at the hands of the political class, the unstoppable greed of businessmen, and the good aim of policemen and soldiers who have no problem sleeping at night.

One of López Cuadras's most endearing and shocking characters is a boy who lives at the bottom of that whale that we customarily call the narco. In a masterful part of *Four Deaths per Chapter*, the boy walks beside his father in the densely forested mountains:

> Around here, by Montoso, there is a lot of coffee beneath the trees. Once I saw a bush and I asked my father: What is that, and he answered me: Coffee. And why is it *colorado*. Because it's green, he said, and I spent many days without understanding, and I even thought that he was making fun of me, but no: after some days I understood. And then I went and I said: Coffee is red when it is green. There, goddamn, he said, since he is an older man he can say bad words, and where did you come up with that about red. Because around here we call red *colorado*. The teacher taught me, I replied, and he stared at me as if I knew more things than he does, and I thought, it is at school where they teach me those things that they don't teach me at home, but I didn't say it.[9]

The boy exceeds the destiny set by his father, a humble marijuana planter, and becomes a successful drug trafficker only because he learns to know the scope of the business and also to respect its limits. The first among them, never challenge the power of the state:

> The problem is that if you kill one, they send ten, and if you kill ten, they send the Army, and then yeah, everyone goes running. Before, when the troops arrived, only the elderly, the women, and the kids stayed in the houses; but ever since the sweeps, the ranches are desolate. Entire families disappear. So, when we know they are coming, or when we hear the rumbling of their helicopter propellers, we run and may Saint Malverde protect us.[10]

This passage is crucial to López Cuadras's political imaginary: the Army is the inescapable power that ends up murdering the citizens, whether civilians or drug traffickers, destroying the social fabric of the town. At his side is the so-called "narco culture" —present in Malverde, the patron saint of narcos—appearing here as a folkloric image just as irrelevant to the Army as the drug trafficking groups themselves.

The irony of the novel peaks near the end of the story when the head of the family, Emanuel Simental, reads in a newspaper that he is accused of being in charge of a cartel. On the verge of being assassinated, Simental reflects: "A cartel, the newspapers say. That's what I'm going to build."[11] This extraordinary moment cannot be exaggerated: the drug trafficker is prey to the same desire for representation as the young *gringa* who seeks to write the screenplay and Caldera who seeks to mythologize the precarious life of the family he serves. Simental fantasizes about becoming that criminal myth claimed by the media, reproducing official information. The trafficker dreams of being a narco and commanding his own cartel. At this point, López Cuadras anticipates the strange Mexican reality: his novel unknowingly recreates the moment when "El Chapo" Guzmán aspires to see his name eternalized, as already seen, in a film starring actress Kate del Castillo. Simental and Guzmán are objects of the same force of representation of official discourse, which ends up seducing even themselves. They never were narcos, but both the fictional character and the real drug trafficker wanted to become one.

López Cuadras's narrative complexity can be summarized in the protagonist of his novel *Cástulo Bojórquez* (2001), who is not the repetitive one-dimensional narco that so many authors of narco novels imagine. Cástulo "was a poppy grower, drug trafficker, highwayman, convict, judicial policeman, party animal, intermittent husband, furtive lover, father of fifteen known children, and prodigal son of a mother who died of lack of sleep with the rosary in hand."[12] Such a character leaves behind the archetypes and can only come to life in a novel constructed with precision and without concessions to the reader, and that by itself, according to Adriana Velderráin, "is enough to place the Sinaloan author among the most distinguished not only of his native state, but of all Mexican letters."[13]

If the demanding reader, like that child imagined by López Cuadras, is interested in discovering why red coffee is green, why Truman Capote can find comfort in Pacífico beer under the Sinaloan sun, why lions sleep in churches, or why drug trafficking is a business between politicians, businessmen, policemen, and a tragedy-prone drug trafficker, then perhaps he will have understood a function of true literature: to imagine the world with a critical intelligence to prevent "reality" —for lack of a better term— from ever letting us down.

DANIEL SADA AND THE RETURN TO THE POLITICAL

Never before has there been such an opening to a book like *Porque parece mentira la verdad nunca se sabe* (Because it seems to be a lie the truth is never known, 1999) the masterpiece by Daniel Sada (1953–2011):

The bodies arrived at 3:00 in the afternoon. They brought them on a truck—piled in a heap, uncovered—all shot to death as expected. Beneath the cruel scorch of the sun surprised looks, since it was no small thing to see, just rolling through the town like that, such a mountain of flesh—belonging to locals? That remained to be seen."[14]

The shocking image of a truck delivering the bodies of victims of state repression takes on a cruel new meaning in these days of political crisis in Mexico. In what follows, I propose to review some aspects of Sada's work as a vehicle for reflection on the national emergency triggered by the disappearance of the forty-three Ayotzinapa *normalistas* in the state of Guerrero. As a privileged space of meaning, one of the possibilities of recent literature is—or should be—to critically approach the historical process that frames our present. I am primarily interested in pointing out how, by setting specific political goals, fictional narrative can generate productive opportunities for intellectual dissent. This dissent is articulated in forms of explicit resistance that, from the symbolic point of view, destabilize the pernicious hegemony of official discourse. In the midst of a literary landscape dominated by depoliticized, frivolous, and irrelevant commercial works, thinking politically through literary work can be a crucial operation to make state violence visible and challenge, as in the case of Ayotzinapa, the most brutal criminal dimension of official state power.

Faced with the so-called War on Drugs, the Mexican narrative has not lived up to the political catastrophe that hides in what we loosely call the narco. As I discussed before, authors such as Élmer Mendoza, Juan Pablo Villalobos, Alejandro Almazán, and Bernardo "Bef" Fernández, among others, have only reproduced the official discourse that attributes violence to a constant drug cartel struggle that simultaneously challenges and even exceeds the power of the state. As replicated in popular music, cinema, and conceptual art in terms of the drug trade, most of the narco novels written in the first decade of the twenty-first century address the phenomenon in a politically neutralized fashion. This is the result of a habitus in the literary world that rewards representations of drug trafficking that are consistent with the official state vision that the mainstream media inside and outside of Mexico reinforce on a daily basis.

Just a few weeks after the Ayotzinapa crime that occurred on September 26, national and international repudiation achieved what was not possible during Calderón's entire administration: a short circuit within the dominant hegemony that blames an abstract narco for state violence. As Óscar de Pablo notes, "[t]he probable collaboration of organized crime with the Iguala police in this attack has contributed to obscuring the specific political nature of this crime."[15] Despite this, the families of the victims, along with numerous intellectuals, journalists, and activists have firmly rejected the official version that attributes the disappearance of the *normalistas* to a happenstance drug trafficking ordeal. They have also resisted the state's attempts to symbolically position itself on the side of civil society, such as when the Movement for Peace and Justice, led by Javier Sicilia, met with President Felipe Calderón, legitimizing him as a still-viable authority.

Along with this extraordinary moment of repoliticization, we now await a literature with the same critical will to bring state violence to trial. While we wait, the work of Daniel Sada provides useful clues to understand our current circumstances. *Because It Seems to Be a Lie the Truth Is Never Known* takes place in the fictional town of Remadrín, in the northern state of Capila in a country called, not without irony, Mágico (Magic). At the center of the story is the blatant electoral fraud perpetrated by Mayor Romeo Pomar, a sinister politician at the service of his party's elites. In plain sight of the citizens, an armed commando steals the ballot boxes on election day. Here begins the critical part of the plot: a mass protest that seeks to bring its outrage to the state capital is suppressed with a bloody massacre planned by the governor.

As he moves along the area's dirt roads, the driver of the truck loaded with corpses becomes disoriented and ends up in a dangerous canyon driving on switchbacks. Meanwhile, the driver and his assistants entertain themselves by telling jokes when a flock of vultures descends on them, rushing to devour the corpses. Everyone begins to pray:

> Suddenly one slams to the ground, and another, but twice as fetid. And from then on, the prayers were more emphatic, since the men praying believed they heard, almost in a chorus, the voices of the corpses saying: Cover us! Cover us! They noticed one of them that fell, but another goddamned curve plainly erased it. Fine: one less problem, because they weren't going to pick it up.[16]

Cowardice and indifference dehumanize the driver and his assistants, who decide to abandon the fallen bodies for the vultures to prey on. To cover up the crime, the state governor forces the resignation and eventual disappearance of the mayor. And to regain control of the distraught people of Remadrín, the governor orders the military to occupy the streets. Detachments of soldiers block the roads and prevent food from entering. The townspeople have no choice but to leave their homes for other communities in the region in order to survive. Trinidad and Cecilia, protagonists of the novel, flee without knowing the whereabouts of their children, Salomón and Papías, who disappeared during the massacre.

In his review, critic Christopher Domínguez Michael considers *Because It Seems to Be a Lie the Truth Is Never Known* as "beyond the ends and means of politics and ethics, manifesting itself in an almost unbearable concert of words, words submitted to all meanings and declensions, where only the appearance is vernacular, for we are faced with the most 'artistic' of prose."[17] This type of reading operates to displace the political and ethical dimensions of Sada's work, privileging a formal analysis only, as if form and politics were irreconcilable extremes of a polar literary object. But there is never a "beyond" of politics in literature: every literary text emerges from a network of ideological significance that always has a political background. The current reader of Sada's novel will find surprising parallels with the Ayotzinapa atrocity: the mayor of Remadrín is charged as the mastermind behind the massacre, like the mayor of Iguala, José Luis Abarca, who along with his wife, María de los Ángeles Pineda, have been blamed for the disappearance of the *normalistas*. The participation of the police and the army resonates equally between the novel and the repression in Guerrero. This can be explained mainly because the Ayotzinapa case is part of the monopoly of legitimate (or made legitimate) violence that the Mexican state exercises at its disposal despite the discontinuity of the policies between its governments, as studied by Carlos Montemayor in his posthumous book *La violencia de Estado en México: Antes y después de 1968* (State violence in Mexico: Before and after 1968, 2010).

There are important political nuances between Tlatelolco in 1968, the Corpus Christi Massacre of 1971, and Ayotzinapa in 2014, but state crime operates in similar ways. However, when returning to the historical context that separates the novel and the present from Ayotzinapa, two differences immediately emerge: the governor of Capila in Sada's novel not only does not resign from his post—as did Ángel Aguirre, the governor of Guerrero—but rather punishes the entire town until he drives its inhabitants into exile. Sada's novel thus responds with precision to an earlier stage in the history of the Mexican state: the last years of the repressive PRI governments. This is why, in the logic of the novel, it is plausible that the state government, protected in absolute impunity and unthreatened by the abundance of information that social networks now provide to the public on the internet, allows the victims' bodies to be handed over to their relatives and then decide it is better to destroy the entire town.

As I have discussed throughout this book, the PRI police state was dismantled and replaced by supposed democratic alternative governments lacking a clear anti-drug policy. The absence of a federal strategy facilitated the creation of regions in which local power structures assumed control of the underground economy with mafia alliances between governors, state attorney offices, and businessmen in states such as Tamaulipas, Chihuahua, Michoacán, and of course, Guerrero. In this context, when Daniel Sada returns to write about violence and official state power, the country finds itself in the middle of the so-called War on Drugs launched by President Calderón. But both in Sada's novel and in reality, the narco has little or nothing to do with state conflicts. Calderón's strategy, less than an attempt to attack "organized crime," can be better understood as the criminal attempt to regain state sovereignty over regional power structures that the PRI unlawfully wielded for decades. In Sada's novel, the governor and his subordinates commit fraud, intimidation, torture, and murder without consequence. The novel and reality meet here in more than one way: state impunity are their common denominators.

With his posthumous novel, *El lenguaje del juego* (The language of the game, 2012), Sada positions language itself as the essential device that makes the narco phenomenon legible, that is, in the sense according to the French philosopher Jacques Rancière: language as the true platform that conditions what is *said* and what is *seen* of drug trafficking. In the US television series *The Wire*, the word *game* is used to designate the distribution and sale of drugs that directly or indirectly become integrated into the power networks of the political and business class and the Baltimore police. In Sada's novel, this game seems indistinctly political and criminal, in which the local bosses, among other trades, are involved in selling drugs under the protection of official, local, and federal power. The language here constructs a reality that determines the conditions of the game, or in other words, the rules of enunciation of the narco that create the illusion of understanding the causes of violence.

The novel takes place in the imaginary northern town of San Gregorio, which pronounced without a pause is—*sangre-gorio*—which makes sense when it becomes the epicenter of a bloody war between criminal groups immediately identified as cartels. The first outbreak of violence suddenly escalates after the murder of the municipal president, a homicide that occurred just after the federal Army occupied the area for several weeks. It is worth stopping at a significant passage:

> It was already obvious that a powerful cartel had the pretense of ipso taking over that town with the sheen of a city, because it suited them so well.

[. . .] Seeing the place, it would soon become a fabulous center for delivering, storing, and distributing drugs. [. . .] and those sonofabitches with the president on their side, well, sure, even easier! Who would be then the interim mayor? Someone they named, of course [. . .] Extensive speculation not so unreasonable.[18]

As with all of Sada's novels, the narrative voice functions as one more character that contributes to producing the general sense of plot while destabilizing it. In the quote it was "obvious" that a new "cartel" will be supported by the new mayor that the narcos themselves would appoint. The "extensive speculation," as the narrator calls it, matches up on a language level with the official narco narrative that the Calderón government defended until the end of his six-year term: powerful cartels fight each other for control of valuable plazas for drug trafficking. In Sada's novel, that's the language of the game. The action itself, however, shows readers a different reality: in the dusty and insignificant San Gregorio, the Army occupation happened before the confrontation between the two criminal groups. In the middle of the war, the so-called cartels are armed groups that attack each other while the Army remains a passive observer, as if waiting for the result of that confrontation in order to finally continue with the game.

It is revealing at this point to compare the mythological notion of the cartel with Virgilio Zorrilla's organization, the businessman and local boss who, among his trades includes local drug trafficking. As in the famous story "House Taken Over" by Julio Cortázar, San Gregorio is occupied by unknown forces that easily defeat Zorrilla's cartel, who is forced to go into exile in the United States with his son, where they die together of a drug overdose: the great drug lord turned drug-den junkie. Meanwhile, the narrator explains: "the acting political party was the one that gave the go-ahead . . ." The suggestive ellipsis alludes to the national political network that supports the new drug lord of San Gregorio, whose provenance is unknown but who had undoubtedly "came in an avalanche of power."[19] That same power is the one that finally decides the replacement of the mayor, as is implied in the following scene:

The interim mayor, for his part, located a protective corner in a banquet hall where a colorful national flag was seen placed in a glass cabinet. That was what the mayor embraced to feel safe: according to him, it was the national banner of a guardian angel. Believing it that way worked, as it was an abstract-artificial covering.[20]

The mayor of a town besieged by drug violence embraces the flag like a disgraced twenty-first century Juan Escutia (the military cadet who jumped from the roof of Chapultepec Castle, wrapped in the Mexican flag, to keep it from the invading US troops in 1847). Just as in the film *El Infierno* (Luis Estrada, 2010), where narcos, the municipal president, and the Federal Police form the same collective that perhaps is deserving of the word "cartel," who at the end of the film stain the Mexican flag red with their own blood, *The Language of the Game* shows a country where, as Juan Villoro notes, "all political parties, the Church, the police, and families promote crime."[21]

The Language of the Game re-politicizes its performative representation of the narco by dramatizing the actions of the characters who face systemic violence in the north of the country. The inertia of language simultaneously constructs and deconstructs the concrete history of a town trapped in an armed conflict in which politicians, the military, businessmen, and drug traffickers participate, but which continues to be narrated under the vague epic of the cartel war. Faced with the gap between language and the reality it symbolizes, the narrator states: "Unfortunately, or fortunately, the mystery belongs to a circuit plagued with assumptions that grows too much, but never breaks."[22] At this point a question arises: does the novel illuminate the conditions of possibility of the official discourse or is it such discourse that conditions and enables the novel's plot? The main literary finding of Daniel Sada is the implicit statement that both phenomena are formed by every contemporary Mexican narrative that approaches the subject of drug trafficking, that in more than one way, the language *is* the game.

The urgency in reconsidering the political has become more relevant since the early 1990s, as has been the agenda to rethink the principle of antagonism conceptualized by Carl Schmitt that the Belgian political scientist Chantal Mouffe considers essential for any democratic social order. Mouffe has warned since then that in the current "process of neutralization and depoliticization" it must be noted that "liberal-democratic capitalism has imposed itself as the only rational solution to the problem of organizing modern societies."[23] In Mexico, the depoliticized regime of representation adopted by most narco novels continues to be epistemologically based on the official discursive matrix that the sociologist Luis Astorga detected almost twenty years ago during the era of the sovereign PRI state. Daniel Sada's work, along with those novels that re-politicize narco representations, reveal the discursive rules of the narco by contrasting them with the less epic reality of drug traffickers immersed in the labyrinths of power in Mexico. That reality, perhaps less striking than the Hollywood life of

"El Chapo" Guzmán, will nevertheless be the raw material of the narco literature that will prevail when the state's recycled language of the game finally ceases to impress us. As in Sada's novel, the complex network of criminality that frames the drug trafficker *within* the state and civil society, among politicians, businessmen, and the police, that is, clearly on the surface of our shared public sphere, will remain.

The political repression perpetrated by the PRI was narrated during the second half of the twentieth century by writers such as Elena Poniatowska in *La noche de Tlatelolco*, (*Massacre in Mexico*, 1971) and Vicente Leñero in *Los periodistas* (The journalists, 1978), who showed, through fiction and testimony, the cruel lethality of state violence. Along with these works, it is also crucial to reread Carlos Montemayor's passionate denunciation, recording the crimes committed by the federal government in order to exterminate revolutionary schoolteacher Lucio Cabañas in *Guerra en el paraíso* (War in paradise, 1991). Our current literature now has the enormous task of picking back up the critical legacy of Mexican literature in the face of the new emergency in the state of Guerrero, to submit the criminal edges of official power to symbolic examination.

In that direction, let's go back to the first page of *Because It Seems to Be a Lie the Truth Is Never Known* to observe that truck's terrible journey distributing the bodies of the victims of state violence. Two decades after the publication of Sada's novel, we are disturbed to read that the plot begins precisely when the bodies, desecrated by impunity and indifference, are returned to their families. Among the horror of this brutal fictional massacre, there were still characters who felt the basic responsibility of returning the dead to their relatives. In the *real* of present-day Mexico, no one has yet been capable of that minimal gesture of humanity that for now only seems possible in the pages of a novel. Let's hope that somewhere in Mexico someone has finally begun to narrate our new reality.

ROBERT BOLAÑO AND THE NARCO'S FACE

In Roberto Bolaño's (1953–2003) posthumous novel, *2666* (2004), there is a scene in a bar that takes place in the fictional city of Santa Teresa, famously based on the border city of Ciudad Juárez. A policeman named Juan de Dios Martínez notices a man on the bar's terrace dressed as a rancher with his back turned to him. Though the policeman can't see him clearly, he speculates that the man is a drug trafficker. Two street musicians try to attract the presumed narco's attention: "The saddest thing, thought Juan de Dios Martínez, was that the narco, or the suited back of the man he thought was a narco, was hardly paying any attention to them, busy as he was talking to a man with the face of a mongoose and a hooker with the face of a cat."[24]

When the musicians finally get the attention of the supposed narco and his companions, something happens that intrigues the policeman:

> The man with the mongoose face rose from his chair and said something into the accordionist's ear. Then he sat down again and the accordionist's mouth screwed up into a pout. Like a child on the verge of tears. The violinist had her eyes open and she was smiling. The narco and the woman with the cat face bent their heads together. The narco's nose was big and bony and aristocratic-looking. But aristocratic-looking how? There was a wild expression on the accordionist's face, except for his lips. Unfamiliar currents surged through the inspector's chest. The world is a strange and fascinating place, he thought.[25]

The assumed narco remains anonymous and faceless, and he is the only one who is not described as an animal (mongoose, cat). His imagined identity immediately assumes a specific social function that transcends that of a normal person. He wields violence and power without having to even do anything: he *is* a narco. When his face appears for a moment, the policeman thinks of the aristocracy, an elite part of society that the policeman fails to place within the construct of his known circles. The scene thus illustrates the problematic way the imagined narco is portrayed in most narco novels in Mexico: stories based on limited reflections of a phenomenon whose reality is inaccessible to us. The identity of the narco is only possible through the imagined construction of certain eruptions of violence seen from an insurmountable distance, where one senses the power of an elite member of society who cannot be truly known.

More than a decade after its first edition, *2666*, Bolaño's most ambitious and complex novel has been read by academic critics through a theoretical lens that attempts to challenge the notion of a national literary tradition. Some critics suggest reading the novel as a reflection on world historical processes that reveal the failure of Western modernity suffered by Mexico, the United States, and Europe. Sharae Deckard, for example, views the structure of *2666* as "systemically world-historical, uniting the aura of a particular semi-periphery (Santa Teresa) and a particular historical conjuncture (late capitalism at the millennium) with a vast geopolitical scope."[26] In the Deckard model, each of the five parts of *2666* explore different forms and literary genres as an attempt to capture the entirety of the Western tradition: "The Part About the Critics" would be a satire on the academic novel; "The Part about Amalfitano" a philosophical thriller; "The Part about Fate" a beat road novel; "The Part about the Crimes" a detective novel; and "The Part about Archimboldi" a Künstlerroman and a historical novel.[27] Similarly, Sergio Villalobos analyzes *2666* as a "planetary articulation of the world through global war," continuing Italian historian Carlo Galli's understanding of the global dynamics that destabilize older concepts of sovereignty, territory, and nation.[28] These approaches, of course valid and productive, are concerned with tracing the historical arc that Bolaño connects to slavery, the Holocaust, and the murders of women in Ciudad Juárez.

However, *2666* also offers a sharp critical representation of twenty-first century Mexico that critics dazzled by globalization have ignored. As I have discussed before, the PRI presidential system dominated entire generations of drug traffickers for seven decades. It was not a relationship of complicity or tolerance, but of total subordination of organized crime to political power. With the democratic transition in 2000, the police state became a security state. And while Bolaño wrote his novel, the country was heading toward a new political order fragmented by the consolidation of neoliberalism as a guiding principle of government. Among its many other qualities, *2666* offers an account of this fragmentation of power.

While some novelists who write about narcos maintain that it's possible to form a critical narrative through renouncing the dominant lexicon (*sicario, plaza, cartel,* the *narco*), others repeat the alleged truism that the writer's only task is to "write well," as if literary praxis could be reduced to a question of endless form, as if the modernist ideal of literary autonomy, "art for art's sake," was feasible. In order to write counterhegemonic literature about the narco it is crucial to understand that the goal of every writer should be to "communicate well," as José Revueltas once said.[29] That is, to crystallize a specific knowledge through literature that critically discusses drug trafficking, by avoiding the official narrative that seeks to break down the drug trade into imaginary cartels that eclipse state power and supposedly control multiple regions of the country.

In the posthumous novel, *Los sinsabores del verdadero policía* (*Woes of the True Policeman*, 2011), Bolaño, via one of his characters, says: "[he] seemed to subscribe to the maxim of De Kooning: *style is fraud.*"[30] More than a mere provocation, Bolaño takes up one of Borges's most famous maxims from his essay, "The Superstitious Ethics of the Reader." Instead of the "perfect page," as if under museum glass, whose delicate order cannot stand alteration, Borges admires the fluid and volatile work that keeps its meaning alive: "The page that becomes immortal can traverse the fire of typographical errors, approximate translations, and inattentive or erroneous readings without losing its soul in the process."[31] Thus, if "style is a fraud," in Bolaño's poetics, this involves literary practices that aim to produce discontinuities that are unafraid to disarm narrative structures, sacrifice plot, and neglect characters as long as critical discovery and transcendent meaning is found in the end.

Bolaño reformulated the Borgesian thesis in his own way, advising:

> "Putting the right words in the right place is the most genuine definition of style," says Jonathan Swift. But obviously Swift also knew that great literature is not a matter of style or grammar. It is a matter of illumination, as Rimbaud understands the word. It is a question of clairvoyance. To say, in one hand is a lucid and exhaustive reading of the literary canon and in the other hand a time bomb. One statement (or a work, as we want to call it) that explodes in the hands of the readers and is projected into the future.[32]

2666 works as an alternative criticism of the narco because, instead of being devoted to pyrotechnics of style, Bolaño *illuminates* the subject of drug trafficking itself. He centers the state and its rationale of power in his analysis: the state is the central signifier of drug trafficking. *2666* enters the labyrinths of official power and discovers the narco always inscribed under the name of employers, policemen, and politicians. Like Lalo Cura's character, the reader is surprised to find narcos who don't seek to quench an insatiable thirst for blood and don't live bizarre and ridiculous lives behind fortified castle walls. The archetype of the narco is dissolved in *2666* with the character of the entrepreneur, who, among other businesses, invests in the drug trade that is always kept under watch by the police and local politicians. The reader sees himself in the political innocence of Lalo Cura:

> Then they talked about Pedro Rengifo, and Lalo Cura asked how it was possible he hadn't realized Don Pedro was a narco. Because you're still an infant, said Epifanio. And then he said: why did you think he had so many bodyguards? Because he's rich, said Lalo Cura. Epifanio laughed. Come on, he said, let's get to bed, you're half asleep already.[33]

Like Lalo Cura, we are more asleep than awake. We base our political understanding on such naive and basic assumptions. We think material success is something legitimate and thus imagine that a narco must be some radical form of a criminal, unable to resemble a respectable member of society, and even less possible, ourselves.

In another part of the novel, we are given further insight through a character's naiveté. In the third of the five parts that make up *2666*, the character of Oscar Fate, a black journalist from New York, suddenly becomes the savior of a young girl who could have been one of the hundreds of female victims in the post-industrial metropolis of Santa Teresa. Drunk and high, Fate follows a group of friends home, where he understands that Rosa Amalfitano, the daughter of a Chilean professor exiled in Santa Teresa, is in danger. In one of the most cinematic action sequences of the novel, Fate punches and knocks out a man who threatened him at gunpoint and escapes with Rosa, whom he barely knows. They cross the border into the United States, where she boards a plane to her native Spain, according to her father's instructions. Rosa knows that her escape was not accidental and explains to Fate, "we are alive because we haven't seen anything and we don't know anything."[34]

Fate's impromptu actions are the fortuitous result of a superficial knowledge and misreading of Santa Teresa. His ignorance of the situation, like Lalo Cura's, is the result of a limited understanding of systemic violence on the border. This idea is seen in a quote often mentioned by critics: "No one pays attention to these killings, but the secret of the world is hidden in them."[35] This paradox is inherent to Fate's character: his inability to understand his surroundings does not change his actions, but, in fact is exactly what allows them to occur. He is caught up in something out of his grasp. His ethical stance is the result of what the French philosopher Alain Badiou calls "an unrelated relationship," i.e., actions that lack a political motive and thus are of no consequence to the criminal border network.[36] In other words, Fate can save Rosa precisely because him doing so is politically harmless. His ignorance of the situation is what allows them to cross the border. He is, so to speak, the man who knew too little.

Certain characters in *2666*, like Fate and Lalo Cura, are effectively neutralized due to their inability to comprehend the terms of the political in Santa Teresa. Jacques Derrida deconstructs Carl Schmitt's political concept, arguing that the enemy's true identity can never be fully established, since its classification remains ambiguous and "accessible only in discourse," since "no politics has ever been adequate to its concept."[37] In his celebrated work, *On the Politics of Friendship*, Derrida states that every individual can independently initiate an act of friendship without necessarily invoking a corresponding friend or antagonistic enemy. Thus, according to Derrida, at the most basic level, material political practice eludes the principle of antagonism proposed by Schmitt. But what happens to those characters who do understand the networks of crime and power? What happens when intervention becomes deliberately political?

Bolaño's representation of the border is structured around a group of characters that politically confront Santa Teresa's femicides. It doesn't come from a depoliticized ethical stance, but from transformative political action. *2666* is, in this sense, a novel about citizens who claim a place in the political battlefield against the corruptive force of politicians, police, military, and businessmen involved in organized crime. The problem with most narco narratives that focus on victims is that they simultaneously leave the political dimension of the crimes out of the narrative. That is why it is crucial to understand the different forms of violence that operate within a given society. Slavoj Žižek points out the importance of discerning systematic violence and not just the anecdotal cases of *subjective* violence, which he defines as acts of violence perpetrated by clearly identifiable individuals. Systemic violence is thus understood as "the most subtle forms of coercion that sustain the relationships of domination and exploitation."[38] Unlike Derrida's critique of Carl Schmitt's concept of politics, Žižek argues that, in a world of systemic violence, the distinction between friend and enemy is "always a performative procedure which brings to light/constructs the enemy's 'true face.'"[39] Refuting academics who are quick to clarify the exhaustion of the political and the triumph of post-national globalization, Žižek argues that "our pluralistic and tolerant liberal democracies remain deeply Schmittean," because they still rely on the binary logic of the friend versus the enemy and are, more than ever, obsessed with the precise demarcation of the world's borders.[40]

Along with other novels that repoliticize narco representations, *2666* poses crucial questions that require our immediate attention. Can a group of people rebuild the political field to once again become, as Jacques Rancière put it, "the part of those who have no part?"[41] Is literature a privileged intellectual practice capable of creating a performative and, at the same time, political discourse? Among scholars who answer no to these questions and who insist on the post-political condition of our times, Brett Levinson argues:

> The more *2666* performs its duty as literature, the more it loses its way as a political and historical declaration. The more it says about history, the more it yields its status as literature. Literature is never political. Attending to politics, it forgets literature; attending to literature, it turns away from politics. It cannot have either without dropping both.[42]

2666, in my opinion, responds to this criticism: literature is always a potentially political performative discourse, and the political is primarily a performative operation of identifying friends and separating them from enemies. Literature can reveal the true symbolic face of power and the equally real possibility of confronting it.

One of the many teachings of Bolaño's work is resisting the temptation to use the complacent narco mythology that has given fame and fortune to many US and Mexican novelists who dreamt of achieving the success of *The Queen of the South*. In this sense, the critics who insist that Bolaño did not write a masterpiece, in my opinion, have not carefully read *2666*. As for me, I point out just *one* of its multiple readings without reducing its scope to merely being a work on narcos. Although Bolaño only tangentially explores the phenomenon of drug trafficking, his treatment is masterful. When we return to the scene with the trafficker whose face is never shown during the novel, we observe the dramatic impossibility of seeing the *real* narco. As the policeman attempts, we need to assume a critical imagination that allows us to narrate the narco beyond the clothes and actions that make him nothing other than himself, nothing more than a cliché. In this way, the novel seeks to shed light upon the networks of power in which the narco operates, and its literary, political, and economic backdrop. It asks, along with Bolaño's policeman, what aristocracy do they represent, to which elite do they really belong?

JUAN VILLORO AND THE COUNTRY TOO FAITHFUL TO ITS OWN IMAGE

At the beginning of his award-winning essay on drug trafficking in Mexico, "The Red Carpet," Juan Villoro (1956) recalls the rituals of secrecy, euphemism, and cryptic signals of official power during the times of the PRI. In those years, a peculiar and subtle slogan was enough for a Mexican president to cypher his national project: President José López Portillo's (1970–1976) slogan, "I will defend the peso like a dog" culminated in Carlos Salinas de Gortari's (1988–1994) attitude toward his opposition in his famous, "I don't see them nor hear them" response. But, as Villoro points out, once the country abandoned the 1929 political pact that put an end to the recurring messy civil war that we customarily call the Mexican Revolution, the political messages in the first decade of the twenty-first century introduced themselves in the thundering of bullets and in the relentless horror of tens of thousands of men and women murdered in unthinkably creative ways. Among other significant changes, the two PAN presidencies transformed the spaces of political violence formerly institutionalized by the PRI: from the solitary executions on unpopulated roads such as those dramatized in Martín Luis Guzmán's *La sombra del caudillo* (*The Shadow of the Strongman*, 1929) the right-wing governments moved the dialectic of brutality to the busy streets and public squares. Villoro notes:

> We have arrived at a new order of fear: we face a diffuse, delocalized war, with no notions of "front" or "rearguard," in which we can't even determine the sides of the conflict. It has become impossible to establish with a reasonable degree of certainty who belongs to the police and who is an infiltrator.[43]

After the War on Drugs ordered by President Felipe Calderón, the mechanisms of power force us to ask ourselves who the members of these factions really are. If the essential notion of the political, as warns Carl Schmitt, consists in distinguishing friend from enemy, today more than ever it must be our first task to overcome the impossibility of representation of the narco and try to discern who is truly part of the groups that tear the country apart and who is really on the side of civil society confronting that threat. Journalism in Mexico has made an effort to chronicle the victims, but the name of the perpetrators is missing. Juan Villoro, over the course of these terrible years, has contributed significantly to the debate and at the same time has generously promoted the work of certain academics, journalists, and writers who have approached the subject with critical intelligence and challenging the usual ways of analyzing the narco that nevertheless predominate in most academic studies, journalistic reports, and novels written in Mexico.

When Villoro won the 2008 Ibero-American Journalism Award for "The Red Carpet," Calderón's alleged war on drugs was just beginning. The reference of the red carpet comes from an art installation where the readymade of Duchamp intersected with the noir tradition of the detective novel: the Sinaloan artist Rosa María Robles covered the ground of her installation space with blood-stained blankets from actual crimes that hitmen used to cover and dispose of their victims.[44] The political comment that Villoro stresses is one of unavoidable cruelty: the drug trafficker has acquired celebrity status before an audience that marvels at the minutiae of their lives and the horror of their death as if they were movie and television stars, a seductive mixture of *The Sopranos*, *Scarface*, and the telenovela *Los ricos también lloran* (The rich also cry). From that early text, Villoro noted the mythical level of the phenomenon:

> Like superheroes, narcos don't have histories or CVs: they have legends. Their counterparts in the United States stay anonymous. In Mexico they are ubiquitous and elusive. It doesn't matter if they're in a maximum-security prison or in a mansion with a mother-of-pearl jacuzzi. They never stop working.

Curiously, the state of denial about the violence has given way to a very informed fear. To certify that the capos are the "others," practically extraterrestrial beings, we memorize their exotic aliases and inventory their culinary habits: jaguar heart with gunpowder, lobster sprinkled with tamarind and cocaine.[45]

Villoro the chronicler could not have overlooked the most pressing issue of our time. A keen and careful reader of the authorities on the subject, Villoro articulates a political critique of the narco that places him alongside few journalists and academics who make up an enlightened minority and who subscribe to two key theses to understand the political dimension of the narco in Mexico. The first thesis indicates that almost every statement of knowledge about the narco is the result of a discursive monopoly held by the Mexican state. This monopoly evolved into a performative discourse matrix that predominates to this day and whose main objective is not to explain the mechanisms of the illegal drug trade, but to determine the parameters of its definition: violent, degenerate, immoral, and psychopathic organizations on the margins of the civil society who challenge the power of the state. Without further evidence to support the narrative that constructs these terms, Mexico speaks of trafficking organizations that are incessantly declaring war, breaking the economic logic of the notion of the cartel that involves different interest groups collaborating for a common goal. The second thesis deconstructs the mythology of the narco and rewrites its history as that of the state disciplining criminal organizations. In other words: the narco in Mexico not only does not antagonize the state, but it is actually the result of a political and judicial operation directed from the same state that structures, and at the same time, puts limits on the illicit drug market. By working with both theses in his essays and narratives, Villoro has established himself in Mexico as one of the last public intellectuals with the clarity and independence necessary to articulate an effective political critique of drug trafficking.

The social echoes of the history of organized crime in Mexico and its forms of representation have fascinated Villoro throughout his literary career. In his novel *El disparo de argón* (Argon's shot, 1991) organ trafficking functions as the ghost that haunts a small community of ophthalmologists who must confront the outbreak of crime in a clinic specialized in improving the eyesight of their patients. Learning to critically see reality is also the motif of *Materia dispuesta* (Arranged matter, 1997) a novel in which a teenager discerns between the nationalist ideology defended by his father, a famous architect, and the rubble that remains when that ideology, together with the corrupt national project manufactured by the PRI, finally collapses literally and symbolically with the earthquake that destroyed the capital in 1985. Then, in *El testigo* (The witness, 2004), Villoro's greatest novel, a self-exiled intellectual in France returns to a democratized Mexico only to discover that the right wing, newly arrived to power, is trying to revamp the country's failed nationalism toward a neoconservatism turn in which the poet Ramón López Velarde is canonized. It is in this new national (dis) order that organized crime covers greater spaces thanks to the power vacuum left by the fall of the PRI in 2000. The narco appears in the novel as a fledgling threat that runs free from the ties of the federal government and that now must make a pact with the emerging regional powers in the northern states of the country. In this sense, *The Witness* is the faithful chronicle of the rebuilding of drug trafficking when the national structure of the PRI was fragmented by new agreements between governors, state police, and both legitimate and illegitimate businessmen.

In 2012, when Villoro published *Arrecife* (*The Reef*), the country had already been through disaster. The plot features two musicians defeated by a brutal and miserable Mexican reality who decide to exploit their country's debacle as part of a unique tourism project. Mario and Tony have squandered their youth in a drug haze and the fleeting rock band that they called Los Extraditables, which reduces the image of the violent Medellín cartel to an insignificant and superficial act in which Pablo Escobar returns to sing the most emotional songs of his life to heavy metal riffs. After the downfall that sooner or later crushes any rock band that prides itself on having tasted stardom, the survivors of Los Extraditables operate a hotel in the Mayan Riviera with the main objective to attract foreign tourists who seek to entertain themselves among the residues of Latin American neoliberalism. Mario, the ex-musician turned hotel manager, explains:

> In all the newspapers of the world there is bad news about Mexico: mutilated bodies, faces sprayed with acid, cut-off heads, a naked woman hanging from a pole, piles of corpses. That causes panic. The strange thing is that in quiet places there are people who want to feel that. They are tired of a life without surprises. [. . .] If they feel fear it means they are alive: they want to *rest feeling fear.*[46]

The extreme vacation experiment is certainly a success. Gringo tourists enjoy being kidnapped by armed commandos with AK-47's breaking the peaceful nighttime tranquility of their penthouse stay. The bureaucrats take pleasure at the guerrilla's bullets saluting them during a daytrip between

Mayan pyramids. Los Extraditables are no longer those criminals who long ago defied the Colombian state: now they are the administrators of a hotel-simulation, the domesticated narco reduced to one more function of the global economy.

The pyramid as a theme appears appropriately accurate within the impoverished Mexican present: it is the last historical artifact to be exploited. Villoro reformulates it with all the coldness of the businessman: The Pyramid is the hotel complex where tourists will pay for a dose of adrenaline, for risking their lives in a country whose best export product is a near-death experience on the polluted Caribbean. Two murders confirm though, that the risk may be too real and that a visit to the hotel is equivalent to playing Russian roulette. In this way, Villoro works with second-degree rubble, the ruins of the ruins, the final exhausted memory of the picturesque Mexico of López Velarde, who demands of the nation in his poem, "La suave Patria" ("The Sweet Homeland"): "Patria, I give you the key to your happiness: be faithful forever to your likeness."[47] Villoro, as the Pyramid manager, refutes: "This country looks too much like itself. It offers past, past and past. Guitars, sunsets and pyramids."[48]

The Pyramid is therefore a hotel that only offers the present and that has clearly understood the two options of the Mexican businessman: either declare bankruptcy and launder drug trafficking money or work with the main raw material of the national landscape—violence. If it's impossible to sell clean sand and run restaurants where no one empties an AK-47 on the dining customers, then you have to capitalize on the danger and collapse, admire the polluted coral, mess up your hair with a burst of bullets, live with the despair of a guerrilla invented in a country where the Zapatistas are busier looking for what to eat than willing to listen to the brilliant speeches of Subcomandante Marcos. "Nature likes everyone and puppies of all kinds stir the heart, but if you don't spoil something, you don't eat. The Pyramid came from plunder, poor people continued to be poor, but they died less or not as soon," notes the creator of the resort.[49] Villoro echoes here Martín Caparrós's thesis in his essay, *Contra el cambio: Un hiperviaje al apocalipsis climático* (Against change: A hypertravel into climate apocalypse, 2010), noting how after destroying the world for their benefit, the world superpowers demand that their subordinate countries build natural reserves and virgin beaches, forcing them to renounce the benefit of the exploitation of mineral wealth and allow no one to access nuclear power except those who prohibit others from building new reactors.

The Reef's narrator, Tony, knows that in a country where history is devoted to counting government-ordered killings, all that remains to be done is to make some profit from it. Tony's father was victimized in the 1968 Tlatelolco student massacre, and as a boy, Tony believed he deserved compensation: "When the apartment buzzer rang, I imagined a government messenger with a color television for having someone in the family die during Tlatelolco."[50] And so, when an elementary school teacher rewards him for his father being disappeared by the state, the narrator claims: "I didn't want a 10 in civics. I wanted the government to give me a television."[51]

A police detective novel, a chronicle of the neoliberal disaster, a subtle and sharp narco novel, *The Reef* addresses the end of that succession of multitudinous misunderstandings that we call the "history of Mexico." *Argon's Shot* taught us how to navigate the fragmented Mexico City neighborhoods in the megalopolis, whose center was everywhere except in Carlos Fuentes's *La region más transparente* (*Where the Air Is Clear*). With *Arranged Matter*, Villoro laid out the attitude of the generation that grew up in the crash of earthquakes who had to learn to break through the rubble of their homeland besieged by tectonic plates and the fissures of nationalist discourses, with its violent forms of masculinity, its families representing the functional illusion of Mexican society. With *The Witness*, Villoro anticipates the trial of recent history and reveals to us the profound failure of the neoconservative turn toward a supposedly newly democratized Mexico: the political suicide that implies letting Televisa (Mexico's largest TV network) dictate the limits of reality and for the business world to transform the whole country into a country club with continuous shootings inside and outside its walls. *The Reef* is an added warning that, after the national apocalypse of more than 121,000 homicides attributed to the narco—that other ghost invented by the state—it is only possible to survive by reproducing the vectors of violence as another exotic product of our international street fair, along with mezcal, petroleum, and telenovelas, whose stars now decorate, with their blonde presence, our criminal but very photogenic political class.

In the last decade, the Mexican literary field has recognized numerous narco narratives that, regardless of their level of realism, are aligned with the coordinates of official state discourse. Far from the mythological representations of the more commercial narcoliterature, Villoro's Mexico only has to sell itself, but not its pastel pink past, which now only exists in the poetry of López Velarde and in the recalcitrant dreams of the PRI dinosaurs. Now, its ruins will exist, as if to say: *come and see us, we are the dark side of the West, here your nightmares can come true, you will find relief to the boredom of always having something to eat, of not fearing an assault on the subway, of living a democracy where Presidents have opened a book once in their life.*

In 2013 Villoro published the essay "La violencia en el espejo" ("Violence in the mirror") in which he examines Felipe Calderón's six-year term, which far exceeds the destruction first described in "The Red Carpet" in 2008. In order to separate itself from the victims of its War on Drugs, the Calderón government tried to reactivate the discursive matrix created by the PRI to give a name to the clandestine public company for drug trafficking in Mexico active until the presidency of Carlos Salinas de Gortari. Justifying the bloodiest program of biopolitics conceived in modern Mexican history, Calderón propelled the official state narrative that claimed that the country was in the hands of dangerous drug cartels much more concerned with annihilating each other than in continuing to generate the unfathomable profits that allegedly put them on the *Forbes* millionaires list. Villoro says in his essay:

> Drug trafficking seems less serious if it is something understandable. For six years, President Felipe Calderón insisted on a combative logic with factions, lines of fire, loyal and enemy troops, where the government stayed out of the problem and fought the others [. . .] The reality is different: drug trafficking forms part of society. Seeing the drug lords as aliens eating an informer's liver for lunch, collecting gold giraffes, and using ivory pistols is reassuring because it confirms that they are different from us. But just like in mirrors, things are closer than they appear.[52]

Here Villoro joins a critical current that, in order to understand the narco, proposes to look back at the state and its anti-drug policies, which, like the extraordinary rhetoric of the PRI, are actually pro-drug policies, that is, in favor of its control and its profitable submission. Perhaps therein lies the secret of the political continuity that has operated in the transition from the PRI to the PAN and back to the PRI, one that Juan Villoro has been able to transfer to literature: the project to effectively manage a post-apocalyptic country that does not blush by profiting from its national tragedy, and rather, makes self-destruction a brilliant economic opportunity; using organized crime for a complexly woven geopolitical plot while always finding the positive side of that same ultra-thin social fabric. That country has been boldly and unambiguously denounced by Villoro's essays as well as his novels. By doing so, Villoro adds his voice to those other writers whose literary political interventions are key to our present and will undoubtedly be the first references of our immediate future: I am referring specifically to Roberto Bolaño and *2666*, which gives narrative form to the new post-PRI political order of Ciudad Juárez and the triumph of the local narco, now regulated by state political elites and their armed police units; to Daniel Sada and his novel *The Language of the Game*, the story of the stubborn owner of a pizzeria in a small northern town who becomes the center of a struggle between local and federal powers for control of the drug market in times of the alleged war against the narco ordered by President Calderón; and finally, to Cesar López Cuadras's *Four Deaths per Chapter*, the playful narrative of a tragic family of drug traffickers whose leader dreamed of becoming a cartel. After the deaths of Bolaño, Sada, and López Cuadras, and the coincidentally posthumous publication of these three novels, it is not easy to locate literary projects which distance themselves from the official narrative that reiterates the narco as the eternal struggle of cartels and their exotic bosses. In a country too faithful to its own image, Villoro's work continues that journey to keep thinking about who we really have been and why it is only in certain moments of our literary imagination that we can reconsider this land that we call Mexico out of habit and nostalgia.

CHAPTER 4

Drug Trafficking, Soldiers, and Police on the Border

IMAGINARY LINES OF POWER: POLITICS AND MYTHOLOGY IN THE LITERATURE ON CIUDAD JUÁREZ

It has become almost customary at this point for critics to quote Roberto Bolaño's well-known answer to an interview question, what is hell like?: "Like Cuidad Juárez, which is our curse and our mirror, the unquiet mirror of our frustrations and of our vile interpretation of freedom and our desires."[1] The image proposed by Bolaño has an evident mythological background that reduces all social space in the city to its most exceptional levels of violence. For some critics, this reduction and other similar images appear mainly in his posthumous novel *2666*. As discussed before, it is about the life of an enigmatic German writer who survives World War II and must travel to the border city of Santa Teresa—based on Ciudad Juárez—to help his nephew in prison accused of the murder of hundreds of women who have disappeared in the area for a decade. Some have negatively judged Bolaño's work based on two complimentary forms: first, as the articulation of a mythologizing narrative that is based on meaning without history, and second, as a literary project devoid of a deliberate political intention, that is, either as a dehistoricized mythology or as a depoliticized narrative. I now want to discuss the scope and limits of these two criticisms, not only when it comes to Bolaño's work, but also in relation to other literary projects that address the border region between Mexico and the United States. This will allow me a brief analysis of what in my opinion are some of the most effective forms of representation of recent violence in Ciudad Juárez, to conclude with a reflection on the general function of literature in the face of armed conflicts in contemporary society.

The Neutralized Critique

The critique that Bolaño represents Juárez in a mythological manner is prominent in the academic work of Ricardo Vigueras Fernández, who starts from "the undeniable fact that Juárez has become an imaginary construction based on realities that, when overstated, acquire a series of connotations that in principle they did not have. In the case of Juárez, all these connotations are misery, labor exploitation, ignorance, political corruption, femicides and, more recently, the high levels of daily violence that causes blood to flow in the streets without the authorities ever solving the crimes nor stopping the guilty."[2] For Vigueras, much of the imagined violence is already present in a city whose sociopolitical daily life is equally imagined. Thus, novelists end up creating their own fictions that their books propose as real.

The mythological representations of Ciudad Juárez, according to Vigueras, are the result of a very peculiar practice that he calls "juárica literature," that is, literature "that is written outside of Juárez about Ciudad Juárez as a mythical space, not as a real location, and with natural ignorance of daily life and death in Ciudad Juárez."[3] Thus, Vigueras explains, Bolaño's work has become the master signifier of this continuous mythologization of Ciudad Juárez present in practically all fields of cultural production about the region, among which 2666 stands out as "the masterpiece of juárica literature."[4] On the contrary, the academic notes, "juarense literature is that which speaks of Ciudad Juárez and is written in Ciudad Juárez."[5] The problematic distinction that Vigueras proposes between "juárica literature" and "juarense literature" categorically depends not only on a deep knowledge of the real border area but also on an ontology of presence that makes physical proximity to the real referent essential. Under this demand, juarense literature can only be written *from* Ciudad Juárez in order to avoid the mythological constructions that supposedly characterize works like those of Bolaño. Vigueras is correct in his critique of the mythological constructions that appear in the exogenous representations of Ciudad Juárez. At the same time, however, he builds a new authoritative myth: writing *in* Ciudad Juárez as the only representation authorized to enunciate reality; the writer *present* on the border as the only legitimate emissary.

Among the mythology of the so-called proper space for formulation and the political impossibility of expressing it, Bolaño's work has produced multiple interpretations that allow for its critical potential. I have already examined Bolaño's narrative, by contrast, as an example of a political demystification of Ciudad Juárez. Now I am interested in highlighting the way in which these criticisms prefigure conditions for analyzing the literature on Ciudad Juárez. Rather than *describing* literary projects like Bolaño's, these agendas *reveal* their own basic limits: in giving his definition of "juarense literature," Vigueras configures a new myth that allows him to arbitrarily designate what he considers mythological literature.

In the criticism that addresses the issue of drug trafficking and femicide in Ciudad Juárez, it is common to find this type of theoretical approach that ends up reproducing the phenomena that were supposed to be analyzed. Faced with this contradiction, it seems appropriate to re-study precisely the forms of literary representation that come into tension with the mythological dimensions of the narrative and the possibility of generating a critical understanding of the political networks that facilitate violence in Ciudad Juárez. I will now discuss two literary works that can be read for this purpose: the theatrical piece *Hotel Juárez* (2003) by Víctor Hugo Rascón Banda (1948–2008), and the novel *Policía de Ciudad Juárez* (Ciudad Juárez police, 2012) by Miguel Ángel Chávez Díaz de León (1962). The two texts, as I will discuss later, are structured as symbolic appropriations of reality that lay out a critical knowledge of border violence. And despite being written with mythological resources, the two works show a political emphasis on their strategies of representation *from* and *about* Ciudad Juárez. This will lead me to point out, toward the end of this chapter, the remarkable political agency present in these textual practices as the essential component for understanding the history of cultural productions around Ciudad Juárez.

Theater and the Materiality of Femicide

One of the first journalists to cover the femicide in Ciudad Juárez was US reporter Charles Bowden, whose article "While You Were Sleeping," published in 1996 in the influential *Harper's* magazine gave international visibility to the phenomenon for the first time. The article discusses femicide as an integral part of a condition of widespread social precarity in Ciudad Juárez, the result of a radicalized process of political and economic breakdown with the implementation of the North American Free Trade Agreement (NAFTA) between Mexico, the United States, and Canada in 1994. According to Bowden, Ciudad Juárez has allowed us to envision the future of post-industrial societies:

This future is based on the rich getting richer, the poor getting poorer, and industrial growth producing poverty faster than it distributes wealth. We have these models in our heads about growth, development, infrastructure. Juárez doesn't look like any of these images, and so our ability to see this city comes and goes, mainly goes.[6]

Bowden's text offers a critical journey through different sectors of the city. His gaze is guided by the journalistic work of local photographers whom Bowden consults to understand the dynamics of violence. Although his style is personal and subjective, in keeping with the tradition of US New Journalism, his comments can hardly be read as a mythological narrative. One of the few times Bowden refers to the murders in a mythical way is when he reads a story in a Ciudad Juárez newspaper about the disappearance of a young woman:

> I turned to a friend I was having breakfast with and said, "What's this about?" He replied matter-of-factly, "Oh, they disappear all the time. Guys kidnap them, rape them, and kill them." Them? Oh, he continued, you know, the young girls who work in the maquiladoras, the foreign owned factories, the ones who have to leave for work when it is still dark. Of course, I knew that violence is normal weather in Juárez. As a local fruit vendor told an American daily, "Even the devil is scared of living here."[7]

This comment, which largely reflects the impressionable average public opinion, appears in the beginning of the article. The rest of the text is presented as Bowden's effort to understand the phenomenon beyond these mythological conditions. Through his visits into the city, his collection and analysis of hard data on the local, national, and international economy, all together with careful first-hand documentation from juarense photographers, and with a critical look at the conditions of possibility of that violence, Bowden's contribution on the subject goes beyond the mere subjective description of violence.

Ironically, the vast majority of investigative journalism books published over the next decade seem to undertake the same operation, but in the opposite direction: from the complex social reality of Ciudad Juárez, a myth starts to form, a myth that radicalizes gender violence in the city. Among these, the most emblematic case is undoubtedly *Bones in the Desert* (2002) by Sergio González Rodríguez. From the first page, González Rodríguez affirms that until the time of his writing—almost a decade after the murders began to be reported in 1993—there had been "a hundred serial murders" in a "misogynistic sacrificial orgy promoted by the authorities."[8] Throughout the book, González Rodríguez insists on the existence of the most prolific serial killer in world history, protected by the most perverse police bureau and political system in memory. In academia, femicide is also the object of the same voluntarist interpretation. When reading 2666, for example, Jean Franco underlines gender violence as a cultural expression inherent in Mexican society. Franco explains:

> Mexico represents, in exaggerated form, a hostility toward women that, despite feminism, despite the partial acquisition of women's rights, is deeply embedded. We are not talking of the werewolf here, of man becoming a wolf, but of extreme forms of masculinity that are backed by society itself.[9]

In view of this type of analysis, which promotes the implausible action of a serial killer and that views gender violence as a cultural practice standardized by society itself, researcher Molly Molloy balances more precise statistical information to conclude that the femicide of Ciudad Juárez is a discursive "myth":

> Of the roughly 400 cases documented in Esther Chavez'[one of the main local activists] files from 1990 to 2005, about three-quarters of the cases were domestic violence, and the cases were essentially resolved. That is, the killer was known as an acquaintance or domestic partner or other relative of the victim. Only about 100 were completely unsolved cases. These are the cases that have received (and continue to receive) most of the media, artistic and academic attention. The only real statistical study on the topic, done in 2008, found that the proportion of female homicides in Ciudad Juárez was lower than Houston's.[10]

Molloy refers here to an article by Pedro H. Albuquerque and Prasad Vemala, who set out to "challenge conventional wisdom and a large share of the existing literature on the US-Mexico border femicide phenomenon."[11] As Molloy notes, this careful statistical study shows that the average rate of femicide in Ciudad Juárez is similar to that of US cities such as Los Angeles and Houston, and even lower than that of several cities in northern Mexico. Against popular opinion, Albuquerque and Vemala explain that the presence of the maquiladoras is not relevant to the phenomenon, since only 10 percent of the victims worked in this sector. The study also reveals that, despite the fact that media and literary works frequently focus on the youngest victims, the reality is that 37 percent of the murdered women were between fifteen and twenty-four years old, while 47 percent of the victims were over twenty-four years of age, many of them unemployed and living with a permanent domestic partner: "The notion that female victims in Ciudad Juárez are young maquiladora workers unfortunately leaves a large number of victims out of the debate who do not fit into this stereotype, contributing to a lack of understanding of the serious problem of femicide in the border region."[12]

This recurring fallacious characterization of the victims serves the myth of femicide that Molloy points elucidates. When forms of representation are articulated from the literary point of view that reproduce the stereotype of the victimized young woman, the most significant conditions of the phenomenon inevitably disappear, such as unemployment, extreme economic inequality, the vulnerability of institutions, institutional corruption. In their place are the machismo and misogyny supposedly inherent to Mexican "culture," the sensationalism of the young woman's corpse assaulted by a fantastical serial killer protected by the highest echelons of power.

The play *Hotel Juárez* by the Chihuahuan writer Víctor Rascón Banda partly responds to that mythological perception of femicide. The drama centers on Ángela, a young woman from the state of Durango who is deported after a season as an undocumented worker in the United States. It is understood that she has been deported to Ciudad Juárez, where she decides to look for her sister Aurora, a young maquiladora worker who disappeared weeks before. Ángela is staying at the Hotel Juárez, located to the south of the Pan-American Highway, between the city limits and the airport. That area of Ciudad Juárez is distinguished by the empty desert, which surrounds lower-middle class residential neighborhoods a considerable distance from the city center.

The hotel is structured as a class system that discriminates according to the political and economic position of its guests. Ramsés, a talkative magician who lives there temporarily, explains to Ángela that, on the second floor, for example, there is the manager's room, the junior and master suites where notable figures stay such as bullfighters, singers, and some ranchers who survive the permanent droughts, and of course drug traffickers, the last of which are "good clients, quiet, out of the way, well-equipped."[13] Human traffickers with groups of undocumented Central Americans are housed on the third floor. Vendors from the informal economy sleep on the following floors: second-hand clothing smugglers, used car importers, back alley synthetic drug dealers. On the sixth and final floor, the upward spiral of misery ends with the poorest guests: retirees, single women, old prostitutes, and among them, Ángela and Ramsés.

The social distribution of the rooms is revealing: the hotel, like the entire city, experiences a radical segregation that discriminates even among the marginal sectors. It is not the same to be a used clothing smuggler as it is to be an unemployed single woman. The characters are fully aware of the layers of misery that surround the city of almost two million inhabitants. This is what Ramsés says:

> Juárez is a floating city. It is a city of passage. But many remain. Here remain the "undocumented," the unsuccessful, the weak, those with doubts. The strong pass. There is an earth-colored belt around the city. Neighborhoods grow and grow without water, without light, without streets. People who build their houses out of cardboard and sheet metal. When they resign themselves to staying, they use cement. Juárez is not September 16 Avenue, nor the Las Américas mall, nor the Santa Fe Bridge, nor the Pan-American highway. There is another Juárez that invades the desert and grows among the dunes, the chaparral, and mesquite. It is like an animal that stretches out, like a living stain that moves forward.[14]

It is significant to note that, despite its squalor, Hotel Juárez is located on the high-traffic Pan-American Highway, which according to Ramsés is still part of the urban area. While the city still maintains relatively functional and inhabitable sectors for the middle class, there are numerous makeshift settlements on the outskirts of the city whose residents live in extreme poverty, for which a stay in the hotel would be an unattainable luxury. Despite the stark realism of the plot, the most radical conditions of poverty in the city are not directly represented. By not including the most precarious regions of the city, Rascón Banda allows the viewer to enter an ambiguous zone that combines survival with dispossession and illegality, where it is possible to visualize the dynamics of oppression and corruption at the hands of the institutional powers in the city: politicians, the police, and businessmen.

Such is the situation for Ángela, who is quickly taken advantage of first by Ramsés and then by El Johnny, a driver who works for the hotel manager and a police chief who is also staying there. The three are in the middle of a political plot led by a *licenciado* who is understood to work for the Institutional Revolutionary Party (PRI), the same one that ruled the country for seventy-one consecutive years. The *licenciado* tries, with little success, to influence local elections where the right-wing National Action Party (PAN) dominates. Later, that *licenciado* asks Ángela, who has been a secretary in the United States, to translate from English what appears to be a written agreement between drug traffickers that establishes the way to send a certain "merchandise," as well as payment by Swiss or Dutch bank account deposits.[15] Ángela makes friends with Lupe, a maquiladora worker who participates in protests over the working conditions of the factory. Lupe tells Ángela that there are video cameras, lights, and a bed in the hotel's backroom. Johnny had offered Ángela to participate in a pornographic film, and so she figures this to be his makeshift studio. It is there that the police chief hits and rapes Rosalba, an undocumented fifteen-year-old girl who was unable to cross into the United States and who stays temporarily with El Johnny. Lupe notes that "woman's cries" are heard over there.[16]

After Ángela translates the agreement between drug traffickers, the *licenciado*, to ensure silence, orders her murder. The police chief and El Johnny break into her room, where they find her asleep next to Ramsés. Threatening the police chief with a pistol, El Johnny decides to let them go, as he yells at the police chief for having raped (and probably murdered) Rosalba. It is also revealed at this point that El Johnny and Ramsés are brothers. When Ángela and Ramsés try to escape, the police chief draws his weapon. Everyone dies except for El Johnny, who leaves the room after closing the eyes of his dead brother's face.

The hotel is not the *natural* site of these types of murders. Instead it represents the *contingent* site of the crimes, since it is located in that liminal zone between the functional city and the slums, with little police surveillance and an abundant flow of migration. Rascón Banda describes the crime as a result of a context in which the corrupted rule of law and vulnerability of migration and poverty flourish. There is no dramatization of a culture of machismo and misogyny in the play, but rather a material experience of those forces facilitated by social conditions that exacerbate them.

Published in 2003, *Hotel Juárez* engages with on the national and international media coverage taking place at that time on the question of femicide. For this reason, it resorts to the figure of the young maquiladora worker as the archetype of the victim. Nevertheless, Rascón Banda also shows other key conditions of the phenomenon: poverty, police corruption, the exploitation of women, and the greed of the business class. By reproducing a real interview that a journalist had with an Egyptian man accused by the Juárez police as the serial killer, Rascón Banda notes how the murders of women continued despite his arrest along with other alleged killers. Of course, machismo and misogyny are also relevant factors in crimes, but these phenomena alone do not explain the violence in Ciudad Juárez. That is why Rascón Banda situates the play in a historical background that represents border violence without suggesting that the entire society is sexist and without the fantasy of a serial killer. *Hotel Juárez* historicizes femicide in its political and economic landscape, in the power dynamics that make poor women one of the most vulnerable social groups on the border.

The Novel and Narco Politics

When describing the presence of the narco in the context of the murders of women in Ciudad Juárez, the anthropologist Rita Segato analyzes the emergence of a "second state," or a "parallel state" made up of criminal organizations that are at the same time the condition of possibility of both femicide and drug trafficking in the border city.[17] According to Segato, the archetypal criminal of the border can be symbolized by the figure of a "feudal and postmodern baron" that dominates the region:

> Nevertheless, in the more than terrible contemporary postmodern, neoliberal, post-state, post-democratic order, the baron has become capable of controlling his territory in an almost unrestricted way as a consequence of the unruly accumulation characteristic of the frontier's expansion, exacerbated by the globalization of the economy and the loose neoliberal market rules in effect. Its only regulating force is the greed and predatory potency of his competitors, the other barons.[18]

Affirming the operational logic of neoliberalism, this type of post-political approach establishes a narrative based on archetypes such as "the baron" that hypothetically act in a context a priori and dehistoricized. Such explanatory models depend on a fragmented, dispersed state in permanent political crisis. Once the presence of the state is erased, these studies *imagine* criminal bosses who overtake the official state power that has been discredited in advance. Thus, by turning the phenomenon into a constant struggle between rival criminals, these analyses, perhaps inadvertently, depoliticize drug trafficking and in return moralize it, assuming it to be a manifestation of evil in contemporary society.

This way of imagining the narco, as I have analyzed in this book, is the direct result of an official state discourse that has permeated society for decades and that positions organized crime as a permanently defiant enemy of state sovereignty. As I have already discussed in detail, Mexican antidrug policy has essentially been transformed into a violent national security strategy that, after the presidency of Felipe Calderón, has consisted of the deployment of tens of thousands of soldiers and federal police in the cities with the highest rate of drug trafficking, Ciudad Juárez the most problematic of all. However, in 2007, Ciudad Juárez registered 320 murders, a figure below the average sustained between 1993 and 2007 with just 0.7 murders per day. After the arrival of the army and the federal police on March 28, 2007, murders increased to more than 1,623 in 2008 (4.4 daily), 2,754 in 2009 (7.5 daily), 3,622 in 2010 (9.9 daily) and finally with a decrease to 2,086 in 2011 (5.7 daily). Thus, at least 10,085 of the more than 121,000 homicides recorded during Calderón's war occurred in Ciudad Juárez.[19]

We can read *Ciudad Juárez Police* by Miguel Ángel Chávez Díaz de León in the context of this convulsive political climate. The novel was published in 2012, immediately after the most combative years of Calderón's drug strategy that turned Juárez into the most violent city in the country. The protagonist is the police officer Pablo Faraón, head of the "Ribbon Brigade," the team of police officers that cordon off crime scenes with yellow tape preventing ordinary citizens to pass. The work of Faraón and his partner Ruth Romo—known as "Chief Yellow" and "Lieutenant Tape"— is constantly interrupted by other police officers, who steal anything of value while they investigate, and the sensationalist press photographers, who rearrange the corpses to improve their shots.[20] Faraón is originally from one of the poor neighborhoods of Ciudad Juárez, the Arroyo Colorado. Through Faraón's memories and his wanderings on the old downtown streets, the novel reconstructs decades of border history in the second half of the twentieth century, when the city was modernized and expanded along with its industrial zones and the dozens of new neighborhoods that began populating the desert outskirts.

Along with the urban explosion, organized crime also increased. According to Faraón, the city was controlled by La Regla (The Ruler), a mafia working for the Paso del Norte cartel (Paso del Norte is the old name of the border city). Suddenly, the Durango cartel and its boss, "Chavo" Gaitán, appear and intend to take over La Regla to control the city's drug trade. The novel clearly operates here as a roman à clef: El Chavo Gaitán is a direct reference to Joaquín "El Chapo" Guzmán, alleged leader of the Sinaloa cartel, while La Regla corresponds to La Línea, which according to the federal government was "the armed wing of the Juárez Cartel." The group called itself that because it forced the alignment of all the drug traffickers in the city, literally to "get in line," subjecting them all under the same control. Until this part, *Ciudad Juárez Police* reproduces the official state narrative on drug trafficking in Mexico point by point: Juárez, like places such as Tijuana, Michoacán, or Monterrey, is being disputed by rival groups of drug traffickers who seek control of the "plaza." Early in the novel, Faraón explains that La Regla controls "half of the Municipal Police and the majority of the Ministerial Police, including its higher ups."[21] Among the bribed officers is Faraón himself, who accepts, along with his salary, a monthly payment of fifteen thousand pesos. And although they have never demanded anything from him in return, "they bought us by force, those of La Regla, if not, you're dead."[22]

As is common in narco noir novels, *Ciudad Juárez Police* uses narrative resources typical of the genre despite the problematic mythology of their intentions. An example of this is the half gallon of milk that Faraón finds "in fifteen-hundred of the two-thousand and something murders" and that functions as a "message left by the sicarios of La Regla."[23] Following the conventions of the police detective novel, the novel introduces a psychopath who leaves a trademark at the scene of the terrible crimes he commits. His name is Atoto (originally from Atotonilco, a town in the state of Guanajuato), an avid milk drinker and ruthless La Regla boss. El Atoto displays his power by assassinating the Municipal Police chief and then killing thirty-five people in a bus, all of whom, according to Atoto, were collaborators of Chavo Gaitán.

From this moment, however, the plot takes a narrative turn away from mythology and into politics: the Municipal Police are deactivated and give absolute control to the Mexican Army and Federal Police, who take to the streets at the orders of the President of the Republic. Desperate for the state violence that awaits the local drug traffickers, Atoto meets with Faraón and explains the real situation in the streets:

> The whole world is taking money from the troubled waters, now any fucking snot-nosed kid can go and ask for a fee, and they all think they're extortionists, they go on kidnaping like if they were going to buy some bread and kill and kill and fuck us all up. [. . .] What you see in the papers is all bullshit, a lot of heavy cargoes are getting here but the feds and the dirty soldiers keep them to themselves and they want to resell them to us as if it were gold.[24]

El Atoto claims that Chavo Gaitán's people are being equally decimated and extorted by federal forces, so he proposes a cease fire between the two sides and even offers "to clean house of the assholes who are working on their own account. If Gaitán's people cooperate, in up to two weeks we will leave Juárez free of dirty rats."[25] Although Faraón continues to believe that it is a cartel war, the state forces maintain their clear upper hand, shown by the two criminal organizations being forced to seek a truce. In exchange for his help, Faraón asks Atoto to locate Ruth's daughter, who disappeared along with her then-husband, a police chief who was assassinated on his own police bureau's orders.

Toward the end of the novel, Faraón asks Atoto who the top leaders are of the criminal organization. The undecisive answer is suggestive: "You can't imagine, better that you don't know."[26] The conflict is resolved when the main members of La Regla are murdered in a bar in the city. Only Atoto escapes alive. In the end, the narco is forced to hand over Ruth's daughter, and the novel ends when she and Faraón head out to find her. Regardless of the explanations of the violence provoked by the novel, La Regla has been destroyed by federal forces with the intermittent collaboration of rival drug traffickers. Despite the unmeasured power that the novel, reproducing official state discourse, attributes to the supposed drug cartels, the final reality of the drug traffickers leads to a critical commentary fundamental to understanding the world of drug trafficking in Mexico—the power of the state always prevails.

From Mythology to Politics

As Ernesto Laclau teaches, all formation of hegemonic discourse is produced from the articulation of a metaphor that essentially summarizes a specific political project. The metaphor works thanks to an erasure of the contingent conditions of its own enunciation, since it is based on links of falsely associated metonymic attributes made invisible by the metaphor itself. Laclau cites the famous study by Roman Jakobson on the structuring of language through two procedures based on the combination and substitution of linguistic elements. Both procedures, Jakobson continues, can be understood respectively as devices of metonymy and metaphor. Laclau takes up Jakobson's theory to apply it to discursive formations in contemporary society, but this analytical methodology is also useful for understanding the representations of violence on the border. Both femicide and drug trafficking are metaphors that erase the contingent history of the power and oppression that produces them to allow for a convenient mythology to prevail. These mythological articulations have supported the thesis that gender violence is the result of a generalized practice of Mexican machismo and serial killers without precedent in world history. Similarly, drug trafficking has been described as the supreme criminal force that surpasses state power and that controls a large part of the national territory. Echoing poststructuralist theoretical thought, Laclau discusses the critical disarticulation of hegemonic discourses to reveal the imaginary lines of power that configure them. To materialize this criticism, "the dissolution of a hegemonic formation involves the reactivation of that contingency: the return from a 'sublime' metaphoric fixation to a humble metonymic association."[27] In the literary works studied here, I have tried to highlight that same narrative of political contingency that manages to dissolve the metaphors of violence that dominate many recent literary productions. This acute political function of literature in contemporary society is also active in the work of authors who have represented the narco outside of the mythological inertia with which we name their violence. In this book I have studied the works of four of them: Roberto Bolaño, César López Cuadras, Daniel Sada, and Juan Villoro. These works take on the political potential that are now beginning to multiply and will renew the critical agendas of Mexican literature in our immediate future.

JULIÁN CARDONA AND CHARLES BOWDEN, HERETICS PREACHING IN HELL

"The border has not always been there," an article in the cultural magazine, *Guaraguao*, notes on Ciudad Juárez.[28] The statement is forceful because, despite the social upheaval that exists on the border, the fact is that Ciudad Juárez, or at least its contemporary version, *appeared* on the horizon of global academic and journalistic thought only since the mid-nineties. Two phenomena have shaped the image that the name Juárez evokes as a transcendent metaphor for late Mexican modernity: the murders of women and drug trafficking. Both problems have become naturalized as symbols of a permissive violence that is constitutive of the social order of the city. The effect of this naturalization is of course problematic: Ciudad Juárez, as I have already discussed, is an empty signifier that is frequently filled with the negative reversal of the country's historical processes. But that imaginary comes into tension with a local journalistic archive whose importance cannot be overstated.

Within that archive, which of course includes the work of numerous border journalists, I highlight the collaboration between US reporter Charles Bowden and the Mexican photographer Julián Cardona. The work of both, which lasted almost two decades of intertwined projects, has become an obligatory reference point for every student of the border. Bowden's essays and Cardona's photojournalism have produced an alternative way of looking at and understanding Ciudad Juárez. In what follows I analyze some of the scope and limits of this collaboration in order to examine that view that has influenced our knowledge of the recent history of the most unusual border events of our time.

Learning to See

I started working as a reporter for *El Diario de Juárez* (now just *El Diario*) in 1996, the same year that Bowden published "While You Were Sleeping" in *Harper's* magazine. That article was one of the first that drew the international attention that transformed Ciudad Juárez into the national bastion of violence and marginalization that it has been known for in the decades since. Like the vast majority of people from the border region, I was not familiar with the reality that is described in that text. The deep social decomposition and systemic corruption of the power structures were delineated to me through Bowden's lyrical and personal gaze. The text was controversial, and I remember the objections of several colleagues who viewed the article as the opportunistic fantasy of a *gringo* reporter trying to make a name for himself by covering a supposedly dangerous city. But, reporting alongside several of the photographers, including Cardona, I soon understood that Juárez was hiding levels of complexity that were just beginning to become visible. The work of Bowden and the photographers was undoubtedly a watershed moment for international opinion, but it also showed people from Juárez unknown aspects of their city whose possibilities of representation were not acknowledged.

Bowden's chronicle was the result of several research trips in Juárez guided by photographers from *El Diario*. Julián Cardona appears in the article as one of the "teachers" who educate Bowden to see the city differently from most foreign journalists who began writing about the border in the late 1990s:

> Julian, about thirty, is a tall, long-legged, thin man with a deep voice. On the street they call him El Compás, the compass. He laughs easily and always seems to be watching. One night at the newspaper, as I plowed through a thick stack of negatives, he watched me like a hanging judge. Finally, I plucked a negative of a cop holding up the shoe of a dead girl found in the desert. Cardona looked at it and for the first time allowed himself a small smile. "This is a good image," he said, almost with relief.[29]

I remember almost identical scenes: Julián literally teaching me to *see* the daily work of the team of photographers, putting my budding journalistic sense to the test before an image that alone offered the essential elements of a chronicle. In Bowden's chosen photograph, a girl's shoe in the hands of a policeman in the dunes of the Juárez desert reveals the capacity for synthesis that Cardona builds in the composition of each image to apprehend the systemic violence of the city. But these compositional codes require an intelligent look and willing gaze from the public in order to discern the various shots captured in each frame. They are the privilege of a gaze that has learned to expand its own limits.

Slavoj Žižek defines the notion of systemic violence that I refer to here as "the violence inherent in a system," constitutive of dominant power relations.[30] Cardona's photographs constantly make the cause and effect of this violence visible in a single image. Without the trappings of the usual sensationalistic photographic work portraying systematic violence (corpse, destruction, misery), Cardona presents multiple aspects of the systems of domination and exploitation that generally operate subtly in contemporary society. In this way, the police officer *discovering* the shoe of the outraged woman in the desert allows for different levels of meaning that lend to multiple readings of the dynamics of violence that are exerted in the most vulnerable sectors of the population, as well as the relationship that this phenomenon has or may have with the police and the other state institutions of the border.

From the beginning of the collaboration, Cardona's photographs with Bowden's prose established an intense intellectual dialogue about the networks of power that are frequently overlooked in most analyzes of Ciudad Juárez. An investigative journalist, author of more than ten books on environmental and political disasters, Bowden found the ideal interlocutor in Cardona, a self-taught photographer with vast Juárez media experience. Paradoxically, their own fierce independence made them a team. The first result of this collaboration was the *Harper's* article, published in 1996. A substantial part of the photographic material that interested Bowden in that text was originally included in an exhibition organized a year earlier by the main press photographers of Juárez. Bowden noted:

> No one in El Paso, separated from Mexico by thirty feet of river, was interested in hanging their work, so they found a small room in Juárez and hung big prints they could not really afford to make. They called their show *Nada Que Ver*, "Nothing to See."[31]

The title *Nothing to See* encoded the ambiguity that the group of photographers represented by showing images of a sinister Juárez, silenced by discourses of power and by an elite that bases its wealth on the exploitation and humiliation of the most vulnerable population: migrants without education, female maquiladora workers, children exposed to all kinds of crime. In Juárez there was *nothing to see* when it came to these phenomena, a society accustomed to ignoring these issues until their images were shown. By making a record of the radical devastation of the neoliberal era materially inescapable, the photographers permanently modified the discourse of representation of domestic and international politics on border areas like Juárez.

FIGURE 2. Hosiery discarded by El Paso shopkeepers is bought, mended, dyed, and dried in the sun by a Ciudad Juárez woman living in Colonia Puerto de Anapra, who then resells the stockings for the equivalent of about one dollar. Julián Cardona, courtesy of the Tom & Ethel Bradley Center at California State University, Northridge.

The Future Among Us

The work of these photographers was the raw material for the book in which Bowden and Cardona's names appear together for the first time: *Juárez: The Laboratory of Our Future*. It was published in 1998, a decade before the city entered the deep crisis of violence and social decomposition that it currently experiences, and years before any authors made the murders of women and drug trafficking into a profitable publishing business. I stop at a photograph from those last years of the twentieth century.

We observe a humble family's clothesline in one of the neighborhoods closest to the border line. Cardona interviewed the mother who bought second-hand stockings in El Paso, Texas. After mending them, the stockings were dyed and dried in the sun over the arid dirt of the patio. The emergence of such survival strategies in the 1990s already demonstrated alternatives to emerging late capitalism in the city.

In *Picture Theory*, W. J. T. Mitchell defines the notion of the "image-text" as the materialization of "writing" in the sense that the French theorist Jacques Derrida conferred on it. Thus, "writing, in its physical, graphic form, is an inseparable suturing of the visual and the verbal, the 'imagetext'

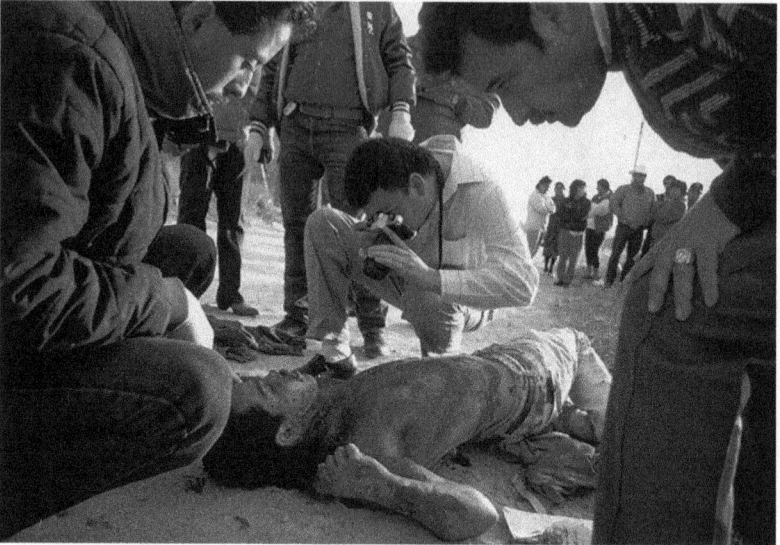

FIGURE 3. Police photographic evidence in the murder of a man who had been stabbed about thirty times. He was found on the territorial boundaries of the La Fama and Los Calaveras gangs, in Colonia 16 de Septiembre. In Ciudad Juárez, an estimated 40 percent of the homicides in recent years can be attributed to gang violence. Julián Cardona, courtesy of the Tom & Ethel Bradley Center at California State University, Northridge.

incarnate."[32] In this tension there is not necessarily a balance, but rather orders of representation that, at times, subject the image to a certain textual enunciation or, on the contrary, a text condensed into a visual composition. According to Mitchell, imagetexts can produce two effects: they generate an *illusion* that deceives the viewer and forces him to accept the simulacrum of its representation in the sensationalism of its resources; or they produce a *realism* that "is associated with the ability of photographs to show the truth of things" without imposing a certain sense of interpretation on the viewer.[33]

Cardona's photographs must be understood as imagetexts that present the effect of realism that Mitchell points out. With his contributions in *Juárez: The Laboratory of Our Future* Cardona decided to refute the globalized economy model defended in the 1990s, among others, by Francis Fukuyama, who at the time stated as fact that "globalization is inevitable" and that "markets are the most efficient drivers of economic development."[34] One photo captures the failure of globalized capitalism on the border. It is the moment that a forensic photographer documents the corpse of a young man stabbed more than thirty times.

Gang violence alone accounted for 40 percent of homicides in the city in the late 1990s. The narrative dynamics of the photograph is effective: Cardona portrays the moment in which a critical eye views a corpse, the moment in which a community learns to see the effects of marginalization and poverty as a result of the economic deterioration of neoliberal Mexico.

Bowden studied the images and surmised with the photographers that Ciudad Juárez was first and foremost the territory with the crudest effects of globalization, the ground zero of the neoliberal government structures that were imposed on Mexico after the North American Free Trade Agreement in 1994. Ciudad Juárez is an experiment of the future to come, Bowden wrote:

> This time we will not even know what to call it, because in the twentieth century we've used up all the names: progress, revolt, revolution, terrorism, wars of national liberation, genocide. We have exhausted our language trying to write over with words what we know will come.[35]

The book jolts you with the prescient signs of the city that had not yet been the subject of the immeasurable media attention that subsequently placed it as one of the most violent cities in the world. The future already reached the corpses of the men and women murdered in an environment of absolute impunity, in a city that was just entering the process of social, cultural and, above all, political transformation.

The first work written in Mexico on the phenomenon of femicide was published in 1999 by an independent publisher in Chihuahua and edited by a group of border journalists and communication specialists who titled the volume *El silencio que la voz de todas quiebra* (The silence broken by the voices of all the women). That same year, the publisher Planeta edited *Las muertas de Juárez* (The dead women of Juárez) by Víctor Ronquillo, a journalist from Mexico City. In the following years, numerous works and reports related to the murders of women appeared, propelling an important debate on gender violence in the neoliberal era, but also feeding a prejudiced imaginary that insists on cultural mythologies that do little or nothing to clarify the real causes of the problem.

Accompanied by images from thirteen Juárez photographers, a foreword by US renowned linguist and social theorist Noam Chomsky, and an epilogue by Uruguayan intellectual Eduardo Galeano, Bowden's book was the first to reflect on the frameworks of local and global hegemonic power that condition the reality of life on the border. Chomsky deconstructs the supposed benefits of the neoliberal project consolidated during the presidency of Carlos Salinas de Gortari (1988–1994) and, together with Galeano, denounces the system of inequity that has exacerbated poverty for most and privilege for a few. In the book's photographs, the murders of women assume a centrality that demands its own space for debate and that instigates unavoidable questions. The victims appear in a specific political, historical, and economic context. Femicide, the book explains, is not but the effect of the systematic dismantling of institutions and rule of law in the country, which accelerates the unraveling of an already reeling social fabric.

Despite the accurate relevancy of *Juárez: The Laboratory of Our Future*, its pioneering interpretation of border problems was affected by editorial decisions that reduced the circulation of the book and its general reception. To date, it still has not been republished. On the contrary, *Bones in the Desert*, by Sergio González Rodríguez, published in 2002 by Anagrama is undoubtedly the most cited reference among intellectual and academic circles. This essay collects interviews, press reports, police and forensic files all complemented by a series of reflections on cultural and political aspects surrounding the murders. Among the different theories on femicide that he proposes, González Rodríguez reproduces the testimony of a subcontracted officer of the State Judicial Police (illegal appointments also known as "madrinas") and speculates that hundreds of murders of women were perpetrated by two individuals, "Alejandro Máynez and his 'cousin' Melchor," who colluded with the head of the Special Anti-Kidnapping Squad of the State Judicial Police and a director of the Ciudad Juárez Municipal Police.[36] Toward the last pages of the book, and as part of a "postscript to the third edition," González Rodríguez presents the argument of a hybrid between the historical novel and noir and affirms that the hundreds of murders of women are actually the result of a political and economic sabotage planned by "a group of businessmen and politicians from Ciudad Juárez, with influence at the highest level in the country."[37] Both explanations are mutually exclusive: while the first theory blames who would be the two most prolific serial killers of all time (Jack the Ripper was accused with certainty of five of the eleven dismembered women attributed to him by the legend), the second theory is so imprecise and vague that it seems more likely to be the plot of a Hollywood blockbuster.

By contrasting *Juárez: The Laboratory of Our Future* with *Bones in the Desert*, I find an essential difference between the two books. In Cardona's photographs and Bowden's text, an immediate reality appears, portrayed without the illusion that one or so theories are able to explain everything. Bowden and Cardona's work moves through the streets of Juárez as if it were the first day for both of them, as if each morning they were

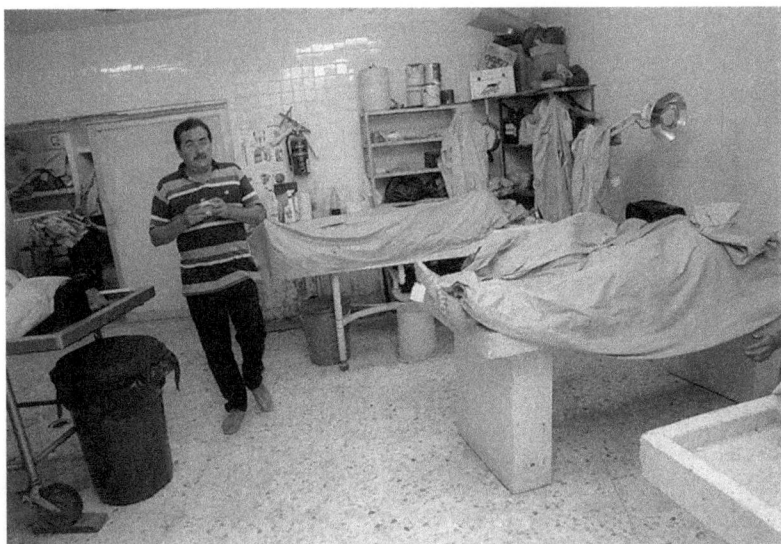

FIGURE 4. The bodies of people killed on August 3, 1997, during a shooting at the restaurant Maxfim in Ciudad Juárez. Police identified Alfonso Corral Oláguez, an alleged trafficker from the state of Durango, as the target of the attack that killed him and five other people inside the restaurant. Julián Cardona, courtesy of the Tom & Ethel Bradley Center at California State University, Northridge.

facing an unknown city that resists being fully deciphered. I particularly remember one of Cardona's photographs, one of the smallest and apparently least striking in the collection. It is the clinical white tile interior of the Ciudad Juárez hospital autopsy room. There are three corpses lying on planks that make me think for a moment of a shared university dormitory. Two nights earlier, six people in total had been killed in a popular restaurant on Avenue Paseo Triunfo de la República. In that year of 1997, public shootings between alleged drug traffickers broke out after the death of Amado Carrillo Fuentes, the head of the so-called Juárez cartel, who according to the authorities died during a plastic surgery procedure that was going to change his face and allow him to evade justice. Local media spent weeks covering the news of the shootings. Upon reaching the morgue, we were immediately barred from entering. Cardona simply walked inside. An official appears in the background of the photograph without reacting in time to stop him. The angle of the shot is slanted, as if the camera was about to fall to the right, as if the corpses are also at risk of sliding off their beds. I wrote the article for *El Diario de Juárez*, but aside for the name of the alleged drug dealer who had been the target of

FIGURE 5. A group of undocumented workers (almost all Mexicans from the state of San Louis Potosí, along with one from Honduras) fix the roof of an apartment building in Gulfport, Mississippi, in 2006. Julián Cardona, courtesy of the Tom & Ethel Bradley Center at California State University, Northridge

the massacre, the identity of the others returned to total anonymity, lost in the newspaper's archives. Studying the brutal effects of gender-based violence has been a necessary, urgent, and dramatic issue for local and foreign journalism, but not even a settling of scores between alleged drug traffickers, in all its extent, can really ever be elucidated, as if the reality of the narco constantly eluded us. The fast pace of questions that need answering always exceeds the possible responses of a roaming reporter and photographer who start over every day without knowing much about what is really happening in the streets in the first place.

Death or Exile

Bowden and Cardona's next book was *Exodus/Éxodo*, an exhaustive cross-border journey following the massive flow of migrants heading north. The project grew out of a collaborative article published in the leftist magazine *Mother Jones*. Cardona's photographs and Bowden's essays span two decades at different points on the Mexico-United States border, as well as US cities (New Orleans, Houston, Phoenix) where migrants have had an important economic and cultural presence. The book also follows them back to their

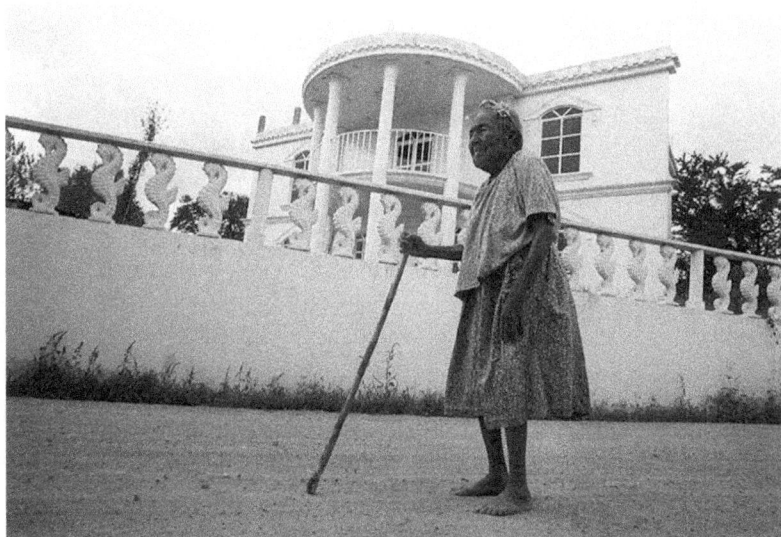

FIGURE 6. Eighty-five-year-old Felícitas Ruiz Ramos stands by her house in the town of San Andrés Ixtlahuaca, Oaxaca, in November 2006. The house was built by her son Gerardo Pérez Ruiz, an immigrant in the United States. Julián Cardona, courtesy of the Tom & Ethel Bradley Center at California State University, Northridge.

places of origin, such as the state of Oaxaca in the south of the country, where Cardona documented the mansions built with money that migrants send to their families, and that has become one of the largest sources of income in Mexico.

Ultimately, the black and white images show the migrants' lonely and dangerous journey through the Sonora desert via the Altar Valley or Sásabe-Nogales corridors, and in other photos showing them stopped by Border Patrol agents or the Minutemen militias waiting to make their own illegal citizen's arrests.

The cover photograph that ran with the *Mother Jones* article (fig. 7) is perhaps one of the most powerful commentaries on the issue of migration that I have ever seen: a desert wasteland turned into a makeshift garbage dump, the land filled with all that is left behind during the migrants' journey. Backpacks, shoes, empty plastic bottles, and clothing for people of all ages almost completely cover the sand that burns during the day and freezes at night.

The continuing migration tragedy has an exact starting date. The endless jobs in the maquiladoras along the border were an illusion that NAFTA dismantled in 1994. The United States hardened its immigration policy a few months earlier. On September 19, 1993, as Cardona accurately notes in the

FIGURE 7. A large trash site in the valley of Altar, Arizona, in April 2006. Undocumented immigrants gather in the area with human traffickers after walking sixty-five kilometers through the desert. They are instructed to dispose of all backpacks and water containers and to replace their clothes with more "American" garments before moving to a safe house. Julián Cardona, courtesy of the Tom & Ethel Bradley Center at California State University, Northridge.

epilogue of *Exodus*, the porous border line between Juárez and El Paso was closed forever. Cardona recalls that before Operation Hold the Line (originally called Operation Blockade) it was possible to cross the Rio Grande on a raft. The two-minute trip cost just two dollars. Many young people from Juárez did it to go to parties or rock concerts in El Paso. Suddenly, that morning in September, Ciudad Juárez was transformed:

> Men who had crossed daily to work construction, farm, or gardening jobs were tossing rocks at Border Patrol agents clad in gas masks and riot gear. A week into the blockade, the price to get smuggled into the United States rose from $20 to $100. Immigrants found more secret and dangerous routes, like the sewer tunnels under the river into El Paso. Three and a half months later, NAFTA went into effect and similar blockades were deployed in urban areas along the entire U.S.-Mexico border.[38]

According to Bowden and Cardona, the migrant wave constitutes the greatest exodus in the history of the world. Mass displacement is perhaps the most obvious sign of the social failure of late capitalism and its most irrefutable dimension of exploitation. Bowden's essay is interspersed with reflections on the Mexican Revolution and its very possibility coming down to those peasants who never received the justice promised by the caudillos of 1910. Migration, Bowden writes, is the only possible way to continue the pending demands of that struggle betrayed by the political and business classes of Mexico.

Starting in 1993, the disappearances of women began to be documented. In 1997, violence broke out in the streets which, among other incidents, included the murder of the six people in the restaurant I mentioned earlier. The laboratory of our future that was Juárez at the end of the nineties became *Murder City* (2010) a decade later, the title of Bowden and Cardona's final book together. The historical arc of criminality that frames the work of both books sealed the prediction of what was anticipated by the cameras of those Juárense photographers: a city on the verge of collapse during an endless wave of violence. *Murder City* picks back up the chronicle of the city that alone had over ten thousand military and Federal Police troops on the ground ordered by Felipe Calderón and his "War on Drugs" in 2007, requiring a state of national siege.

That year, the total number of murders in Ciudad Juárez did not exceed four hundred victims. In 2010 the reality was different: 3,622 murders. According to a study done by the NGO Citizen's Council for Public Security and Criminal Justice, the more than 800 percent increase in the murder rate made Juárez "the most violent metropolis in the world."[39] Between 2009 and 2010, more than 190 murders per 100,000 inhabitants were committed in Juárez, according to that document. Following that same ratio, in 2009, Juárez was followed by San Pedro de Sula, Honduras and San Salvador, with 119 and 95 murders, respectively. "It has a lot to do with the fact that some soldiers have been co-opted by drug trafficking, so it is necessary to analyze their departure from Juárez," declared José Antonio Ortega Sánchez, president of that civil association.[40]

In those years, the phenomenon of femicide was only a fraction of the chaos. As Bowden argues in *Murder City*, the number of murders of women represents only 10 to 12 percent of the homicides recorded in the city each year. Along with the need to denounce the systemic crimes against women, it is important to note that the homicides of men occur in the same void of judicial order and in an environment of the deepest impunity. Bowden writes:

> ignoring the dead men enables the United States to ignore the failure of its free-trade schemes, which in Juárez are producing poor people and dead

FIGURE 8. A poster of a young woman used for shooting practice in the backyard of the so-called House of Death in Ciudad Juárez. In January 2004, Mexico's Federal Police unearthed twelve bodies from this yard. An undercover informant on the payroll of U.S. Immigration and Customs Enforcement (ICE) is implicated in the killings. At the least, the first homicide committed in this home was transmitted to ICE agents in El Paso through a recording. These events only came to light when DEA agents in Juarez were mistakenly attacked by police working with drug traffickers. Julián Cardona, courtesy of the Tom & Ethel Bradley Center at California State University, Northridge.

people faster than any other product. Of course, the murders of the women in Juárez are hardly investigated or solved. Murders in Juárez are hardly ever investigated, and so in death, women finally receive the same treatment as dead men.[41]

One of Cardona's photographs included in *Murder City* summarizes the extreme reality of those years: the poster of a beautiful woman, a model with voluminous and wavy hair, her face cracked by the battered paper and with a bullet hole passing through the corner of her parted lips. Inside the hole you can see the brown earth. It appears that the poster was shot off a wall and thrown onto the dirt.

Julián found it in a house where the Federal Police unearthed the bodies of twelve people in 2004. An informant transmitted news of one of the homicides in a recording to the US Immigration and Customs Enforcement (ICE), who chose not to do anything until DEA agents were attacked by the friendly fire of police officers who worked with the drug traffickers involved. In another photograph, that same house appears in disarray, with cracked walls, garbage and scraps.

The image of the bullet-riddled poster was the cover for the first issue of the British magazine *Frontline*, founded by foreign correspondents. That first edition featured a two-page spread with a selection of Cardona's photographs accompanied by his text entitled "J-war-ez." Emulating the typical accent of a native English speaker, Cardona turns the very name of Ciudad Juárez into the site of an alleged war. But, in photography, border violence is always a double layered subject: material and symbolic. Juárez, we may say in a first instance, is the place where even the printed face of a woman is subject to being shot at. But, in a second interpretation, the photograph lays out a commentary on the forms of representation of violence itself. The criminal responsibility of the US agents who chose not to act stays *outside* the frame and instead only appears to be a symbol of gender violence that informs the superficial work of many journalists and academics. Cardona's photography does not capture then the supposed generalized machismo in the border society, as the hastiest opinions would suppose, but the finished process of reification of a metaphor whose historical contingency has been erased. There is literally *nothing to see* in the photograph, as the power relations that produced the murders in that house remain beyond our reach. The photographer arrived late to the scene of the crime, when the different factors that produced the murders had already been condensed into the metaphor of femicide. With all the force of its realism, photography reminds us that we are dealing with a prefabricated image, and that the true protagonists of the plot are still covered in the invisibility of impunity. After understanding, paradoxically, that *there is nothing to see*, our gaze searches the edges of the photograph. There, Julián Cardona's work tells us, the conditions that have created our present are yet to be uncovered.

Documented Heresy

In the *Frontline* text, Cardona speaks with a human rights activist who doesn't give his name but refutes one of the federal government's justifications for its supposed War on Drugs in Juárez. It is not about the Sinaloa cartel and its boss Joaquín "El Chapo" Guzmán trying to seize the plaza from the Juárez cartel. Nor is there even a fight between cartels in the first place. What happened was a confrontation between federal forces that arrived to wrest control from drug traffickers and local drug dealers from La Línea, an organization made up of corrupt Municipal and State Police. Juárez is no longer just one of the favorite corridors for drug trafficking.

In the last decade it became an area of high consumption as well, replete with criminal organizations that no longer accepted the historical subjugation from federal forces in the 1970s and 1980s. The dramatic increase in reports of all kinds of crimes and offenses committed by soldiers and Federal Police is significant, as well as by commandos of armed hitmen who operated without the slightest hindrance in a city taken over by ten thousand soldiers and Federal Police. Julian's text concludes:

> And if El Chapo is not behind this, then who is? "It's the army, stupid." This is what you hear on the street. The search for a true answer to this question is reason enough to continue writing the history from here.[42]

The ideas of Cardona and Bowden establish a corresponding analysis. According to Bowden, there are two discursive versions of Mexico. On the one hand, there is the Mexico of the brave President Calderón who has decided not to tolerate drug trafficking organizations any longer, risking his political capital for the good of the nation. Seen from the United States, this Mexico appears as a "sister" republic where there is a functional civil society, laws and its corresponding rule of law. But that Mexico simply "does not exist."[43] In the second version of Mexico, Bowden writes:

> the war is for drugs, for the enormous money to be made in drugs, where the police and the military fight for their share, where the press is restrained by the murder of reporters and feasts on a steady diet of bribes, and where the line between government and the drug world has never existed.[44]

No such line exists in the US, we may add, where drugs and laundered money flow, where the gun trade fuels violence on both sides of the border. And where the "War on Drugs" provides for a politically useful governing resource against minorities and dissidents and where fighting cartels has proven to be a highly lucrative public policy for security contractors and each country's armed forces.

The two journalists subscribe to a critical current that explores the centrality of the political class, the Army, and the police bureaus within the evolution of the drug trade. During his time as a correspondent in Ciudad Juárez, the British reporter Ed Vulliamy met with Cardona, who detailed the journalistic work he was doing at that time in collaboration with the Juárense reporter Ignacio Alvarado. Both of their theses, Vulliamy notes, then appeared as what he called a "heresy":

The Mexican military, they suspect, could be using the crisis to facilitate, or even get involved in a campaign of what they call "social cleansing" of the human dump: the undesirables, the drug addicts, the vagrants and the petty thieves or more than the petty thieves. The Army practically did not dispel this idea when, in a press conference on April 1, 2008, Jorge Juárez Loera, the general in charge of the eleventh military district (of which Juárez is a part), described each death that occurred under his surveillance as "one less criminal."[45]

The work of Cardona and Bowden, along with that of other reporters such as Ignacio Alvarado, receives little media attention when compared to the works of journalists that, as in the case of Diego Enrique Osorno, Anabel Hernández, and Alejandro Almazán, to mention some of the most visible, reproduce the official state logic that insists that violence is the direct product of an alleged struggle between cartels that dominate certain areas of the country and that surpass the power of the state. Going against the opinion of renowned journalists legitimized by their own official discourses, the work of Bowden and Cardona is in fact the closest thing to a journalistic heresy because it refutes the credo that the majority of Mexico holds so dear.

That being said, it is fair to recognize the validity of certain critiques that have rightly pointed out limitations in Bowden and Cardona's work. For the scholar, journalist and activist from Juárez, Willivaldo Delgadillo, for example, books such as *Juárez: The Laboratory of Our Future* have been responsible for the construction of a vision that has generated a dark legend around the border region. "Bowden pretends that we gauge exactly the Comanche territory that he has dared penetrate. For the author, Juárez is the heart of darkness," writes Delgadillo. Juárez is "that place where people sleepwalk, that gulag where the ghost of Bowden lives."[46] Journalistic investigations like *Murder City* certainly run the risk of generalizing a problem that is produced under very precise historical and political conditions, and at certain moments of its reading, the book makes the problems seem inherent and constitutive of the border society itself. Such vision is perhaps brought to its extreme in the book *Dreamland: The Way Out of Juárez*, in which Bowden uses the ahistorical and depoliticized notion of a dream as a metaphor to explain the dynamics of crime in the city and thus it is not surprising then to see the crimes in Ciudad Juárez described "as a deviation from the natural order of things."[47] Bowden's analyses can also be contradictory and even reiterate the official mythology of the cartel wars and go so far as to point out, as occurs in that same book, that "the power of the drug industry has exceeded the power of the state."[48]

However, setting aside the exaggerated and sensationalistic claims, Bowden and Cardona's books have a solid foundation in immediate lived experience. In its 2009 report, *Mexico: New Reports of Human Rights Violations by the Military*, Amnesty International makes it clear that, in the context of the alleged war against the narco, it should be understood that:

> crime cannot be fought with crime. Neither should the severity of a crisis become justification for the use of illegal methods or a pretext for turning a blind eye when abuses are committed. The aim of this report is to highlight a grave pattern of recent human rights violations perpetrated by members of the Mexican military and to call on the civilian and military authorities to take immediate and effective steps to halt and remedy such abuses.[49]

The NGO documents hundreds of reports of cases in which citizens of Juárez and other parts of the country were kidnapped, tortured, and murdered at the hands of soldiers sent by Calderón in what was known as the Joint Operation Chihuahua (later called Coordinated Operation Chihuahua) to attack alleged drug cartels. In those years, the State Commission of Human Rights received more than 1,450 complaints of disappearances, torture, and illegal searches.[50] The worst thing about the Amnesty International report, however, is what it fails to document: "Amnesty International believes these figures are conservative and that the real number of cases of torture, enforced disappearance, and unlawful killings is much higher.[51]

In the beginning of this chapter, I quoted the pointed phrase "the border has not always been there" and I explained how Ciudad Juárez appeared on the horizon of the contemporary world circa 1996, among other reasons, because journalists like Charles Bowden and Julián Cardona walked its streets together and wrote what they saw. But it is necessary to recognize the imprecise determinism of my interpretation, the reductive force of that phrase. Ciudad Juárez has always been there, but its intermittent visibility throughout border history has dazzled us with its key relevance to the transformation of that part of the country, whose very invention has only spanned barely two centuries and has already been forced to guard itself at the border when the storms are unleashed. I would like to recall two transcendent historical episodes: the roving carriage (that Alejo Carpentier would call "the marvelous real") that on August 14, 1865 brought Benito Juárez to Paso del Norte (which would be renamed after the President in 1888), the only indigenous president in the history of our country, who moved with him the capital of the country, relocating it at the border, so that it would not be left in the hands of the French who were occupying Mexico City at the time; and the morning of May 8, 1911, when the brave soldiers of the first revolution of the twentieth century carried out the orders of Pancho Villa and Pascual Orozco (the same orders that the fearful Francisco I. Madero wanted to halt) to take control of Ciudad Juárez from federal forces and thereby force dictator Porfirio Díaz's unconditional resignation. Almost a century later, Ciudad Juárez burns down again for the fate of the country, in the name of the supposed war against the narco, through the violent biopolitical program of a neoliberal state regaining sovereignty over energy-rich lands and in the face of emerging criminal pacts among police officers, businessmen, and local politicians who, as in Michoacán or Tamaulipas, have tried to create autonomous territories under federal jurisdiction. Among committed journalists such as Ignacio Alvarado, José Pérez Espino, Bárbara Vázquez, Jaime Bailleres, Alfredo Carbajal, and Sandra Rodríguez Nieto, Julián Cardona and Charles Bowden taught us to see this burning city through their work and *despite* their work. I don't know if they have understood it completely. I don't know if you can truly understand a city, but I know that their work has managed to *signify it*, which is just a more awkward way of saying that you have known its streets, that you have spoken with its people, and that you have asked the right questions.

Coda with Guts and Poetry

Bowden and Cardona worked together on various photo exhibitions accompanied by narrative essays. One of the most successful was the exhibition, *The History of the Future*, which included an essay by Cardona himself. In this text, Cardona concludes: "Juárez blows like cold wind through the windows of our souls and demands our attention. We embrace its images as if they could fill our own empty spaces, but we cannot hold on. We do not discover Juárez: Juárez discovers us."[52] They did not wait long for international recognition. Cardona received the 2004 Cultural Freedom Fellowship from the Lannan Foundation.[53] In 2013, California State University, Northridge's Institute for Arts and Media acquired more than 8,500 digitized images and around more than nine thousand photographs on film from Cardona's personal collection.[54] Bowden's prolific work has frequently appeared in US mainstream media. He has received numerous distinctions and, as the *New Yorker* recalls, for his "austere lyricism" he was considered "a journalist of blood and guts with a poet's sensibility."[55] During the journey through the territories most affected by migration, Bowden wrote down biographical sketches of Cardona, his career as a photographer on the border, and some of the most defining features of his personality. At times he observed his traveling companion from those years and noted: "He will capture that eternity, that beauty amid the stench and dust and dirt and broken glass and painted lips on the young girls soliciting in the doorways."[56] Wrapping up his last collaboration for *Murder City* in 2008, Bowden added a final note telling how Molly Molloy, research librarian and border and Latin American specialist at New Mexico State University, ended up exasperated by the "torrent of death" that she struggled to record that year on her ongoing website, "Frontera List" which has provided key information to books like *Murder City*. Bowden writes:[57]

> This fatigue with recording the deaths is a common experience. I remember my friend, photographer Julián Cardona, in early June after the machine-gunning of the twelve-year-old girl, telling me, "I can't do this anymore, it is hopeless." And so for a spell, he stopped taking photographs. And then, of course, resumed. I kept a running file of newspaper stories until around May or June, when it hit fifteen hundred pages single-spaced. And I threw in the towel. I crossed the bridge from Juárez to El Paso in June or early July swearing I would never return. But I did. And Julián Cardona and Molly Molloy also resumed their work."[58]

Charles Bowden died in his sleep on August 30, 2014. I visited him at his home in Tucson in 2009. He introduced me, via email, to Julián Cardona. What I remember most from our conversation was his constant outrage at the violence in Juárez and all the journalistic work that *we* still needed to do. He included me in that sentence and actually tried to convince me to research some issues. Julián Cardona, my friend and mentor for more than two decades, died unexpectedly on September 21, 2020, walking on the streets of Juárez toward a local coffee shop. The last time I saw him, he was finishing the last revisions of *Abecedario de Júarez: An Illustrated Lexicon* (University of Texas Press, 2022, in collaboration with illustrator Alice Leora Briggs), a work of etymological erudition about the border semantics that emerged with the so-called War on Drugs. His photographic intervention completed his survey of a border vocabulary in times of violence. His final lesson is to point at the radical relevance of language as the condition of possibility of our understanding of our immediate present. There is yet so much to see.

WHO CONTROLS THE PLAZA? THE CITY, THE STATE,
AND ORGANIZED CRIME

In 2014, during the most critical stage of the armed conflict in the state of Michoacán, which forms part of the Tierra Caliente region of Southern Mexico, reporter José Gil Olmos, from the political magazine *Proceso*, summed up the dire situation by noting that "there were at least twelve heavily armed legal and illegal organizations willing to shoot at any moment: the community police, the self-defense groups, the criminal groups the Familia Michoacana, the Knights Templar, the Zetas, the Jalisco New Generation Cartel, and the Gulf Cartel, in addition to the Army and the State, Municipal and Federal police."[59] Such an array of armed forces stimulated the critical imagination of journalists, intellectuals, and academics from very different perspectives. Anthropologist Claudio Lomnitz, for example, highlighted the breakdown of order in the community caused by the different drug trafficking organizations that operated within the Tierra Caliente of Michoacán. In his interpretation, "through an anthropological lens," Lomnitz advocates for a rebuilding of community relations, since the social fabric itself has been damaged by the itinerant control exercised first by the Zetas, then by the Familia Michoacana, and finally by the Knights Templar.[60] Sociologist Rossana Reguillo echoed an unfounded but very widespread opinion about "the possibility of narcos and guerrillas forming some kind of alliance in Mexico."[61] At the opposite extreme, Antonio Navalón observed the self-defense groups as a positive force, since, according to him, they had initiated a revolution that positioned themselves as "the Zapatistas of the twenty-first century."[62] With greater gravity, Héctor Aguilar Camín explained the cause of the conflict as part of "the second war in Mexican territory that the United States has imposed on Mexico" and that "it allowed the formation of a parallel state in a territory where the governing force is organized crime."[63] Thus, the region is supposedly under the simultaneous control of United States, the Mexican state, and the parallel state of "organized crime," whose cartels also govern the region while fighting each other. If we stick to the aforementioned opinions, in Michoacán everyone and nobody controlled the "plaza," the word of preference used by the media to name the cities and regions under the alleged control of drug cartels. With so many different violent forces at play, each interpretation cancels out the previous one. Then, who did control the Michoacán "plaza"?

Two facts further complicate a possible answer. First, the May 18, 2014, cover of *Proceso* magazine ran with the headline, "The Domesticated Self-Defense Groups," which discusses the conversion of "the Zapatistas of the twenty-first century" into a rural police force by order of the federal government after only fifteen months of being on the political scene of the conflict. In previous investigations, *Proceso* had reported that the self-defense groups were being supported, protected, and finally neutralized by the federal government. On June 27, 2014, the government dealt the greatest symbolic blow to the self-defense groups with the capture and imprisonment of their main leader, Dr. José Manuel Mireles, accused of illegally carrying weapons reserved for the Armed Forces. As has been pointed out in the media, there are official documents that prove that the federal authorities authorized Mireles to personally carry these types of firearms. According to the former Governor of Michoacán, Leonel Godoy, then-President Enrique Peña Nieto's strategy was selective when capturing Mireles. "The real self-defense groups," Godoy said in an interview, "were imprisoned and some others were killed by those who are now part of organized crime groups."[64] Mireles was released on bail on May 12, 2017, almost three years after his arrest. He was acquitted in 2018, but died on November 25, 2020, from COVID-19 symptoms.

The second of these events, and even more important, was the March 2015 capture of Servando Gómez Martínez, alias La Tuta, leader of the Knights Templar at the time, repeating the rise and fall storyline of Mexico narco bosses since the 1970s. In one of the last statements after his arrest, La Tuta defined the activities of the Knights Templar as follows: "This isn't organized crime. If anything, this is disorganized crime." And not without irony, he added: "I led a gang of fuckups."[65]

La Tuta, who had been hiding in a cave full of bats for months, was arrested at a hot dog stand just before President Peña Nieto's official visit to England. The arrest also coincided with the questionable appointments of Arely Gómez as the Attorney General of Mexico and of Eduardo Medina Mora as Minister of the Supreme Court of Justice of the Nation. One of the criticisms of Gómez was that she is the sister of Leopoldo Gómez, vice president of media conglomerate Televisa, while Medina Mora was accused of serious human rights violations as a public official, and also was close friends with Bernardo Gómez, another vice president of the same company, Televisa, generating claims of serious conflicts of interest.[66] The coincidence between the police mobilizations and the questionable political appointments at that time was reminiscent of Joaquín "El Chapo" Guzmán's second arrest in 2014, three days after Barack Obama's visit to Mexico where he highlighted the national security policy of the Peña Nieto government.

Surprisingly, critical agendas still view drug trafficking in Mexico through a model that explains it as a complex transnational economic structure that goes beyond state structures in the neoliberal era. Saturated with a theoretical lexicon from anthropology, sociology, economics, philosophy, and even religion, drug trafficking remains studied by these specialists as the result of a structural fall of the state, the latter being replaced by "oligopolistic television stations or criminal transnational companies," as the academic and security expert Edgardo Buscaglia warned.[67] It is due to these "power vacuums," as Buscaglia calls them, that the Mexican drug traffickers, according to the Secretariat of Foreign Affairs, have supposedly been able to extend their operations to "at least 46 countries, as far away as North Korea, Togo, Ivory Coast, Egypt, Turkey, Malaysia and New Zealand."[68]

How is it possible that the capture of the capos and the permanent state of relentless war in which the alleged cartels operate does not interrupt the alleged dominance of Mexican criminals at the national and global level? As I believe I have already made evident, the notion of *plaza* operates as an empty signifier structured as a narrative function devoid of specific content in which you can fill in the blank. It takes the place of chaos, community breakdown, neoliberal control of transnational criminals, the dominance of media monopolies, US imperialism, and even a second Mexican Revolution.

Historically, however, the organized crime plaza appeared on the scene with a very different political significance. The notion emerged in the late 1970s as the concession that the Mexican state gave to certain groups of traffickers that allowed them to operate under official control. In the following two decades, that same notion has been redefined as the center of meaning of the so-called drug cartels: criminal structures that are thought of as alternatives to the state. To conclude this book, I am interested in analyzing the representational strategies that turned the plaza from a notion of drug trafficking organizations regulated *under* state control into drug trafficking organizations operating *beyond* state control, as read about in journalistic investigations and fictional narratives about drug trafficking in cities like Juárez, Culiacán, and Tijuana. Against those who consider plazas as areas where drug trafficking has overtaken the power of the state, I will discuss how these cities actually designate contingent spaces in which a multiplicity of actors, organizations, and institutions come together through alliances between politicians, police corporations, military branches, businessmen, and drug traffickers. In such a contingent space, an effective definition of the sovereignty of the Mexican state in the face of the criminal world, especially of its judicial-police system after two decades of neoliberal transformations, will be at stake. In this way, I propose then to reinsert the drug trafficking plaza into a complex historical and political context. With this

I will point out finally that every plaza, that is, every city and region where the state of emergency is visible over the country's underground economies, is the necessary location of the judicial-police system of sovereignty that, although fragmented in the various conflict regions of the country, reaffirms itself as the expression of state hegemony over organized crime. Thus, we will understand finally that what we call narco is politically located *within* state structures and not outside the global economy nor the immoral agency of drug traffickers.

For more than a decade beginning in 1975, as I explained at the outset of this book, the governments of Mexico and the United States carried out Operation Condor to destroy the marijuana and poppy fields in what is called the golden triangle, the mountain range that crosses the states of Sinaloa, Chihuahua, and Durango. Until then, those mountains were the natural growing place for drug crops for the peasant farmers in Mexico since the late nineteenth and early twentieth centuries. However, far from dismantling drug trafficking in rural areas, Operation Condor had two counterproductive effects. First, the massive exodus of around one hundred thousand peasants toward the bigger cities of Sinaloa, in particular Culiacán, Guasave and Guamúchil.[69] And second, the realignment of the main drug trafficking bosses to form the so-called federation of drug trafficking based in Guadalajara, in the state of Jalisco, the first modern drug trafficking plaza of the PRI era. In that city, strategically located in the center of the country and relatively close to Mexico City, a national criminal structure was installed and administered by former Sinaloa police officer Miguel Ángel Félix Gallardo, among other drug traffickers, and under direct management of the Federal Security Directorate (FDS), the political police that operated with impunity under the authority of the Secretariat of the Interior. This strategic rearrangement allowed the state to control drug trafficking throughout the country. This is how Sergio Aguayo explains it:

> This city (Guadalajara) offered not only good weather and an excellent geographical location, but also the presence of a police force willing to protect them and a long-standing culture of violence that guaranteed the constant stream of recruits for their organizations.[70]

But it wasn't until the publication of *Druglord: The Life and Death of a Mexican Kingpin* by US reporter Terrence Poppa, that the crucial question about Mexican drug trafficking was posed: "Who's running the plaza?", which is to say: "Who's running the show?"[71] This book, perhaps the first "owner's manual for the Mexican drug cartels," is the first journalistic investigation into the operational dynamics of criminal organizations in the main pla-zas.[72] Poppa came to the subject from a series of news articles on official corruption in the border state of Chihuahua that, in part, led to the arrest of a local drug trafficker. It was at that moment, Poppa writes, that his "edu-cation about the true nature of the Mexican political system was just begin-ning."[73] When his investigations led him to the border city of Ojinaga to interview the drug trafficker Pablo Acosta, his degree of knowledge of the Mexican state had only, until then, been matched by a few Mexican journal-ists, such as Julio Scherer, who had been defamed and expelled from *Excél-sior* newspaper due to his confrontation with President Luis Echeverría; and Manuel Buendía, who was assassinated in retaliation for his revelations regarding the deep corruption of the DFS and its opaque relationship with the CIA in Mexico. Lacking familiarity with the Mexican political system, Poppa gained privileged knowledge about drug trafficking by following the chain of causality between the rise of certain traffickers in their plazas, their apparent control of the business within the limits of those cities, and their resounding fall at the hands of the police and military.

But the question "who's running the plaza?" is deceptively simple. According to Poppa, the plaza in those years was not the domain of a drug trafficker, but rather the concession that the Mexican political system had made to a certain group to administer drug-related operations. When investigating the criminal history of the drug trafficker Pablo Acosta in the city of Ojinaga, Poppa deduced the two main responsibilities of the owner of the plaza: to maintain a constant flow of money and to provide informa-tion to the Federal Police about any other illegal activity outside the autho-rized criminal organization. Poppa writes:

> Usually, the authorities would protect their man from rivals; other times they would not, preferring a variety of natural selection to determine who should run the plaza. If the authorities arrested or killed the plaza holder, it was usually because he had stopped making payments, or because his name had started to appear in the press too frequently and the trafficker had become a liability. Sometimes international pressure became so strong that the gov-ernment was forced to take action against a specific individual regardless of how much money he was generating for his patrons.[74]

It is key here to understand that *managing* the plaza did not mean *control-ling* the plaza. The trafficker then was only the administrator of a structure and a space that he could lose at any moment, even in spite of his own suc-cess in the business. Poppa's revelations ran in a long feature article in the

Boston Globe on March 29, 1987, unprecedented in the journalistic context of the time. It contributed decisively to draw the attention of the federal government and national and international opinion to such a degree that Pablo Acosta was murdered through a military operation on April 24, 1987, and his organization destroyed. As Poppa himself understood through his journalistic investigations, the political system thus eliminated drug traffickers who attracted too much public attention within the discreet official control over the plazas.

Despite its profitable effectiveness, this disciplinary regime was abruptly interrupted in the late 1980s. The hegemony exercised by the Mexican political system over drug trafficking underwent a profound transformation with the incorporation of the new national security agenda during the PRI neoliberal era that altered the vertical discipline on the plazas to the point that a multiplicity of actors claimed their own agency in tension with the police and political institutions. And although this balance of forces undoubtedly modified the scope of state sovereignty, the drug plaza has not ceased to be the disciplinary space of official sovereignty.

I would like to summarize, by way of conclusion, the main arguments of this book. The emergence of the narco security discourse in the public sphere accompanied the symbolic dismantling of state sovereignty brought on by the rise of neoliberalism starting in the late eighties. But what is crucial to understand here is that this security discourse did not arise from the threat of the narco, but to a large extent, how the new security agenda *configured* the narco as a discursive object. Beyond the materiality of drug trafficking, what we often call narco is the *discursive invention* of a state policy that responds to specific geopolitical interests.

This transition toward the supposed national security emergency can be understood within three stages in profound discontinuity that evolved as the very notion of national security was introduced. In the first stage, decades before the introduction of neoliberalism in the region and rather during the dawn of the Cold War, the appearance of the security agenda in 1947 came about in Mexico with the creation of the Federal Security Directorate (DFS) under the presidency of Miguel Alemán and with the assistance of the US Federal Bureau of Investigation (FBI). It is not a simple coincidence, as I discussed at the beginning of this book, that this is the same year that the United States Congress passed the National Security Act to lay out their anti-communist strategy that would define global geopolitics for the following forty years, and in addition to that, the same year the Central Intelligence Agency (CIA) was also founded. In this context, Canadian academic and diplomat Peter Dale Scott explains, "the prime purpose of the DFS was not to contain drug violence, but on the contrary to manage it and unleash violence against the pro-communist left."[75] In a few years, the DFS attacked and neutralized guerrilla movements, student organizations, and trade unions at the very same time that it dominated drug trafficking organizations. The DFS, in fact, preceded the DEA (which was not created in the United States until 1973) as an agency whose essential function was both the neutralization of political dissent and the creation of a new anti-drug policy. Those were the years when the political system and Federal Police absolutely and brutally controlled the drug trafficking plazas.

Faced with the shifting biopolitics that came with the disintegration of the Soviet Union during the Cold War, the neoliberal era gave new meaning to the United States security agenda. It was then that President Ronald Reagan signed National Security Directive 221 in 1986 to designate drug trafficking as the new national security threat. This event had at least two correlated landmarks in Mexico. First, the closure of the DFS in 1985 after the murder of DEA agent Enrique "Kiki" Camarena, allegedly ordered by Mexican drug traffickers but with the consent of the CIA, according to recent journalistic investigations.[76] And second, the creation of the Center for Investigation and National Security (CISEN) in 1989 to replace the DFS. The disappearance of the DFS implied the dismantling of the political and police structures that, until then, had subordinated drug trafficking groups to federal power, while the creation of CISEN led the Mexican political system to consider drug trafficking as a permanent national security threat that required immediate police and military action.

The various emergencies attributed to drug trafficking since the securitarian turn of the late 1980s in Mexico have been conflicts built from the strategies of representation deliberately devised by the political systems of the United States and Mexico. The narco has never been a *stricto sensu* threat to either of the two countries. Astorga writes: "Attributing tens of thousands of members to a given organization is a simple fantasy of the authorities, which in turn feeds popular fantasies and mythologies."[77] This fantasy has served a specific political use: it allowed the federal government in Mexico during the Calderón and Peña Nieto years to exponentially expand the security apparatus under the fallacious discourse of national security, seeking to reestablish police controls in different cities of the country where political and business groups previously dominated underground economies by denying the federal government any privileges and gains.

The third and final phase of this national security emergency is expressed in the unprecedented wave of violence with the militarization initiated by then-President Calderón in 2006. The strategy consisted of the mobilization of thousands of soldiers and Federal Police to cities with increased drug trafficking in what was undoubtedly a violent reconfiguration of "plazas" throughout the country. In other words, Calderón's "War on Drugs" did not respond to violence caused by the so-called "cartels." Lacking real causes, the violence broke out *after* the arrival of the military and police units to those "plazas." Their presence was the determining factor of change, the true condition of possibility of the violence in cities like Juárez.

Without the police work of the DFS, the CISEN and its security agenda have turned the drug trafficking phenomenon into the object of a permanent military and police campaign that made us accustomed to its disproportionate amounts of violence. The official explanation about the supposed wars between cartels persist, but the exercise of sovereignty only reaffirms the Mexican political system's state of exception. Although discontinuous and fragmented in different areas of power in the neoliberal era, this state of exception continues to be the condition of possibility for organized crime. As the philosopher Giorgio Agamben points out, the state of exception is the result of a principle of anomie, or state of suspension of the law, which is based on the dialectical imposition of the sovereign decision (*auctoritas*) and legal action (*potestas*) of the state. This dual legal-political system, intermittently based on a principle of sovereignty and an active legal framework, is what appears when we look through the fog of the discursive security strategy. In the armed conflict in Michoacán, for example, it was the federal government that maintained control of the state of exception. The same can be extrapolated to the rest of the country: on the issue of drug trafficking, the state has lost neither its sovereignty nor the power to apply, when it deems it politically convenient, the rule of law.

To understand the scope of security geopolitics, we can recall that in a 1986 text, Noam Chomsky considered the US national security policy in Central America during the Cold War "a system of global management."[78] And by 1989, the same year that CISEN was created in Mexico, the political scientist Waltraud Morales stated that the "the war on drugs has been most effective as a principle of public legitimation within the USA."[79] So effective, in fact, that "the average US citizen, whether he has accepted the official ideological linkage of drugs with terrorism as a global communist conspiracy or as a valid national security threat in its own right, is mobilized against international drug trafficking."[80] Anti-drug security policy, as we have already seen, has also served as a principal public legitimizer of the Mexican political system and has been assimilated into the most recent reconfigurations of cultural imaginaries surrounding drug trafficking in the hemisphere. Contrary to common liberal critiques, the War on Drugs is far from being a failure: it is perhaps one of the most successful geopolitical power structures advancing the interests of political and business elites against the rest of the people in either country, disenfranchised by their own governments.

The anthropologist and geographer David Harvey notes that Henri Lefebvre's call to claim the "right to the city" is actually "an empty signifier" that can only be activated from different contingent spaces of political impulse, that is to say, "everything depends on who gets to fill it with meaning."[81] The political and cultural imaginaries that I have studied throughout these pages have managed, at times, to give meaning to the notion of the plaza that is manipulated by an official state discourse as the place of the unlimited power of the narco. These narco imaginaries, of course, erase the official state history of the plazas, the long incursions of state sovereignty over our precarious society. The agenda yet to come from our best journalists, academics, writers, filmmakers, musicians, and conceptual artists is to imagine that still-pending urban revolution in our cities in order to regain a more legitimate democratic control, alien to the groups of drug traffickers, and certainly beyond the criminal political systems that govern us.

The New "Cartel War" Is Not New, nor a War, nor between Cartels

When the reporter Miroslava Breach was murdered with impunity in the city of Chihuahua on March 23, 2017, the mainstream media immediately jumped to the alleged cartel war and the little to no protection that the Chihuahua state authorities offered the journalist after being repeatedly threatened. The news coverage, in part, reflected rushed and contradictory official versions of the crime. The governor of Chihuahua, Javier Corral, for example, affirmed in a press conference hours after the murder that the preliminary investigations blamed "organized crime" and local "narcopolitics."[1]

What went unnoticed though, was that the authorities determined the motive for the murder unusually quickly. Furthermore, this information functioned as the guiding principle for the case. According to the authorities, Breach was murdered by that chimera, "organized crime," and it was now up to those same authorities to solve the crime, as if this were a detective novel. In other words: no one among the authorities could be responsible. Only "organized crime" members are murderers, the ones who plotted it and carried it out. The authorities who said so took the opportunity to distance themselves from any link to the murder and were automatically exempt from the very same crime they were trying to solve. With appalling laziness, the media took it upon themselves to legitimize the official version. The day after the murder, on Friday March 24, 2017, reporter Alberto Nájar published on *BBC Mundo*, the apparent context in which Breach reported: "The mountains of Chihuahua became a battlefield between the Sinaloa and Juárez cartels. The dispute was to control one of the most important drug corridors in northern Mexico."[2] That "context," it is worth noting, was the recurring explanation that Felipe Calderón's government used during his six-year term in order to attribute the 121,000 homicides and more than 30,000 forced disappearances committed between 2008 and 2012 to "cartels."

In the same *BBC Mundo* article, Nájar recalls that Breach also covered ecological issues, such as illegal logging in the Sierra Tarahumara, and the way in which entire communities had been violently displaced from their homes. With questionable logic at best, Nájar immediately claimed that these communities were attacked by drug trafficking gangs. It is not explained why these cartels, who are supposedly engaged in a bloody war in the mountains, may be interested in cutting down trees and moving onto remote Tarahumara community land. Are the trees and the Tarahumara an obstacle to the "most important drug corridor in northern Mexico"?

As journalists Ignacio Alvarado, Dawn Paley, and Federico Mastrogiovanni have reported, much of the violence attributed to the "cartels" often has to do with official strategies of illegal appropriation and exploitation of lands rich in natural resources. It would serve us well to think beyond the narco politics of Chihuahua and consider this possibility in greater depth.

This is what Olga Alicia Aragón did in a March 31, 2017, *Newsweek en Español* article. Aragon considered the official statements, but did not take them as fact:

> Miroslava Breach Velducea was murdered for her investigative journalism work that allowed her to document the illicit enrichment of former governor César Duarte and expose some of the criminal networks of drug traffickers and politicians, both from the Institutional Revolutionary Party and from National Action Party, who control government structures and large areas of the state.[3]

Even more important, in my opinion, is to review what the governor of Chihuahua said about the alleged responsibility of narco politics in the region. Aragón continues:

> Corral Jurado has referred, above all, to the story that Breach published in *La Jornada* on Friday, March 4, 2016, "Organized Crime Installs Representative Candidates in Chihuahua." But the journalist not only documented the PRI's

ties to drug trafficking, but also expanded her investigation to the political structure of the National Action Party [of then governor Corral Jurado].[4]

If, as the human rights organization Article 19 has reported, seven out of ten attacks against journalists in Mexico are perpetrated by state agents, how can we accept the official narrative that public officials make about narcos who murder journalists? Since its creation in 2010, the Special Prosecutor for Attention to Crimes Against Freedom of Expression (FEADLE) has only dealt with forty-eight cases and has only obtained three convictions. As Ana Cristina Ruelas, Article 19 regional director in Mexico and Central America affirms, "the state does not want to investigate itself."[5]

Of course, in the case of Miroslava Breach, it is possible that criminals who act in complicity with state authorities are involved. But this complicit relationship is often purported as the action of organized crime allegedly spreading its corruption to a few officials, while maintaining that the political system in general remains safe from such corruption. On April 17, 2017, Governor Corral stated that the "material perpetrator, accomplices, and of course the mastermind" of the crime "had already been found."[6]

Without even having to prove anything, the outward appearance of the "perpetrators" as criminals imply that same narrative that conveniently separates them (the "bad hombres," President Donald Trump would say) from us (the ruling class). In 2020, during court proceedings against the alleged assassin, the FEADLE informed that all evidence pointed to Crispín Salazar Zamorano, the leader of Los Salazares, a criminal branch of the Sinaloa cartel, as the man who ordered the hit. The group has been linked to the forced displacement of hundreds of families in the Chihuahua sierra between 2014 and 2015, but it all came down, according to the authorities, to the drug trade.[7]

I want to end this book by looking critically at the true political context in which this crime occurred: the supposed new cartel war that would have started in the state of Chihuahua in mid-2016. In one of his weekly columns, published on March 6, 2017, in the newspaper *El Universal*, the well-known security analyst Alejandro Hope presented an alarming outlook of Ciudad Juárez, based on the number of murders rapidly accumulating that year. Hope recorded 138 murders between January and February 2017, which represented, according to his data, an increase of 146 percent compared to the same period in 2016. The analyst categorically interpreted the information and directly titled his article, "The War Returns to Ciudad Juárez." What is going on? Hope wondered. "What explains this wave of violence in this city, which until a few months ago was presented as a model of pacification?"[8] His analysis, allegedly based on "sources from Juárez" that he did not identify, pointed to a "combination of four factors." First, an alleged conflict over control of the Sinaloa cartel after the arrest and extradition of Joaquín "El Chapo" Guzmán; second, the reappearance of La Línea, "the armed wing of the Juárez cartel" in the streets, but this time supplemented by a "cross-border" gang called Barrio Azteca; third, the alleged arrival of the Jalisco New Generation cartel, which sought to control methamphetamine trafficking from Juárez to the United States; and finally, Hope attached importance to the political tension between the PAN governor Javier Corral and the municipal president of Ciudad Juárez, Armando Cabada. As a possible solution, Hope's judgement was that "a little more troops and a little more will and a dose of accountability" could pacify Juárez again, as happened before, according to him, in violent cities such as Tijuana, Monterrey, and Juárez itself.[9] The column circulated on social media, even among journalists and intellectuals from Juárez, as a warning in the face of the escalating violence taking place in the city.

The number of murders in Ciudad Juárez during those weeks was indeed a worrying matter. It is also important to observe the short historical memory that allows us to forget the brutal effects of the supposed War on Drugs, the security agenda motto used by President Felipe Calderón during his six-year term. It should not surprise us that Hope, an official at the Center for Investigation and National Security (CISEN) between 2008 and 2011, that is, during the peak years of the War on Drugs, made use of official vocabulary to consider the possibility of a new war in Ciudad Juárez starring the usual suspects, the drug cartels. The presence of the Army and the Federal Police, certainly "a little more troops" as Hope requests, did not pacify the city in those years of extreme violence, but rather was the factor of change that precipitated the wave of unprecedented murders in those years. In Juárez, there was no war until the arrival of the federal units sent by Calderón to stop a cartel war that no one could see on the streets and that did not produce any increase in the number of murders in all the previous decade.

The acritical position of researchers such as Alejandro Hope can be explained in part by the fact that their arguments regarding the imminence of a supposed new cartel war reproduce information originating in federal and state institutions and then circulated in the media. Let's review them one by one. The tension between the governor Corral and the mayor of Juárez was aired publicly since the state elections that year, with a recurring exchange of accusations of links with drug trafficking organizations, and through the almost folkloric *narcomantas*, those messages attributed to cartels written on bedsheets or blankets and hung in public view.[10] Evidence of a new cartel war is a bit more difficult to track, but the information is also a public matter. The supposed war within the Sinaloa cartel was first announced by the Sinaloa State Public Security Minister, General Genaro Robles Casillas, during the first week of February, when El Chapo's sons said in a letter, reportedly signed by them and sent to the media, that they had been attacked by another member of the organization.[11] In October 2016, the former Chihuahua Attorney General, and also former Juárez secretary of Public Security, Jorge González Nicolás, confirmed that a new confrontation between La Línea and the Sinaloa cartel was about to begin. According to him, "the [drug trafficking] groups have not yet left Chihuahua and they are not going to." González offered this statement to the reporter Luis Chaparro, complementing an interview that this reporter did with an alleged sicario from La Línea who also predicted a new war between the narcos from Juárez and Sinaloa. According to the hitman, anticipating Hope's analysis, "the period of peace in Ciudad Juárez is about to end."[12]

But the coming war was actually announced three months earlier with an important difference: on July 5, 2016, then Chihuahua Attorney General González Nicolás told the media that, according to military intelligence, Rafael Caro Quintero, one of the most notorious drug traffickers in Mexico history—accused of killing DEA agent Enrique "Kiki" Camarena—freed in 2013 after twenty-eight years in prison, allied with the Beltrán Leyva cartel, and planned to attack Ciudad Juárez to dispute control of the city that, according to the state government, was still under Sinaloa cartel control.[13] The news matched up with previous information: on May 11, 2016, the United States Department of the Treasury declared that it had detected "criminal activity" by Caro Quintero and his girlfriend in Mexico.[14] The threat materialized on July 11, 2016, by means of a *narcomanta* signed with Caro Quintero's name that warned of an upcoming "cleansing" and imposed a period of one week on Attorney General González Nicolás to resign from his position.

The construction of this official state narrative line, however, went into question with an unexpected interview that the sixty-four-year-old Caro Quintero gave to *Proceso* magazine the same month, July 2016, that the *narcomanta* appeared in Chihuahua signed with his name. In the *Proceso* interview, Caro Quintero denied that he was planning a new cartel war and apologized to Mexico and the United States for his past crimes.[15] With the old narco denying the plan of invasion, a new threat appeared in early February: according to Will R. Glaspy, former Special Agent in Charge of DEA's

El Paso Division, the Jalisco New Generation Cartel (CJNG, in Spanish) was going to let loose another war in Ciudad Juárez: "We are beginning to make some seizures and arrests linked to the CJNG in this Juárez-El Paso corridor," said the DEA agent during an interview with another reporter from *Proceso* magazine.[16]

The inconsistencies between the alleged threats from drug traffickers and cartels that alternately plan to attack Ciudad Juárez expose the questionable information that comes mostly from official sources. I have already analyzed the effect of the dissemination of official information among journalists supposedly critical of the government. I am now interested in ending by noting some recent movements in the official state strategy that seem to manufacture a new consensus of public opinion to justify another wave of violence in which the country's armed forces are likely to be involved. But the official narrative is contradictory in its multiple reinventions, to say the least, so let's go over its failed logic. In July 2016, the Chihuahua Attorney General told us that Ciudad Juárez was in the hands of the Sinaloa cartel since it had defeated La Línea during the war during Calderón's administration and that Caro Quintero was ready to invade the city, as confirmed by the drug trafficker with his own signed *narcomanta*. In October of that same year, the Chihuahua Attorney General gave up in blaming Caro Quintero after the drug trafficker's personal denial of this invasion and chose then to seek a new invading force: a war between La Línea, which was now rising from the ashes, and the occupying Sinaloa cartel. Ever since February of 2017, however, we are now supposed to fear the imminent siege of the Jalisco New Generation cartel. And, to add to our confusion, on March 7, 2017, the security consulting US company Stratfor Global Intelligence— the so-called "shadow CIA"—published a report predicting an increase in violence because the cartels were no longer actually fighting each other like agitated giants, but have fragmented into smaller, out of control gangs. At the end of the day, according to US intelligence, neither La Línea, nor the Sinaloa cartel, nor the Jalisco New Generation cartel, nor Corral against Cabada, nor Caro Quintero, nor his girlfriend, would be the protagonists of the new war: it will be mini-cartels without a drug lord leading them, according to Stratfor, a "balkanization" of violence, alluding to the collapse of former Yugoslavia in the 1990s.[17]

Since Calderón's war, Mexico's security agenda has mobilized the military and police to confront wars between cartels that had never existed before but that, according to the official discourse, are solely responsible for the tens of thousands of killings across the whole country. This new cartel war isn't new, nor a war, nor between cartels. It is the political system's permanent state of exception that has been exercising its violent control and sovereignty over organized crime in Mexico for more than half a century. Among other possible undercurrents, is the line of investigation that journalists such as Ignacio Alvarado, Dawn Paley, and Federico Mastrogiovanni have pointed out: the cartel wars most likely hide the federal government's strategy to facilitate the illegal appropriation of territories of the country rich in natural resources now open for the exploitation by transnational companies with acquiescence of various political and business interest groups in Mexico.

Faced with the permanent crisis of legitimacy at all levels of government, our leaders insist on implementing the same discursive strategy that generates the *virtual explanation* of a climate of uncontrolled violence. This explanation is nothing more than a political control of public opinion to facilitate the collective tolerance of these waves of violence that would otherwise be unacceptable. My interest here is not to determine the factuality of virtual threats to cities like Juárez, but to understand that the political success of these strategies lies precisely in the indistinction between the real and the merely discursive. As the sociologist Phillip Abrams teaches, what we call the "state" legitimizes its monopoly on violence and its criminal use by the Army and the police through a mythologization of its power that silences all protest. Thus, Abrams writes, the myth of the state "excuses force and convinces almost all of us that the fate of the victims is just and necessary."[18]

In the discursive clumsiness of our political system, the narco myth should fall under the weight of its ridiculous incoherence. But the virtual explanation of the cartel wars, always starting over again with volatile protagonists changing identities, prevails precisely because of its coordinated, albeit illogical, insistence: prosecutors, police chiefs, DEA agents, and security analysts all in unison, repeating the essential structure of the plot: that the cartels, no matter which ones, will enter a war and cause an indeterminate but high number of homicides. It is inexplicable that confused intelligence constantly and mistakenly names warring cartels, but not the predictions of their capacity for destruction. Although the cartel war is virtual, the corpses it leaves behind are not, nor is the illegal exploitation of our natural resources where the violent drug traffickers supposedly reign. And neither are the military and police forces whose deployment coincides with massacres precisely in the places where they arrive.

Faced with our bewilderment and horror at the violence, the official discourse knows how to get us used to the central line of its plot. What begins as mere statements by some officials soon becomes, as has happened in the last two decades, a whole field of cultural production: novels, music, cinema, conceptual art, narrative journalism, and most of the academic work that studies and gives meaning to the drug phenomenon; they accept the cartel wars as something real. While the militarization of our cities keeps destroying families and entire communities and appropriating our most important natural resources, our intellectual class entertains itself by imagining endless wars between drug traffickers that the political system has astutely invented in order to evade any critical examination. What will our *intelligentsia* tell us about the new war that is coming to Ciudad Juárez and, with certainty, in other parts of the national territory? Our intellectual class has a new opportunity to learn to distinguish whether the combatants are only that endless line of drug traffickers with interchangeable faces, or the political system that names them.

Afterword
for the English Edition

On January 30, 2018, newly elected President Andrés Manuel López Obrador (also known as AMLO) shocked the country with an announcement during his daily press conference: the immediate cancellation of the War on Drugs, that is, the termination of the militarization ordered by President Felipe Calderón (2006–2012) and that continued in the government of President Enrique Peña Nieto (2012–2018). While the circulation of drugs within Mexico and to the US seemed unaffected by the militarization, as we know, the deployment of thousands of soldiers and federal agents was linked to the surge in violence, as I argued in this book through various credible studies and journalistic investigations. "Officially, there is no war anymore," said López Obrador. "We want peace and we are going to get it."[1]

The announcement followed a campaign proposal and a specific agenda of AMLO's government, when his transition team presented its National Plan for Peace and Security. This document argued that drug prohibition was the result of a US national security policy that should not continue to be enforced in Mexico. In turn, AMLO's team pointed at a general process of pacification in which the circulation and sales of illegal drugs would now be seen only as a public health issue.

The only realist action to be taken to reduce the levels of drug use resides in reorienting in a bilateral and negotiated way the resources currently appropriated to fight drug trafficking and to apply them in programs —massive, but individualized— of social reinsertion and detoxification.[2]

The creation of a National Guard to suspend the militarization of security tasks became the material component of the end of the drug war. After an intense debate in Congress, the National Guard was approved on February 28, 2019, with only one vote against in the Chamber of Deputies. Two constitutive aspects of the National Guard were key for a paradigmatic change in Mexico's security policy. First, the army, still partially in charge of security operations in the country, is scheduled to fully return to its headquarters in no more than five years from the vote in Congress. And second, the National Guard is structured to obey a civil command within the Secretariat of Public Security and Citizen Protection and without military jurisdiction. This meant that the 99,946 soldiers and former police agents enlisted in the National Guard (as of July 2021) would submit themselves to a civil jurisdiction. The reached consensus in Congress was recognized even by its harshest critics.[3]

From the official perspective, the cancellation of the War on Drugs pushed indeed for a reversal of the violent strategy of militarization of the last two governments. By July 2019, *Proceso* magazine reported that according to the US Department of Justice the Mexican government maintained "the collaboration with the United States on the fight against drug cartels deactivated."[4] At the same time, President López Obrador began an aggressive revision of the 2013 energy reform, indicting former government officials involved in bribe schemes to fast track foreign investment in oil, electricity and natural gas and moving forward with plans to expand oil, gas and electricity production.

On December 27, 2018, less than a month after taking office, AMLO redirected the country's attention to Mexico's most significant "national security and homeland security" conflict: the massive theft of hydrocarbons from Petróleos Mexicanos (PEMEX). On that day, a national strategy was announced to safeguard PEMEX's six refineries, thirty-nine supply terminals, and twelve fuel pumping stations with four thousand soldiers of the Mexican Navy and Army. According to AMLO, the annual theft of hydrocarbons was estimated at 66 billion pesos (about $3.2 billion USD) and was perpetrated in complicity with employees and executives of the parastatal.

Let us understand the importance of this strategic shift: first, the AMLO government proposes to dismantle the "War on Drugs" not through demilitarization but by stripping bare the fallacy of the domestic enemy constructed by official discourse. By designating the use of illegal drugs as a public health issue, the federal government is making the legitimacy of state violence exercised in the last decade in the name of the War on Drugs outright impossible.

By redesignating oil theft as the central problem for the federal government, however, AMLO took a major step that exposed the fallacy of the more pervasive "national security" agenda: the problem is not the use of drugs outlawed by the US prohibitionist discourse, but the looting of PEMEX for the benefit of transnational corporations and Mexico's political-business elite. In other words, the AMLO government has understood that the false War on Drugs had to be dismantled in order to set up a plan to rebuild national sovereignty over the real object of transnational dispute: the country's natural resources.

Since the presentation of the national strategy, AMLO pointed out that the problem is not concentrated in the *huachicol*, as the clandestine drilling and "milking" of fuel pipelines is popularly called. In fact, as the work of journalist Ana Lilia Pérez has demonstrated, 80 percent of hydrocarbon theft in past governments occurred *inside* refineries, in the supply terminals and even at the PEMEX naval stations.[5]

"We are not talking about the so-called *huachicol*, the milking of pipelines," AMLO explained. "This is upper-class *huachicol*. How is it possible that over one thousand gas trucks [with stolen gasoline circulate] daily? There are hypotheses that only 20 percent of gasoline theft is by milking pipelines; it is a smokescreen; most of it has to do with the complicity of the authorities and with a distribution network."[6]

But the hegemonic narrative of national security persists because it is anchored on a symbolic structure that can be easily modified, since it operates as an abstract form. It is, in other words, a war with a variable enemy that, since the 1980s, has been the Latin American narco but is not going to stay as such. In fact, this has been the complex discursive process mediating the recent iterations of Mexico's national security policies. In the same press conference in which President López Obrador announced the end of the drug war on January 31, 2019, the secretary of the Mexican Navy, José Rafael Ojeda, told reporters of the threat posed by the Santa Rosa de Lima cartel, a new organization heading a violent network devoted to oil and fuel theft in the central state of Guanajuato. As he explained, this new cartel already controlled the clandestine extraction sites where criminals seize fuel from government pipelines. Also in Guanajuato, as was common during the War on Drugs, local police reported sudden *mantas* left by the thieves hanging on bridges with threatening messages against AMLO and his proposed strategy to put an end to fuel theft. According to the authorities, alleged *huachicoleros* drove a pick-up truck loaded with explosives to the entry of a refinery. This cartel also has its own boss with his own nickname: José Antonio Yépez Ortiz, alias "El Marro" (The Hammer).[7] And as a strategy to complete the refurbishing of the national security threat, the media reported on the local veneration of the "*Huachicolero* Holy Child," a curious variation of the popular Jesús Malverde, the Sinaloan "saint" followed by Mexican drug dealers.[8] With *corridos* and even a new soap opera about *huachicoleros* already available as variations of narco culture, how long will we wait before the first novel about the "war against *huachicol*" appears in Mexican bookstores?

More recently, pressured by then-President Donald Trump, AMLO ordered thousands of troops of the newly created National Guard to the Mexican borders, north and south, to curb the increasing wave of undocumented migrants from Central America, expected to rise to 700,000 in 2019 alone.[9] This shocking new militarization includes the illegal detention of migrants on the northern border, de facto operating as a virtual wall for the aggressive anti-immigrant policy pushed by Trump from the beginning of his presidency in 2016. In other words, AMLO has accepted to use the new Mexican security force to undertake what could potentially become an extension of Trump's permanent campaign against migrants, often criminalized as traffickers, rapists, and even terrorists, with little evidence to support those claims.[10] It is telling that on June 14, 2019, a week after a binational agreement to increase anti-immigrant militarization efforts south of the Rio Grande, AMLO accepted the resignation of the Mexican head of the National Institute of Migration, Tonatiuh Guillén López, who led the federal government's initial strategy of encouraging the "human right to migrate." In his place, AMLO named Francisco Garduño Yáñez, a former official with Mexico's Attorney General and former secretary of public security in Mexico City, to promote "the toughening of the federal government's strategy to stop migration and comply with its commitment to U.S. President Donald Trump."[11] This new enemy offers the synthesis of the history of the national security agenda by combining, in a single persona, the illegal, the narco, and the terrorist. The expanding role that AMLO is assigning to the armed forces does not amount to a new state of war, but it has alarmed many of his critics as soldiers now control Mexico City's new international airport, the northern and southern borders, all customs checkpoints and even the construction of the Mayan Train, a tourism infrastructure project for the Yucatán peninsula.[12]

As the Mexican government contests with uneven success the validity of the US-led anti-drug policy, numerous violent incidents have led public opinion back to the War on Drugs state of mind. On October 17, 2019, AMLO's security cabinet aborted a military operation to capture Ovidio Guzmán, the son of the drug lord Joaquín "El Chapo" Guzmán, after armed groups took to the streets of Culiacán terrorizing civilians and even taking relatives of some of the participating soldiers hostage. As I argued elsewhere, it was the right decision to avoid high civilian casualties, as the Mexican forces outnumbered the traffickers and could have easily turned the operation into a massacre.[13] On Nov. 4, 2019, nine members of the Lebaron family (from a Mormon community established in northern Mexico) were brutally assassinated in Sonora state. Although the crime has been attributed to drug traffickers, it is now reported that in the same region is found the world's largest lithium reserve —about 243 million tons, eleven times bigger than Bolivia's reserves—where increasing unrest is constantly reported as another form of a "drug war."[14] President Trump, unsurprisingly, offered President López Obrador his full support in the form of a military intervention.

Colombian journalist Germán Castro Caycedo, one of the leading voices against the anti-drug militarization of his country, famously described US intervention in the region as "our foreign war," in which "the interests and the geopolitics that determine it, are neither ours."[15] As we face a new era of militarization beyond the drug war, we may be witnessing the beginning of a new foreign war on Mexican soil. Mexico's intellectual class is once again put to the task of observing this new reality. Will they question those working from official institutions to ignite a new armed conflict? Have they learned the lessons brought about narco culture? Will they see past the articulation of these new "national security" myths and seek those responsible for the continuation of war? We are yet to test the limits of our critical imagination.

Notes

INTRODUCTION

1. Luis Astorga, *¿Qué querían que hiciera? Inseguridad y delincuencia organizada en el gobierno de Felipe Calderón* (México: Grijalbo, 2015), 139.

2. For example, in the museum there is a gold-plated gun with the initials "AFC" that SEDENA attributes to Amado Carrillo Fuentes, the supposed head of the Juárez Cartel. The gun, reported in the museum, was a gift from Carrillo Fuentes to Joaquín "El Chapo" Guzmán, which was seized when he was first arrested in 1993. See Jesús Aranda, "Museo del Enervante exhibe 'trofeos' del Ejército en su lucha contra el narco," *La Jornada,* March 12, 2017, http://www.jornada.unam.mx/2017/03/12/politica/010n1pol.

3. This figure is from the National Institute of Statistics and Geography (INEGI), which collected information from 4,700 civil registry officers and 1,107 public ministry agencies. See "Más de 121 mil muertos, el saldo de la narcoguerra de Calderón: Inegi," *Proceso,* July 30, 2013, https://www.proceso.com.mx/nacional/2013/7/30/mas-de-121-mil-muertos-el-saldo-de-la-narcoguerra-de-calderon-inegi-121510.html.

4. See Leticia Ramírez de Alba, "Indicadores de víctimas visibles e invisibles de homicidio," México Evalúa, Centro de Análisis de Políticas Públicas (November 2012): 37–38.

5. Waltraud Morales, "The War on Drugs: A New U.S. National Security Doctrine?," *Third World Quarterly* 11, no. 3 (July 1989): 147–69.

6. Miguel Ángel Félix Gallardo, Ernesto Fonseca, and Rafael Caro Quintero were integral parts of a transnational structure sanctioned by "senior DFS officials, the federal police, and Mexican and US banks responsible for laundering profit." See Peter Watt y Roberto Zepeda, *Drug War Mexico: Politics, Neoliberalism and Violence in the New Narcoeconomy* (London: Zed Books, 2012), 83.

7. Luis Astorga, *El siglo de las drogas* (México: Espasa, 1996), 160.

8. Ioan Grillo, *El Narco: Inside Mexico's Criminal Insurgency* (New York: Blooms-bury, 2011), 61.

9. Among other key contributions, Alvarado has reported on the root of violence in states like Coahuila and Tamaulipas. Where trafficking groups such as the Zetas or the Gulf cartel are supposedly disputing territory, it is also where natural resources are concentrated and are being exploited by local oligarchies together in collusion with transnational conglomerates. "But as with much of the violence in Mexico in recent years," writes Alvarado, "the police, the army, and public officials are often involved in enforced disappearances, kidnapping, torture, and the murder of thousands of citizens." See Ignacio Alvarado, "Terror in Coahuila: Up to 300 disappeared in Mexico's forgotten massacre," *Al Jazeera America*, March 9, 2015, http://america.aljazeera.com/articles/2015/3/9/hundreds-disappeared-in-allende-massacre-in-mexico.html.

10. Luis Astorga, *Mitología del "narcotraficante" en México* (México: Plaza y Val-dés, 1995), 10.

11. Astorga, *Mitología*, 12.

12. Morales, "The War on Drugs," 148.

13. Morales, "The War on Drugs," 167.

14. Gary Webb, "America's 'Crack' Plague has Roots in Nicaragua War," *San Jose Mercury News*, August 18, 1996. The series of the three reports, as they appeared in the newspaper, are available in their original format arranged by that newspaper in the internet archive Web.Archive.com. See http://web.archive.org/web/19961220021036/http://www.sjmercury.com:80/drugs/start.htm.

15. Alfred McCoy, *The Politics of Heroin: CIA Complicity in the Global Drug Trade, Afghanistan, Southeast Asia, Central America, Colombia* (New York: Harper-Collins Publishers, 2003), 495–96.

16. Nick Schou, *Kill the Messenger: How the CIA's Crack-Cocaine Controversy Destroyed Journalist Gary Webb* (New York: Nation Books, 2006), 8.

17. Terrence E. Poppa, *Druglord: The Life and Death of a Mexican Kingpin* (El Paso, TX: Cinco Puntos Press, 2010), xix.

18. Fernando Escalante Gonzalbo, "Homicidios 2008–2009: La muerte tiene permiso," *Nexos*, January 3, 2011, http://www.nexos.com.mx/?P=leerarticulo&Article=1943189.

19. Luis Astorga, *Seguridad, traficantes y militares* (México: Tusquets, 2007), 54.

20. Óscar Castelnovo, "México: entrevista con Ignacio 'Nacho' Alvarado, periodista especializado en violencia," *Red Eco Alternativo*. March 3, 2016, http://www.redeco.com.ar/masvoces/entrevistas/18173-mexico-entrevista-con-ignacio-nacho-alvarado-periodista-especializado-en-violencia. The Mérida Initiative is a US government aid package to provide training and military equipment for the "War on Drugs." It originally consisted of $1.5 billion in funding and it has increased ever since. I will discuss this program in detail later.

21. Federico Mastrogiovanni, *Ni vivos ni muertos: La desaparición forzada en México como estrategia de terror* (México: Penguin Random House, 2016), 40.

22. Dawn Paley, *Drug War Capitalism* (Oakland, CA: AK Press, 2014), 16.

23. Juan Villoro, "Inventando al enemigo," *El País*, January 13, 2017, http://internacional.elpais.com/internacional/2017/01/13/mexico/1484342636_332727.html.

CHAPTER 1

1. Images of this mural and other works of Yescka are available on the following facebook page: https://business.facebook.com/Yescka-Guerrilla-Art-14539389 54910528/?ref=page_internal&path=%2FYescka-Guerrilla-Art-1453938954910 528%2F.

2. José Luis Pardo Veiras and Íñigo Arredondo, "Una guerra inventada y 350,000 muertos en México," *Washington Post*, June 15, 2021, https://www.washington post.com/es/post-opinion/2021/06/14/mexico-guerra-narcotrafico-calderon-homicidios-desaparecidos.

3. Carlo Galli, *Political Spaces and Global War*, trans. Elisabeth Fay (Minneapolis: University of Minneapolis Press, 2010).

4. Gareth Williams, *The Mexican Exception: Sovereignty, Police, and Democracy* (New York: Palgrave, 2011), 154.

5. Elmer Mendoza, *Silver Bullets* trans. Mark Fried (New York: Hachette Book Group, 2016), 20.

6. Mendoza, *Silver Bullets*, 227.

7. Mendoza, *Silver Bullets*, 253.

8. Mendoza, *Silver Bullets*, 200.

9. Margolles's work can be thought of as the symbolic condensation of the narco mythology. In her exhibition "What Else Could We Talk About?" at the Mexican pavilion during the 2009 Venice Biennale in, Margolles presented five objects: a flag dyed with blood obtained in places where murders were committed, fabrics marked with human figures of murdered people like those found dead wrapped in a blanket, fabrics embroidered with gold thread with supposed "narco-messages," blood mixed with water to mop the floor of the pavilion and "cards to chop cocaine" with images of corpses, all coming from cities in the north of the country. That same year, Margolles unveiled a piece that is now part of Mexico City's Tamayo Museum collection: a wall pierced with "bullet interventions" brought from Ciudad Juárez. In all this paraphernalia, the violence is directly related to drug trafficking and the little additional information that accompanies it is limited to an association with the symbols and official vocabulary used to explain the "wars between cartels." Though, due to lack of space I cannot delve into this interpretation, it is enough to remember that Margolles's work, which began in the 1990s, only achieved international celebrity when the violence attributed to the narco during the Calderón government became the immediate context that allowed her conceptual pieces to be readable in a global context. And although it was surprising that the

Mexican pavilion at the Venice Biennale, financed with public money since 2007, was dedicated to the work of Margolles, it is important to understand that the exhibition did not in any way refute the official explanation of Felipe Calderón's government that prevailed concerning narco violence. Far from criticizing the Calderón government and its strategy to fight organized crime, Margolles's conceptual pieces consolidated the hegemonic imaginary by blaming the violence on drug traffickers. The title "What Else Could We Talk About?" can be understood as an intellectual abdication in the face of the powerful official narrative that urges us to repeat that the narcos are the main forces responsible for the violence in Mexico.

10. Mendoza, 62.

11. Geney Beltrán Félix, "Ceder," *Letras Libres* (July 2011), 85–86.

12. "Froylán Enciso, "Periodismo y narcoficción: El más buscado, de Alejandro Almazán," *Vice*, May 21, 2012, http://www.vice.com/es_mx/read/periodismo-y-narcoficcin-el-ms-buscado-de-alejandro-almazn.

13. Juan José Rodríguez, *Mi nombre es Casablanca* (México: Plaza & Janés 2005), 30.

14. Rodríguez, *Mi nombre es Casablanca*, 80.

15. Rodríguez, *Mi nombre es Casablanca*, 52.

16. Rodríguez, *Mi nombre es Casablanca*, 52

17. Rodríguez, *Mi nombre es Casablanca*, 53.

18. Rodríguez, *Mi nombre es Casablanca*, 111–12.

19. Luis Astorga, *Mitología*, 10–11.

20. Fernando Escalante Gonzalbo, *El crimen como realidad y representación* (México: El Colegio de México, 2012), 56.

21. Max Weber, *The Vocation Lectures*, eds. David Owen and Tracy B. Strong, trans. Rodney Livingstone (Indianapolis: Hackett Publishing Company, 2004), 33. Carl Schmitt, *Political Theology*, trans. George Schwab (Chicago: University of Chicago Press, 2005), 13.

22. Francis Fukuyama, *The Origins of Political Order* (New York: Farrar, Straus and Giroux, 2011), 477.

23. Carolina Moreno, "Enrique Peña Nieto's TIME Cover Sparks Outrage In Mexico," *Huffington Post*, February 17, 2014, http://www.huffingtonpost.com/2014/02/17/enrique worth grandson time_n_4803677.html.

24. "Remarks by President Obama before Restricted Bilateral Meeting." National Archives and Records Administration, February 19, 2014, https://obamawhitehouse.archives.gov/the-press-office/2014/02/19/remarks-president-obama-restricted-bilateral-meeting.

25. Randal C. Archibold and Ginger Thompson, "El Chapo, Most Wanted Drug Lord, Is Captured in Mexico," *New York Times*, February 22, 2014, http://nyti.ms/1fIf3Dl.

26. Brian Bow and Arturo Santa-Cruz, eds., *The State and Security in Mexico: Crisis and Transformation in Regional Perspective* (New York: Routledge, 2013), 7.

27. Bow and Santa-Cruz, *The State and Security in Mexico*, 7.

28. Carlos Montemayor, *La violencia de Estado en México: Antes y después de 1968* (México: Random House, 2010), 179.

29. Julio Scherer y Carlos Monsiváis, *Los patriotas: De Tlatelolco a la guerra sucia* (México: Aguilar, 2004), 11, 147. In an effort to delegitimize the struggle for social justice mobilizing armed groups, the minister of Defense Félix Galván López —under president José López Portillo— said in a rare press conference that Marxist-Leninist guerrilla movement known as "Liga Comunista 23 de Septiembre" simply did not exist: "There exists the Liga 23 de Septiembre, but those are not guerilla fighters but offenders of common order, who kill public servants, who rob banks and murder innocent people that have nothing to do with their objectives." Paz Muñoz, "La 'Liga' no existe," *Al Día* (February 9, 1977). Denying the existence of the armed guerrilla movements attempted the opposite critical operation of my argument. By understanding that "cartels" don't exist, we can clearly see state violence operating against various sectors of civil society. Claiming that guerrilla groups did not exist allowed the military in the 1970s to engage in brutal repression, torture and forced disappearance tactics.

30. Luis Astorga, *Seguridad*, 31.

31. Jorge Castañeda, *La herencia: Arqueología de la sucesión presidencial en México* (México: Alfaguara, 1999), 207.

32. CISEN continued operating until 2018, when President Andrés Manuel López Obrador (2018–2024) renamed it the National Intelligence Center (CNI), with the objective to undo its close relation to the US national security interests in Mexico.

33. Jorge Alejandro Medellín, "El narco es sólo un problema policiaco," *El Universal* (July 25 2000), http://www.eluniversal.com.mx/primera/2394.html.

34. Astorga, *Seguridad, traficantes y militares*, 36.

35. Fernando Escalante Gonzalbo, "Homicidios 2008–2009: La muerte tiene permiso," *Nexos*, January 3, 2011, http://www.nexos.com.mx/?P=leerarticulo& Article=1943189.

36. Fernando Escalante Gonzalbo, *El crimen como realidad y representación* (México: El Colegio de México, 2012), 240.

37. Gonzalbo, *El crimen como*, 240.

38. Astorga, *Seguridad*, 276.

39. Ricardo Gutiérrez Mouat, "Monsiváis y la crónica de la violencia" en *El arte de la ironía: Carlos Monsiváis ante la crítica*, eds. Mabel Moraña e Ignacio Sánchez Prado (México: Era, 2007), 235–41, 239.

40. Carlos Monsiváis, "Notas sobre la violencia urbana," *Letras Libres* (May 1999), 34–39.

41. Carlos Monsiváis, *Los mil y un velorios: Crónica de la nota roja en México* (México: Grijalbo y Proceso, 2013), 212.

42. Monsiváis, *Los mil y un velorios*, 214–15.

43. Monsiváis, *Los mil y un velorios*, 216, 217, 219.

44. Felipe Calderón, *Decisiones difíciles* (México: Debate, 2020), 310.

45. Susana Rotker, *La invención de la crónica* (México: FCE y Fondo Nuevo Periodismo Iberoamericano, 2005), 133–34.

46. Tom Wolfe, *The New Journalism* (New York: Harper & Row, 1973), 34.

47. Juan Villoro, *Safari accidental* (Mexico: Joaquín Mortiz, 2005), 14. Fabrizio Mejía Madrid, *Salida de emergencia* (Barcelona: Random House, 2007), 11.

48. Pierre Bourdieu, *On the State: Lectures at the Collège de France, 1989–1992* (Cambridge, UK: Polity, 2014), 3.

49. Bourdieu, *On the State*, 4 (emphasis from the original).

50. Mabel Moraña, *Bourdieu en la periferia: Capital simbólico y campo cultural en América Latina* (Santiago de Chile: Editorial Cuatro Propio, 2014), 123.

51. Moraña, *Bourdieu en la periferia*, 123.

52. Jesús Martín-Barbero, *Oficio de cartógrafo: Travesías latinoamericanas de la comunicación en la cultura* (México: Fondo de Cultura Económica, 2002), 82–83 (emphasis in the original).

53. Martín-Barbero, *Oficio de cartógrafo*, 79.

54. Sergio González Rodríguez died on April 3, 2017, while the original Spanish-language edition of this book was in the revision process. Although my analysis disagrees with his interpretation of the violence attributed to drug trafficking, I would like to offer my admiration for the essays and literary works of González Rodríguez, which have had a deserving central place in the last three decades of intellectual debates in Mexico.

55. Ignacio Sánchez Prado, "Sergio González Rodríguez: literatura y pensamiento en la edad de la catástrofe," *Hispanic Review* (Winter 2014), 285–306, 287.

56. Sánchez Prado, "Sergio González Rodríguez," 290.

57. Sánchez Prado, "Sergio González Rodríguez," 286.

58. Sergio González Rodríguez, *El hombre sin cabeza* (México: Anagrama, 2009), 15.

59. González Rodríguez, *El hombre sin cabeza*, 71.

60. Bernardo Esquinca, "Mensajeros del lado oscuro," *Letras libres* (May 2009), 84–85.

61. González Rodríguez, *El hombre sin cabeza*, 22.

62. González Rodríguez, *El hombre sin cabeza*, 27–28.

63. Octavio Paz, *Labyrinth of Solitude and Other Writings*, trans. Lysander Kemp (New York: Grove Press, 1985), 291.

64. Umberto Eco, *The Limits of Interpretation* (Bloomington: Indiana University Press, 1990), 15.

65. Diego Enrique Osorno, *El cártel de Sinaloa: Una historia del uso político del narco* (México: Random House Mondadori, 2009), 41–42.

66. Guillermo Valdés Castellanos, *Historia del narcotráfico en México* (México: Aguilar, 2013), 15.

67. Valdés Castellanos, *Historia*, 131.

68. Valdés Castellanos, *Historia*, 222, 466.

69. Valdés Castellanos, *Historia*, 211.

70. Valdés Castellanos, *Historia*, 305.

71. Anabel Hernández, *Narcoland* (London: Verso, 2013), 16.

72. Hernández, *Narcoland*, 414.

73. Hernández, *Narcoland*, 583.

74. Valdes Castellanos, *Historia*, 467–68.

75. Valdes Castellanos, *Historia*, 431.

76. Andrés Lajous, "El periodismo que el narco nos dejó," *Nexos*, July 1, 2013, http://www.nexos.com.mx/?p=15386.

77. Diego Enrique Osorno, *La guerra de los Zetas* (México: Grijalbo, 2012), 34. Osorno has even written a "Manifesto of Infrarrealist Journalism" that can be consulted on the page of the Gabriel García Márquez Foundation for New Ibero-American Journalism, one of the main journalistic institutions promoting the Mexican journalistic chroniclers who write about the "narco" using literary narrative strategies: http://nuevoscronistasdeindias.fnpi.org/el-mani fiesto-del-periodismo-infrarrealista-de-diego-osorno. It can also be accessed in English here: https://www.narconews.com/Issue67/article4489.html.

78. El Debate, "¿Cómo hicieron el túnel por donde escapó El Chapo?" *El Debate*, July 17, 2015, http://www.debate.com.mx/mexico/Como-hicieron-el-tunel-por-donde-escapo-El-Chapo-20150717-0119.html.

79. NPR, "'Cartel' Author Spins a Grand Tale of Mexico's Drug Wars," National Public Radio, July 15, 2015, http://www.npr.org/2015/07/15/423203008/cartel-author-spins-an-grand-tale-of-mexicos-drug-wars.

80. NPR, "'Cartel' Author Spins a Grand Tale."

81. Don Winslow, "An Open Letter to the Congress and the President," *Washington Post*, June 28, 2015, B8.

82. The accusation that the government of Felipe Calderón favored the organization of Joaquín "El Chapo" Guzmán was documented in a news report by National Public Radio. The story found that traffickers linked to Chapo were detained in significantly fewer numbers than those of any other criminal organization. See John Burnett, Marisa Peñaloza and Robert Benincasa, "Mexico Seems to Favor Sinaloa Cartel in Drug War," National Public Radio, May 19, 2010, www.npr.org/2010/05/19/126906809/mexico-seems-to-favor-sinaloa-cartel-in-drug-war.

83. See Carlo Galli, *Political Spaces and Global War*, and Wendy Brown, *Walled States, Waning Sovereignty* (New York: Zone Books, 2010).

84. For a more complete discussion of the Mérida Initiative, see Brian Bow, "Beyond Merida? The Evolution of the US Mexico's Security Response to Crisis" in *State and Security in Mexico: Crisis and Transformation in Regional Perspective*, eds. Brian Bow and Arturo Santa-Cruz (New York: Routledge, 2013), 77–98.

85. Valeria Espinosa and Donald B. Rubin, "Did the Military Interventions in the Mexican Drug War Increase the Violence?," *American Statistician* 69, no. 1 (2015): 17–27.

86. Laura Miller, "The System," *New Yorker* (July 6 and 13, 2015), 84–87. A complete analysis of the novel *The Power of the Dog* can be found here: www.newyorker.com/magazine/2015/07/06/the-system-books-laura-miller.

87. Miller, "The System," 84.

88. Miller, "The System," 87.

89. Rossana Reguillo, "The Narco Machine and the Work of Violence: Notes Toward its Decodification," *E-misférica* 8, no. 2 (2011), https://hemi.nyu.edu/hemi/en/e-misferica-82/reguillo.

90. Héctor Hoyos, *Beyond Bolaño: The Global Latin American Novel* (New York: Columbia University Press, 2015), 126.

91. Nazih Richani, *Systems of Violence: The Political Economy of War and Peace in Colombia* (Albany, NY: State University of New York Press, 2013), 52.

92. Richani, *Systems of Violence*, 53.

93. Richani, *Systems of Violence*, 53.

94. Michel Foucault, *Security, Territory, Population: Lectures at the College of France, 1977–1978* (New York: Picador, 2007), 261, 266.

CHAPTER 2

1. The Peña Nieto government reversed the decentralization of the presidential power and the federal government that split the state structures during the Fox and Calderón presidencies. Two of the most significant changes in this regard were: 1) the reconcentration of police power in the Secretariat of the Interior with the creation of a "national gendarmerie" that functioned as a single police force with 10,000 agents; and 2) the foreign policy that at the time forced US agencies such as the DEA and the CIA to use a single channel of communication with the federal government—the Ministry of the Interior itself—preventing Army or Federal Police commanders from having direct exchanges with their US counterparts, as happened during the PAN presidencies of Fox and Calderón. See Randal C. Archibold, Damien Cave and Ginger Thompson, "Mexico's President Limits US Role in Fighting Drug Trade," *New York Times*, April 30, 2013, www.nytimes.com/2013/05/01/world/americas/friction-between-us-and-mexico-threatens-efforts-on-drugs.html.

2. Winslow synthesizes decades of the history of drug trafficking in the hemisphere and combines real characters such as Pedro Avilés and other fictitious ones, such as the case of Barrera, based on the drug trafficker Miguel Ángel Félix Gallardo, known as "the boss of bosses", after a celebrated drug ballad composed by norteño band Los Tigres del Norte.

3. Luis Astorga, "Los corridos de traficantes de drogas en México y Colombia," manuscript read in the congress of the Latin American Studies Association (LASA), in Guadalajara, México (April 17–19, 1997), 2.

4. Luis Astorga, *El siglo de las drogas* (México: Espasa, 1996), 89.

5. Astorga, *El siglo de las drogas*, 21–122.

6. Quoted in Diego Enrique Osorno, *El cártel de Sinaloa: Una historia del uso político del narco* (México: Grijalbo, 2009), 161.

7. Dan Baum, *Smoke and Mirrors: The War on Drugs and the Politics of Failure* (New York: Back Bay Books, 1996), 107–8.

8. Carl Schmitt, *Political Theology*, trans. George Schwab (Chicago: University of Chicago Press, 2005), 5.

9. Baum, *Smoke and Mirrors*, 21. Michelle Alexander argues that the War on Drugs instituted in the United States is a continuation of the racial policies of the early twentieth century and that it creates a caste system that designates the African-American population as a criminal sector of society with the aim of neutralizing their political agency and making it impossible for them to rise up the social ladder. See Michelle Alexander, *The New Jim Crow: Mass Incarceration in the Age of Colorblindness* (New York: The New Press, 2012), 2–3.

10. Ioan Grillo, *El Narco: Inside Mexico's Criminal Insurgency* (New York: Bloomsbury Press, 2011) 51. It is at this point that what happened with Operation Condor in Mexico intersects with the multiple military and paramilitary actions of espionage, repression, and counterinsurgency that were carried out during the 1960s, 1970s, and 1980s with greater visibility in Chile, Argentina and Uruguay, with the advice of the United States government. Although these actions are also known as Operation Condor, in Mexico they focused mainly on drug trafficking and later spread into the so-called "dirty war" against radical left groups between the late 1960s and early 1970s. See J. Patrice McSherry, *Predatory States: Operation Condor and the Covert War in Latin America* (Lanham, Maryland: Rowman and Littlefield Publishers, Inc., 2005).

11. Judith Butler and Gayatri Chakravorty Spivak, *Who Sings the Nation State?* (New York: Seagull Books, 2010), 40.

12. Ed Vulliamy, *Amexica: War along the Borderline* (New York: Farrar, Straus and Giroux, 2010), 23.

13. Charles Bowden, *Down by the River: Drugs, Money, Murder, and Family* (New York: Simon & Schuster, 2004), 136.

14. Fernando Escalante Gonzalbo, "Homicidios 2008–2009."

15. Víctor Hugo Rascón Banda, *Contrabando* (México: Mondadori, 2008), 9.

16. Rascón Banda, 21.

17. Rascón Banda, 209.

18. Fernando García Ramírez, "Literatura contra el horror," *Letras Libres* (May 2011), 84–85, 80.

19. Leopoldo Mendívil, "Buscaglia y el narco mexicano," *Crónica* (February 11, 2013), http://www.cronica.com.mx/notas/2011/602201.html.

20. García Ramírez, "Literatura contra el horror," 84.

21. Luis Astorga, *Seguridad*, 51.

22. Giorgio Agamben, *Homo Sacer: Sovereign Power and Bare Life*, trans. Daniel Heller-Roazen (Stanford, CA: Stanford University Press, 1998), 28.

23. Roberto Bolaño, *2666*, trans. Natasha Wimmer (New York: Farrar, Straus and Giroux.), 302.

24. Bolaño, 372.

25. Bolaño, 365.

26. Astorga, *Seguridad*, 306.

27. Leticia Ramírez de Alba, "Indicadores de víctimas visibles e invisibles de homicidio," México Evalúa, Centro de Análisis de Políticas Públicas (November 2012).

28. Manuel Hernández Borbolla, "Guerra contra el narco 'perfeccionó' letalidad de fuerzas armadas," *Huffington Post*, February 1, 2017, http://www.huffington post.com.mx/2017/02/01/guerra-contra-el-narco-de-calderon-perfecciono-letalidad-de-fu.

29. See Marcela Turati, "Los muertos de Calderón: asesino y asesinado, rostros en un espejo," *Proceso*, December 30, 2020, 16–19. Gustavo Castillo y corresponsales, "A la fosa común, 97% de los cuerpos no identificados en la guerra antinarco de Calderón," *La Jornada*, January 2, 2013, http://www.jornada.unam.mx/2013/01/02/politica/002n1pol.

30. Carlo Galli, Political Spaces and Global War; Wendy Brown, Walled States, Waning Sovereignty, 182.

31. Carl Schmitt, *The Concept of the Political*, 32.

32. Gabriela Polit, "La persuasiva escritura del crimen: literatura y narcotráfico," *Nuevos hispanismos: Para una crítica del lenguaje dominante*, ed. Julio Ortega (Madrid y Fráncfort: Iberoamericana, 2012), 337–51, 347.

33. Alain Badiou, *The Century* (Malden, MA: Polity Press, 2007), 52.

34. Jacques Rancière, *The Politics of Aesthetics*, trans. Gabriel Rochill (London and New York: Continuum, 2004), 38.

35. Schmitt, *The Concept of the Political*, 30–31.

36. Associated Press, "Cartels Winning Mexico Drug War; Sinaloa Kingpin Controls Key Ciudad Juárez Trafficking Routes," *New York Daily News*, April 9, 2010, http://www.nydailynews.com/news/world/cartels-winning-mexico-drug-war-sinaloa-kingpin-controls-key-ciudad-juarez-trafficking-routes-article-1.166306.

37. Chris Matthews, "Fortune 5: The biggest organized crime groups in the world," *Fortune*, September 14, 2014, https://fortune.com/2014/09/14/biggest-organized-crime-groups-in-the-world.

38. David Agren, "Authorities haven't found 'even a dollar' of El Chapo's $1bn drug fortune," *Guardian*, May 3, 2017, https://www.theguardian.com/world/2017/may/03/el-chapo-drug-fortune-1-billion-mexico.

39. Sean Penn, "El Chapo speaks: A secret visit with the most wanted man in the world," *Rolling Stone*, January 10, 2016, https://www.rollingstone.com/politics/politics-news/el-chapo-speaks-40784.

40. Sean Penn, "El Chapo speaks."

41. Michael Crowley, "Saving Mexico: How Enrique Peña Nieto's Sweeping Reforms Have Changed the Narrative in His Narco Stained Nation," *Time*, Febru-

ary 24 2014, http://content.time.com/time/covers/pacific/0,16641,20140224,00. html.

42. Azam Ahmed and Randal C. Archibold, "Mexican Drug Kingpin, El Chapo, Escapes Prison through Tunnel," *New York Times*, July 12, 2015, https://www. nytimes.com/2015/07/13/world/americas/joaquin-guzman-loera-el-chapo-mexican-drug-kingpin-prison-escape.html.

43. Azam Ahmed, "El Chapo How Was Captured Finally, Again," *New York Times*, January 16, 2016, https://www.nytimes.com/2016/01/17/world/americas/mexico-el-chapo-sinaloa-sean-penn.html.

44. Ahmed, "El Chapo."

45. Natalia Mendoza, "Un triunfo de la antropología," *Milenio*, January 18, 2016, http://www.milenio.com/tribunamilenio/que_aprendi_del_chapo_guzman/entrevista_Chapo_Sean_Penn-aportes_entrevista_Chapo-vida_Chapo_Guzman_entrevista_13_669063089.html.

46. Steven Dudley, "5 Reasons Sean Penn Failed as a 'Journalist' in 'Chapo' Interview," *InsightCrime*, January 16, 2016, https://insightcrime.org/news/analysis/5-reasons-sean-penn-failed-as-a-journalist-in-chapo-interview.

47. Francisco Goldman, "El Chapo, Episode III: The Farce Awakens," *New Yorker*, January 14, 2016, www.newyorker.com/news/news-desk/el-chapo-episode-iii-the-farce-awakens.

48. Guillermo Valdés Castellanos, "Leyendo entre líneas," *Milenio*, January 18, 2016, http://www.milenio.com/tribunamilenio/que_aprendi_del_chapo_guzman/Chapo-captura_Chapo-recaptura_Chapo-Chapo-Kate_del_Castillo_13_666663328.html.

49. Valdés Castellanos, "Levendo entre lineas."

50. Julio Scherer, "Proceso en la guarida de 'El Mayo' Zambada," *Proceso*, April 3, 2010, https://www.proceso.com.mx/reportajes/2010/4/3/proceso-en-la-guarida-de-el-mayo-zambada-8150.html.

51. Sean Penn, "El Chapo speaks"

52. Juan Villoro, "Un célebre desconocido," *Reforma*, January 15, 2016, http://www.reforma.com/aplicacioneslibre/editoriales/editorial.aspx?id=79969&md5=c8577cf8905d2ae14125be15e770d627&ta=0dfdbac11765226904c16cb9ad1b2efe.

53. It should be remembered that O'Reilly, the famous conservative Fox News host, was fired by the television network after several accusations of sexual harassment against him that ended with the payment of compensation of damages of 13 million dollars to the women who reported him.

54. "Trump humilló a Peña vía telefónica: Reporte de Dolia Estévez," *Aristegui Noticias*, February 1, 2017, http://aristeguinoticias.com/0102/mundo/trump-humillo-a-pena-nieto-el-presidente-mexicano-balbuceo-dolia-estevez.

55. See the full transcript of the interview: https://www.sbnation.com/2017/2/5/14516156/donald-trump-interview-transcript-bill-orcilly-super-bowl-2017.

56. Katherine Faulders, "Trump signs three executive actions on crime against police, drug cartels," *ABC News*, February 9, 2017, https://abcnews.go.com/

US/trump-signs-executive-actions-crime-police-drug-cartels/story?id=
45375771.

57. Valeria Luiselli, "Así acaba el mundo," *El País*, November 14, 2016, https://
elpais.com/elpais/2016/11/13/opinion/1479052343_462253.html.

58. Guadalupe Correa and Tony Payán, "Energy Reform and Security in Northeastern Mexico," *Issue Brief*, Baker Institute of Rice University (May 6, 2014).

59. Steve Horn, "Exclusive: Hillary Clinton State Department Emails, Mexico Energy Reform and the Revolving Door," *Huffington Post* (August 9, 2016), www.
huffingtonpost.com/steve-horn/exclusive-hillary-clinton_b_7963596.html.

60. The video is available on YouTube: https://youtu.be/nMPWhn8HEJk.

61. Amy B. Wang, "Donald Trump Plans to Immediately Deport 2 Million to 3
Million Undocumented Immigrants," *Washington Post*, November 14, 2016,
https://www.washingtonpost.com/news/the-fix/wp/2016/11/13/donald-trump-
plans-to-immediately-deport-2-to-3-million-undocumented-immigrants.

62. Rebecca Harrington, "Obama Deported 3 million immigrants during his
presidency—here's how Trump's new immigration order compares," *Business
Insider*, February 22, 2017, www.businessinsider.com/whats-the-difference-
between-trump-obama-immigration-orders-2017-2.

63. Faye Hipsman, Bárbara Gómez Aguinaga and Randy Capps, "DACA at
Four: Participation in the Deferred Action Program and Impacts on Recipients," Migration Policy Institute (August 2016), www.migrationpolicy.org/
research/daca-four-participation-deferred-action-program-and-impacts-
recipients.

64. Sahil Kapur and Jennifer Jacobs, "Trump Obama Floats Like Deportation
Plan, and Fans Do not Mind," Bloomberg, August 23, 2016, https://www.bloom
berg.com/news/articles/2016-08-23/trump-floats-obama-like-deportation-
plan-and-fans-don-t-mind.

65. Wilbert Torre, *Narcoleaks: La alianza México-Estados Unidos en la guerra contra el crimen organizado* (México: Grijalbo, 2013), 24.

66. Guadalupe Correa and Tony Payán, *La guerra improvisada: Los años de Calderón y sus consecuencias* (México: Océano, 2021), 180.

67. "Denuncian a Calderón ante la Corte Internacional por crímenes de guerra," *Proceso* (November 25, 2011), http://www.proceso.com.mx/289224/denuncian-a-
calderon-ante-la-cpi-por-crimenes-de-guerra.

68. Milli Legrain, "EE.UU. debe decidir si entrega fondos para polémico plan de
seguridad en México," Univisión, July 22, 2016, http://www.univision.com/
noticias/relaciones-internacionales/eeuu-debe-decidir-si-entrega-fondos-para-
polemico-plan-de-seguridad-en-mexico.

69. Nina Lakhani, "El apoyo de Hillary Clinton al golpe de Estado marcó un
camino de violencia en Honduras," *El Diario* and *Guardian*, September 3,
2016, http://www.eldiario.es/theguardian/Hillary-Clinton-camino-violencia-
Honduras_0_554695049.html.

70. Oliver Milman, "Biden Administration Reinstates Trump-era 'Remain in Mexico' Policy," *Guardian*, December 2, 2021, https://www.theguardian.com/us-news/2021/dec/02/remain-in-mexico-biden-administration-immigration.

71. Jacobo García, "El muro de Trump se puede tocar y está frío," *El País* (November 4, 2016), http://internacional.elpais.com/internacional/2016/10/30/mexico/1477843472_939946.html.

72. Todd Miller and Nick Buxton, "Biden's Border: The Industry, the Democrats and the 2020 Elections," Transnational Institute (February 17, 2021).

73. Zack Budryk, "Deportations Lower under Trump Administration than Obama: Report," *The Hill*, November 18, 2019, https://thehill.com/latino/470900-deportations-lower-under-trump-than-obama-report.

74. Roberto Aguilar and Noé Torres, "Cementera mexicana GCC podría vender materiales para muro de Trump: Directivo," *Reuters*, November 22, 2016, http://mx.reuters.com/article/topNews/idMXL1N1DN1CU.

CHAPTER 3

1. Cesar López Cuadras, *Cuatro muertos por capítulo* (México: Ediciones B, 2013), 9.

2. López Cuadras, *Cuatro muertos por capítulo*, 139.

3. López Cuadras, *Cuatro muertos por capítulo*, 11.

4. López Cuadras, *Cuatro muertos por capítulo*, 193–94.

5. Geney Beltrán Félix, "Una de narcos," *Confabulario*, May 25, 2013, http://confabulario.eluniversal.com.mx/107.

6. In 2013, during the International Book Fair at the Palacio de Minería in Mexico City, I saw the remaining copies of that single edition for a fragment of its original price among the book stalls for editorial clearance sales in a popular alley next the palace.

7. López Cuadras, *La primera vez que vi a Kim Novak: Cuentos y relatos de Guasachi* (1996, México: Universidad Autónoma de Sinaloa, 2010), 24.

8. López Cuadras, *La novela inconclusa de Bernardino Casablanca* (1996, México: Ediciones Arlequín, 2007), 223.

9. López Cuadras, *Cuatro muertos por capítulo*, 32.

10. López Cuadras, *Cástulo Bojórquez*, 160.

11. López Cuadras, *Cástulo Bojórquez*, 179.

12. López Cuadras, *Cástulo Bojórquez* (México: Fondo de Cultura Económica, 2007), 9.

13. Adriana Velderráin, "Cesar López Cuadras (1951–2013)," Feria del Libro de Hermosillo 2015, October 2015, http://isc.gob.mx/flh2015/cesarlopezcuadras.html. That the large commercial publishers are not fighting for the work of López Cuadras will remain a mystery. For now, it is possible to read *Four Deaths per Chapter* because Ediciones B had the right to publish it without expecting immediate sales success (although its only edition is apparently

already out of print). We owe Ediciones Arlequín for the new and well-done editions of *The Unfinished Novel* by Bernardino Casablanca and the controversial short novel *Macho profundo* (1999), a double diatribe against extreme machismo and feminism. And although not always available in its bookstores, the Fondo de Cultura Económica (FCE) still reprints *Cástulo Bojórquez*. Finally, the magnificent stories of *La primera vez que vi a Kim Novak* (The first time I saw Kim Novak) still exist on paper thanks to the Autonomous University of Sinaloa, who also published, with the FCE, a co-edition of *El delfín de Kowalsky* (Kowalsky's dolphin), López Cuadras's last unpublished work.

14. Daniel Sada, trans. Jen Hofer, Excerpt of *Because It Seems to Be a Lie the Truth Is Never Known*, *Bomb Magazine*, January 1, 2006, https://bombmagazine.org/articles/because-it-seems-to-be-a-lie-the-truth-is-never-known.

15. Oscar de Pablo, "Iguala: Crimen de estado, crimen de clase," *Gkillcity* 178 (November 17, 2014), http://gkillcity.com/articulos/el-mirador-politico/iguala-crimen-estado-crimen-clase.

16. Daniel Sada, *Porque parece mentira la verdad nunca se sabe* (México: Tusquets, 1999), 413.

17. Christopher Domínguez Michael, "La lección del maestro," *Letras Libres*, I.10 (1999), 90–91, http://www.letraslibres.com/mexico/libros/porque-parece-mentira-la-verdad-nunca-se-sabe-daniel-sada.

18. Daniel Sada, *El lenguaje del juego* (Barcelona: Anagrama, 2012), 72.

19. Sada, *El lenguaje del juego*, 82.

20. Sada, *El lenguaje del juego*, 82.

21. Juan Villoro, "La violencia en el espejo," *El País* (August 3, 2013).

22. Sada, *El lenguaje del juego*, 185.

23. Chantal Mouffe, ed., *The Challenge of Carl Schmitt* (New York and London: Verso, 1999), 2, 3.

24. Roberto Bolaño, *2666*, trans. Natasha Wimmer (New York: Farrar, Straus and Giroux.), 300.

25. Bolaño, *2666*, 300.

26. Sharae Deckard, "Peripheral Realism, Millennial Capitalism, and Roberto Bolaño's 2666," *Modern Language Quarterly* 73:3 (2012), 351–72, 353.

27. Deckard, "Peripheral Realism," 356.

28. Sergio Villalobos-Ruminott, "A Kind of Hell: Roberto Bolaño and The Return of World Literature," *Journal of Latin American Cultural Studies* 18, no. 2–3 (2009), 193–205, 194.

29. José Revueltas, "Réplica sobre la novela: el cascabel al gato," *Visión del Paricutín (y otras crónicas y reseñas)* eds. Andrea Revueltas y Philippe Cheron (México: Era, 1983), 206–14, 213.

30. Roberto Bolaño, *Woes of the True Policeman*, trans. Natasha Wimmer (New York: Farrar, Straus and Giroux, 2012), 219

31. Jorge Luis Borges, "The Superstitious Ethics of the Reader," trans. Suzanne Jill Levine, *On Writing* (London: Penguin, 210).

32. Roberto Bolaño y Rodrigo Fresán, "Dos hombres en el castillo: Una conversación electrónica sobre Philip K. Dick," *Letras Libres* (June 2002), 38–40, 40.

33. Bolaño, *2666*, 372.

34. Bolaño, *2666*, 274.

35. Bolaño, *2666*, 276.

36. Alain Badiou and Slavoj Žižek, *Philosophy in the Present* (Cambridge: Polity Press, 2009), 11.

37. Jacques Derrida, *The Politics of Friendship*, trans. George Collins (New York and London: Verso, 2005), 114.

38. Slavoj Žižek, *Violence* (New York: Picador, 2008), 9.

39. Slavoj Žižek, "Homo Sacer in Afghanistan," *Lacanian Ink* 20 (2002), 100–113.

40. Žižek, "Homo Sacer in Afghanistan," 101.

41. Jacques Rancière, *Disagreement: Politics and Philosophy* (Minneapolis: University of Minnesota Press, 1999), 77.

42. Brett Levinson, "Case Closed: Madness and Dissociation in *2666*," *Journal of Latin American Cultural Studies*, 18 no. 2–3 (2009), 177–91, 187.

43. Juan Villoro, "The Red Carpet," trans. David Noriega, *N+1* 105 (Spring 2010), https://nplusonemag.com/issue-9/translation/the-red-carpet.

44. The eight blankets that were used for the installation, "The Red Carpet" mounted in 2007 at the Sinaloa Art Museum were later claimed by the Attorney General's Office (PGR) as part of ongoing investigations. Robles later used her own blood to continue the installation. On September 10, 2010, Robles presented her exhibition Navajas at the Centro de Arte Contemporáneo Wifredo Lam, in Havana. See Merry MacMasters, "Rosa María Robles stars in her photographic version of the Angel of Independence," *La Jornada*, August 26, 2010, http://www.jornada.unam.mx/2010/08/26/cultura/ a05n1cul.

45. Villoro, "The Red Carpet."

46. Juan Villoro, *Arrecife* (Barcelona: Anagrama, 2012), 63.

47. Ramón López Velarde, "La suave Patria," *Obras*, comp. José Luis Martínez (México: FCE, 2004), 260–65, 264.

48. Villoro, *Arrecife*, 62. Villoro also parodies here one of Octavio Paz's most famous poems, "Hymn Amon the Ruins," referring to one of its most celebrated stanzas: "Night falls on Teotihuacán./ On top of the pyramid the boys are smoking marijuana,/ harsh guitars sound,/ What weed, what living waters will give life to us,/ where shall we unearth the word,/ the relations that govern hymn and speech,/ the dance, the city and the measuring scales?" Read the poem, translated by Williams Carlos Williams: https://voetica.com/voetica.php? collection=1&poet=45&poem=5592.

49. Villoro, *Arrecife*, 61.

50. Villoro, *Arrecife*, 25.

51. Villoro, *Arrecife*, 25.

52. Juan Villoro, "La violencia en el espejo," *El País* (August 3, 2013).

CHAPTER 4

1. Roberto Bolaño, *Between Parentheses*, trans. Natasha Wimmer (New York: New Directions, 2004), 365.
2. Ricardo Vigueras-Fernández, "Edmond Baudoin y Troub's en Ciudad Juárez: del mito a la vida cotidiana," *Fronteras metafóricas*, comps. Magali Velasco Vargas y Guadalupe Vargas Montero (Ciudad Juárez: Universidad Autónoma de Ciudad Juárez, 2012), 143–59).
3. Vigueras-Fernández, "Edmond Baudoin," 147.
4. Vigueras-Fernández, "Edmond Baudoin," 147.
5. Vigueras-Fernández, "Edmond Baudoin," 147.
6. Charles Bowden, "While You Were Sleeping," *The Charles Bowden Reader*, eds. Erin Almeranti y Mary Martha Miles (Austin: University of Texas Press, 2010), 105–21.
7. Bowden, *The Charles Bowden Reader*, 105.
8. Sergio González Rodríguez, *Huesos en el desierto* (Barcelona: Anagrama, 2006), 11.
9. Jean Franco, *Cruel Modernity* (Durham, NC: Duke University Press, 2013), 244–45.
10. Christopher Hooks, "Q&A with Molly Molloy: The Story of the Juárez Femicides is a 'Myth,'" *Texas Observer*, January 9, 2014, http://www.texasobserver.org/qa-molly-molloy-story-juarez-femicides-myth.
11. Pedro H. Albuquerque y Prasad Vemala, "Femicide Rates in Mexican Cities along the US-Mexico Border: Do the Maquiladora Industries Play a Role?" Social Science Research Network, June 3, 2014, http://ssrn.com/abstract=1112308 and http://dx.doi.org/10.2139/ssrn.1112308, 5.
12. Albuquerque y Vemala, "Femicide Rates," 13.
13. Víctor Hugo Rascón Banda, *Hotel Juárez*, en *Umbral de la memori: Teatro completo de Víctor Hugo Rascón Banda. Tomo III. El teatro del crimen*, comp. Enrique Mijares (Chihuahua: Instituto Chihuahuense de la Cultura, 2010), 433–77, 442.
14. Rascón Banda, *Hotel Juárez*, 457–8.
15. Rascón Banda, *Hotel Juárez*, 460.
16. Rascón Banda, *Hotel Juárez*, 463.
17. Rita Laura Segato, "Territorio, soberanía y crímenes de segundo Estado: la escritura en el cuerpo de las mujeres asesinadas en Ciudad Juárez" (Brasilia: Departamento de Antropología, Universidad de Brasilia, 2004), 16.
18. Segato, "Territorio," 13.
19. These figures come from *Frontera List*, the information site on drug trafficking and violence directed by researcher Molly Molloy: http://fronteralist.org/category/murder-rate. For a statistical analysis of the murders attributed to the narco during Calderón's presidency in Ciudad Juárez and other entities in the country, see Escalante Gonzalbo, "Homicidios 2008–2009: La muerte tiene permiso."
20. Miguel Ángel Chávez Díaz de León, *Policía de Ciudad Juárez* (México: Océano, 2012), 8.

21. Chávez Díaz de León, *Policía de Ciudad Juárez*, 33.

22. Chávez Díaz de León, *Policía de Ciudad Juárez*, 34.

23. Chávez Díaz de León, *Policía de Ciudad Juárez*, 33.

24. Chávez Díaz de León, *Policía de Ciudad Juárez*, 82.

25. Chávez Díaz de León, *Policía de Ciudad Juárez*, 84.

26. Chávez Díaz de León, *Policía de Ciudad Juárez*, 119.

27. Ernesto Laclau, *The Rhetorical Foundations of Society* (London: Verso, 2014), 63.

28. Daniel Gamper y Luis Alfonso Herrera Robles, "Editorial," *Guaraguao: Revista de cultura latinoamericana*, 34 (Winter 2010), 5–6.

29. Charles Bowden, "While You Were Sleeping," in *The Charles Bowden Reader*, eds. Erin Almeranti y Mary Martha Miles (Austin: University of Texas Press, 2010), 105–21, 109.

30. Slavoj Žižek, *Violence* (New York: Picador, 2008), 9.

31. Bowden, "While You Were Sleeping," 106.

32. W. J. T. Mitchell, *Picture Theory* (Chicago: The University of Chicago Press, 1994), 95.

33. Mitchell, *Picture Theory*, 325.

34. Francis Fukuyama, "Fukuyama revisa su Fin de la historia," *Milenio semanal* 112 (October 25, 1999).

35. Charles Bowden, *Juárez: The Laboratory of Our Future* (New York: Aperture, 1998), 117.

36. Sergio González Rodríguez, *Huesos en el desierto* (2002, Barcelona: Anagrama, 2006), 172. This version was criticized by the juarense journalist José Pérez Espino, who points out inconsistencies in *Bones in the Desert*: "González Rodríguez preferred to imagine rather than to investigate. Some of the unsolved murders were likely perpetrated by mafia hitmen. But the version that the nearly 300 cases [now more than 500] are 'ritualistic' crimes committed by 'two people' is untenable. His statements to the press contradict what was published in his own book, from which it can be inferred that homicides in Ciudad Juárez have occurred for the most varied causes: passionate motives, for intra-family violence or clashes between gangs, for example." See José Pérez Espino, "La invención de mitos en los medios y la lucrativa teoría de la conspiración," *Derechos humanos: Órgano informativo de la Comisión de Derechos Humanos del Estado de México*, 12.73 (May–June 2005), 63–70, 64.

37. González Rodríguez, *Huesos en el desierto*, xx.

38. Charles Bowden y Julián Cardona, *Exodus/Éxodo* (Austin: University of Texas Press, 2008), 265.

39. Martha Elba Figueroa, "De lejos, siguen a Juárez otras ciudades violentas," *El Diario*, January 11, 2010, http://demojado.blogspot.com/2010/01/de-lejos-siguen-juarez-otras-ciudades.html.

40. Figueroa, "De lejos."

41. Charles Bowden, *Murder City: Ciudad Juárez and the Global Economy's New Killing Fields* (New York: Nation Books, 2010), 14.

42. Julian Cardona, "J-war-ez" *Frontline* (Summer 2009), 9–12, 9.

43. Bowden, *Murder City*, 18.

44. Bowden, *Murder City*, 18 (emphasis in original).

45. Ed Vulliamy, "As Juárez Falls," *The Nation*, December 9, 2010, https://www.thenation.com/article/archive/juarez-falls.

46. Willivaldo Delgadillo, *Fabular Juárez: Marcos de Guerra, memoria y los foros por venir* (Juárez: Bown Buffalo Press, 2020), 62–63.

47. Charles Bowden and Alice Leora Briggs, *Dreamland: The Way Out of Juárez* (Austin: University of Texas Press, 2010), 10.

48. Bowden and Briggs, *Dreamland*, 2.

49. Amnesty International, *Mexico: New Reports of Human Rights Violations by the Military* (London: Amnesty International Publications, 2009), 7, https://www.amnesty.org/download/Documents/44000/amr410582009en.pdf.

50. Luis Carlos Cano, "Suman mil 450 quejas vs. Ejército," *El Universal*, September 10, 2009, https://archivo.eluniversal.com.mx/estados/73044.html.

51. Amnesty International, *Mexico*, 6.

52. Julián Cardona, "World Class City," *The History of the Future / La historia del futuro*, ed. Nancy Sutor (Santa Fe, NM: Lannan Foundation, 2008), 24. One phrase from this quote was the seminal idea for the documentary "If Images Could Fill Our Empty Spaces" by journalist Alice Driver, an approach to violence in Ciudad Juárez based on the work of Bowden and Cardona among others. The documentary is available on the following website: https://velamag.com/documentary-if-images-could-fill-our-empty-spaces.

53. For details of the prize on the official Lannan Foundation website: https://lannan.org/cultural-freedom/detail/julian-cardona-awarded-2004-cultural-freedom-fellowship.

54. See the official announcement of the acquisition of the archive: csunshinetoday.csun.edu/arts-and-culture/csun-acquires-works-by-mexican-photographer-julian-cardona.

55. Meredith Blake, "The Exchange: Charles Bowden on Juárez, 'Murder City,'" *New Yorker*, May 24, 2010, http://www.newyorker.com/online/blogs/books/2010/05/the-exchange-charles-bowden-on-jurez-murder-city.html.

56. Bowden, *Exodus*, 186–87.

57. Bowden, *Murder City*, 319.

58. Bowden, *Murder City*, 319–20.

59. José Gil Olmos, "El fatídico experimento de Peña Nieto," *Proceso*, March 3, 2015, http://www.proceso.com.mx/?p=397455.

60. Claudio Lomnitz, "Tierra Caliente: lectura en clave antropológica," La Jornada, January 22, 2014, https://web.archive.org/web/20201112011224/https://www.jornada.com.mx/2014/01/22/opinion/021a2pol.

61. Rossana Reguillo, "Algunas razones para mi 'aparente rendición,'" Nuestra aparente rendición, August 29, 2011, http://nuestraaparenterendicion.com/

index.php/nuestra-aparente-rendicion/primer-aniversario/item/483-algunas-razones-para-mi-"aparente-rendición"-rossana-reguillo#.VPvpTUJGjdk.

62. Antonio Navalón, "Los zapatistas del siglo 21," El País, February 3, 2014, https://elpais.com/internacional/2014/02/03/actualidad/1391398145_430792.html.

63. Héctor Aguilar Camín, "La guerra perdida de México," Milenio, March 6, 2015, http://www.milenio.com/firmas/hector_aguilar_camin_dia-con-dia/guerra-perdida-Mexico_18_476532362.html.

64. Francisco Castellanos J., "Liberación de Mireles evidencia que el gobierno actuó de manera selectiva: Leonel Godoy," Proceso, May 12, 2017, https://www.proceso.com.mx/nacional/estados/2017/5/12/liberacion-de-mireles-evidencia-que-el-gobierno-actuo-de-manera-selectiva-leonel-godoy-184138.html.

65. Andrea Noel, "'La Tuta' vivía en una cueva cuando fue capturado," Vice, March 4, 2015, www.vice.com/es_mx/read/la-tuta-viva-en-una-cueva-y-fue-atrapado-gracias-a-un-pastel-que-le-llevo-su-novia.

66. Eduardo Medina Mora was director of the Center for Investigation and National Security (CISEN) and Public Safety Secretary under President Vicente Fox (2000–2006). Later, he was the Attorney General of Mexico under President Felipe Calderón (2006–2012). His appointment as Minister of the Supreme Court of Justice of the Nation was denounced by civil organizations, academics, activists and journalists, in addition to a petition on Change.org that collected almost 45,000 signatures. See Tania L. Montalvo, "Five arguments against Medina Mora in court and the responses of the former Attorney General," Animal Politico, 10 March, 2015, http://www.animalpolitico.com/2015/03/5-razones-por-las-que-organizaciones-y-academicos-se-oponen-que-medina-mora-sea-ministro-de-la-corte.

67. Edgardo Buscaglia, Vacíos de poder en México (México: Debate, 2013), 13.

68. Buscaglia, Vacios de poder en Mexico, 49.

69. Javier Cabrera Martínez, "Operación 'Cóndor' causó éxodo de capos y civiles," El Universal, December 22, 2006, http://archivo.eluniversal.com.mx/estados/63346.html.

70. Sergio Aguayo, La charola: Una historia de los servicios de inteligencia en México (México: Grijalbo, 2001), 222.

71. Poppa, Druglord, 42.

72. Poppa, Druglord, xi.

73. Poppa, Druglord, xvi.

74. Poppa, Druglord, 43.

75. Peter Dale Scott, "Drugs, Anti-Communism and Extra-Legal Repression in Mexico," Government of the Shadows: Parapolitics and Criminal Sovereignty, ed. Eric Wilson (Nueva York: Pluto Press, 2009), 173–94, 178.

76. See in particular Charles Bowden's posthumous narrative report, "Blood on the Corn." In that text, Bowden interviews the DEA official in charge of investigating Camarena's murder. According to the official, the CIA ordered the kidnapping

and assassination of Camarena because he obtained information that linked President Ronald Reagan's government to the sale of crack cocaine in California to finance the Contra guerrillas in Nicaragua during the peak years of the Cold War. See Charles Bowden, "Blood on the Corn," *Matter*, (November 17, 2014), https://medium.com/matter/blood-on-the-corn-52ac13f7e643#.hb14eozep.

77. Luis Astorga, *Seguridad*, 52.

78. Noam Chomsky, *On Power and Ideology: The Managua Lectures* (Chicago: Haymarket Books, 2015), 134.

79. Waltraud Morales, "The War on Drugs: A New US National Security Doctrine?," *Third World Quarterly* 11, no. 3 (July 1989), 147–69, 167.

80. Morales, "The War on Drugs," 147–69, 167.

81. David Harvey, *Rebel Cities: From the Right to the City to the Urban Revolution* (New York: Verso, 2012), xv.

EPILOGUE

1. See, for example, Carmen Aristegui's interview with the governor of Chihuahua, Javier Corral, less than twenty-four hours after Breach's murder. Without any police investigation, Corral immediately establishes the narrative that the journalist was murdered in a narco context: https://aristeguinoticias.com/2403/multimedia/miroslava-breach-recibio-amenazas-tras-reportajes-sobre-narco-politica.

2. Alberto Nájar, "Miroslava Breach, la periodista 'incómoda' asesinada en México cuando llevaba a su hijo a la escuela," *BBC Mundo*, March 24, 2017, http://www.bbc.com/mundo/noticias-america-latina-39376671.

3. Olga Alicia Aragón, "La trama en el asesinato de Miroslava," *Newsweek en español*, March 31, 2017, https://www.noroeste.com.mx/internacional/la-trama-en-el-asesinato-de-miroslava-MVNO1076912.

4. Aragón, "La trama en el asesinato de Miroslava.

5. EFE, "Artículo 19: Funcionarios, la mayor amenaza para prensa mexicana," *La Opinión*, April 6, 2017, https://laopinion.com/2017/04/06/articulo-19-funcionarios-la-mayor-amenaza-para-prensa-mexicana.

6. Editorial, "Identificados, autores intelectuales y materiales del asesinato de Miroslava Breach: Corral," *Proceso*, April 17, 2017, http://www.proceso.com.mx/482623/identificados-autores-intelectuales-materiales-del-asesinato-miroslava-breach-corral.

7. "Líder de 'Los Salazares' ordenó el asesinato de la periodista Miroslava Breach: fiscalía," *El Financiero*, February 17, 2020, https://www.elfinanciero.com.mx/nacional/lider-de-los-salazares-ordeno-el-asesinato-de-la-periodista-miroslava-breach-fiscalia.

8. Alejandro Hope, "La guerra regresa a Ciudad Juárez," *El Universal*, March 6, 2017, http://www.eluniversal.com.mx/entrada-de-opinion/columna/alejandro-hope/nacion/2017/03/6/la-guerra-regresa-ciudad-juarez.

9. Hope, "La Guerra regresa."

10. Gabriela Minjáres, "Aparecen panorámicos contra Javier Corral," *El Diario*, May 9, 2016, https://diario.mx/Estado/2016-05-09_4d83ffd2/aparecen-panoramicos-contra-javier-corral.

11. EFE, "Heridos los hijos de 'El Chapo' en una emboscada en plena guerra interna del cártel de Sinaloa," *La Vanguardia*, February 9, 2017, http://www.lavanguardia.com/internacional/20170209/414176267650/heridos-hijos-chapo-emboscada-plena-guerra-interna-cartel-sinaloa.html.

12. Luis Chaparro, "Jefe sicario: Viene otra 'guerra' en Ciudad Juárez," *El Universal*, October 20, 2016, http://www.eluniversal.com.mx/articulo/periodismo-de-investigacion/2016/10/20/jefe-sicario-viene-otra-guerra-en-ciudad-juarez.

13. Newsroom, "Caro Quintero, liberado en este sexenio, se une a la guerra: va a pelearse Chihuahua, dice Fiscal," *Sin embargo*, July 5, 2016, http://www.sinembargo.mx/05-07-2016/3062898.

14. Reuters, "Caro Quintero sigue operando, dice EU," *La Jornada de San Luis*, May 11, 2016, https://lajornadasanluis.com.mx/ultimas-publicaciones/caro-quintero-sigue-operando-dice-eu.

15. Newsroom, "Caro Quintero: 'No estoy en guerra con El Chapo; ya no soy narco,'" *Proceso*, July 25, 2016, https://www.proceso.com.mx/proceso-tv/2016/7/25/caro-quintero-no-estoy-en-guerra-con-el-chapo-ya-no-soy-narco-167828.html.

16. J. Jesús Esquivel, "El cártel de Jalisco se cierne sobre Ciudad Juárez," *Proceso*, February 1, 2017, https://www.proceso.com.mx/reportajes/2017/2/11/el-cartel-de-jalisco-se-cierne-sobre-ciudad-juarez-178807.html.

17. Juliana Henao, "Fragmentación de cárteles desata la violencia," *El Diario de El Paso*, March 7, 2017, http://diario.mx/El_Paso/2017-03-06_2d6df576/fragmentacion-de-carteles-desata-la-narcoviolencia.

18. Philip Abrams, "Notes on the Difficulty of Studying the State (1977)," *Journal of Historical Sociology* 1, no. 1 (March 1988), 58–89, 77.

AFTERWORD

1. Rubén Mosso and Jannet López, "Ya no hay guerra: AMLO," *Milenio*, January 31, 2019, https://www.milenio.com/politica/ya-no-hay-guerra-amlo.

2. Andrés Manuel López Obrador, "Plan nacional de paz y seguridad: 2018–2024," Transición.mx (2018), 8–9.

3. Catalina Pérez Correa, "Un dictamen para celebrar," *El Universal*, February 21, 2019, https://www.eluniversal.com.mx/columna/catalina-perez-correa/nacion/un-dictamen-para-celebrar.

4. Jesús Esquivel, J. "Queja en Washington: no tenemos interlocutores en México." *Proceso*, July 7, 2019, 16–17.

5. Ana Lilia Pérez, "Huachicoleo a escala multimillonaria: dentro de Pemex, toda una 'industria paralela," *Proceso*, December 30, 2018, 7.

6. Mathieu Tourliere, "Cuatro mil militares evitarán robo de combustible en 58 puntos estratégicos de Pemex: AMLO" *Proceso*, December 27, 2018, https://diariotribunachiapas.com.mx/?p=28013.

7. Chris Dalby, "Mexico's Santa Rosa de Lima Cartel Risks Burning Too Bright, Too Fast," *InSight Crime*, February 15, 2019, https://insightcrime.org/news/analysis/mexicos-santa-rosa-de-lima-cartel-el-marro.

8. Rodrigo Vera, "La iglesia católica censura el culto al Santo Niño Huachicolero," *Proceso*, January 21, 2019, https://www.proceso.com.mx/nacional/2019/1/21/la-iglesia-catolica-censura-el-culto-al-santo-nino-huachicolero-218941.html.

9. Stephanie Leutert and Sarah Spalding, "How Many Central Americans Are Traveling North?" *Lawfare*, March 14, 2019, https://www.lawfareblog.com/how-many-central-americans-are-traveling-north.

10. Julia Ainsley, "Only six immigrants in terrorism database stopped by CBP at southern border from October to March," *NBC News*, January 7, 2019, https://www.nbcnews.com/politics/immigration/only-six-immigrants-terrorism-database-stopped-cbp-southern-border-first-n955861.

11. Mathieu Tourliere, "El modelo represivo se reimplanta en migración," *Proceso*, June 17, 2019, https://www.proceso.com.mx/reportajes/2019/6/17/el-modelo-represivo-se-reimplanta-en-migracion-226523.html.

12. Rolando Ramos, "Amnistía Internacional alerta de mayor militarización con AMLO," *El Economista*, April 7, 2021, https://www.eleconomista.com.mx/politica/Amnistia-Internacional-alerta-de-mayor-militarizacion-con-AMLO-20210407-0007.html.

13. Oswaldo Zavala, "La tentación de la guerra: Una lectura sobre la jornada violenta de Culiacán," *Perro crónico*, November 5, 2019, https://perrocronico.com/la-tentacion-de-la-guerra.

14. Ricardo Raphael, "Hay una guerra por los recursos naturales en Sonora," *Washington Post*, June 15, 2021, https://www.washingtonpost.com/es/post-opinion/2021/06/15/sonora-asesinatos-lebaron-rojo-valencia-yaqui.

15. Germán Castro Caycedo, *Nuestra guerra ajena* (Bogotá: Planeta, 2014), 12.

Index

www.ingramcontent.com/pod-product-compliance
Lightning Source LLC
Chambersburg PA
CBHW030331270326
41926CB00010B/1582